QUOTATION
FINDER

By Everett McKinley Dirksen and Herbert V. Prochnow

QUOTATION FINDER

By Herbert V. Prochnow and Herbert V. Prochnow, Jr.

A TREASURY OF HUMOROUS QUOTATIONS
THE SUCCESSFUL TOASTMASTER
THE PUBLIC SPEAKER'S TREASURE CHEST
A DICTIONARY OF WIT, WISDOM, & SATIRE

By Herbert V. Prochnow

THE FEDERAL RESERVE SYSTEM
THE NEW SPEAKER'S TREASURY OF WIT AND WISDOM
SPEAKER'S HANDBOOK OF EPIGRAMS AND WITTICISMS
DETERMINING THE BUSINESS OUTLOOK
1001 WAYS TO IMPROVE YOUR CONVERSATION & SPEECHES

QUOTATION FINDER

EVERETT McKINLEY DIRKSEN
and HERBERT V. PROCHNOW

HARPER & ROW, PUBLISHERS

New York

Evanston

San Francisco

London

FIRST EDITION

STANDARD BOOK NUMBER: 06–011033–3

LIBRARY OF CONGRESS CATALOG CARD NUMBER: 70–95950

Contents

Preface

With its well over 2,000 items, this book is meant to be useful to many groups of people. It contains almost 1,000 epigrams and witticisms by distinguished persons, hundreds of quotations from the great minds of the present and past.

Quotation Finder also offers 500 quotations from literature, almost 600 from the Bible and other sources, and many American proverbs. In addition, there are 300 examples of the wit and wisdom of statesmen. Excerpts from addresses by the authors and TV interviews of Senator Everett McKinley Dirksen are included. Here is a collection of not only the humor and wit of great figures in history, but also inspiring and wise statements by modern world leaders.

Many of the illustrations, stories, epigrams, and quotations will be recalled by the reader for use in conversation, informal discussions, and meetings.

Sooner or later every person in charge of a meeting searches frantically for a humorous or other pertinent quotation. He needs assistance, and he needs it promptly. This book should be helpful to him. Occasionally it's possible to introduce a speaker with humor that is extemporaneous, but there is a great risk of making a dull introduction. It is infinitely better to take a few minutes to select appropriate material.

Selections from the Bible and from literature were often used with great effect by Senator Dirksen. They exemplify what are perhaps the most profound and classic expressions available to us on subjects of vital concern to man.

The Senator also enlivened his speeches with frequent quotations from great statesmen and leaders of all nations. It seemed especially appropriate to include in this book many such inspiring excerpts, including some from his own addresses.

It is hoped that those who make speeches will find in these pages a wealth of illustrative material, useful to them on many occasions. Even daily conversation can be made more interesting, as Senator Dirksen often illustrated, when it contains wit, humor, and apposite quotations. Instead of vague generalities, a speaker may begin to use with greater frequency and effectiveness epigrams or illustrations that make conversation colorful.

This book had its beginning when I suggested to Senator Dirksen in a letter of November 1968 that we might cooperate in editing a book of inspiring selections from great addresses, quotations from the Bible and literature, proverbs, illustrations of the wit and wisdom of statesmen, and utterances of distinguished philosophers and leaders of all ages. Following a correspondence in which we arrived at an understanding of what the book would contain, I began its preparation.

During the following year, the Senator wrote me that his workload had been so heavy that he had not been able to make any progress on the book, which at that time chiefly involved taking speech outlines from his notebooks and putting them into readable text. I continued the preparation of the manuscript along the lines of our understanding of its contents.

With Senator Dirksen's unfortunate death, I took on the responsibility of selecting the excerpts from his addresses, TV interviews, and other sources.

Although it was my privilege to know this distinguished statesman for many years, I did not know until we undertook this book the full extent of his heroic struggle to live greatly, the courage with which he met the problem of his eyesight, his humility, his love of his country, his deep religious convictions, the esteem with which he was held by his associates, and his dedication at all times to what he believed was right and good for the United States and the American people. He was a great American.

I hope especially that I have chosen at least some of the excerpts he would have selected from his own addresses in the Senate and from his utterances on other occasions.

HERBERT V. PROCHNOW

...1...

Selections from Speeches, Letters, and Remarks of Everett McKinley Dirksen

DIDN'T SPEAK UP

1 A man bought a beautiful parrot. It spoke four languages. Even so the guy was reluctant to pay the thirty-five dollars plus fifteen dollars for the cage. It seemed a lot, but after all, *four* languages.

"Deliver it to this address," the buyer said, paying the money. When he got home that night, his wife met him at the door.

"Did the bird arrive?" he asked excitedly.

"Yes, he did," she answered.

"Where is he?"

"In the oven."

"What? My beautiful bird! Thirty-five dollars gone. And he spoke four languages."

"Well, why didn't he?" she said.

THANKS

2 I am reminded of the North Dakota farmer who went out to the barn one morning when it was about forty degrees below zero. He sat down on a milk stool and took hold of the animal. She turned to him and said, "Thanks for the warm hand."

HONEST COW

3 A farmer was unable to tell the Agriculture Department representative how much milk his cow produced. "I just know that she's an honest cow and she'll give you all the milk she's got."

IN DOUBT

4 I can now appreciate the widow with her young son, while her late lamented husband lay in state in the front of the church, and the minister was doing quite a good job in the eulogistic field. But at a certain point she couldn't take it any longer. Finally she said, "Johnny, you go up and see if that's your pa in that casket."

OPENING A SPEECH
(The Executives' Club of Chicago, 1965)

5 Well, I'm delighted to see you. I have been a captive a long time, and the captivity seems to know no bounds; but those are the woes and distresses of a leader, and you are expected to be as you're posed. So the only time I get away from Washington is when I put on my hat and walk out of the office.

I feel like that young mother with two children who received a playpen for Christmas. She sent the donor a letter. She said, "My dear, it's a godsend. I can sit in it every afternoon and the children can't get near me." So my colleagues can't get near me for a little while.

I am delighted to come and break bread and enjoy this thoroughgoing fellowship.

I have no speech. What I have in my pocket looks like something that has been belabored by the chickens. That's as far as it goes. Maybe I don't even have it in my pocket [searching pockets]. If I don't have it, it's too bad.

But now what do you make of that [indicating sheet of paper]? That's supposed to be this speech. I did tell you on one occasion, I am sure, about the husband with a nagging wife, who nagged him from the day they were married, and then the Lord saw fit to gather her up into Abraham's bosom, which is the courteous way of saying she died.

And when they were at the graveside there came a great roll of thunder and a jagged bolt of lightning in the sky. The husband contemplated this phenomenon a moment and said to the preacher, "Parson, I think she made it."

CONSTITUTIONALITY VERSUS COMPASSION

6 The mind is no match with the heart in persuasiveness; constitutionality is no match for compassion.

PARAPHRASING JOHN DONNE

7 Whatever the color of a man's skin, we are all mankind. So every denial of freedom, of equal opportunity for a livelihood, or for an education, diminishes me. There is the moral basis for this legislation.

A FIRM DUTY

8 To those who have charged me with doing a disservice to my party because of my interest in the enactment of a good civil rights bill—and there have been a good many who have made that charge—I can only say that our party found its faith in the Declaration of Independence, in which a great Democrat, Jefferson by name, wrote the flaming words: "We hold these truths to be self-evident: that all men are created equal."

That has been the living faith of our party. Do we forsake this article of faith now that equality's time has come or do we stand up for it and ensure the survival of our party and its ultimate victory? There is no substitute for a basic and righteous idea. We have a firm duty to use the instruments at hand—namely, the cloture rule—to bring about the enactment of a good civil rights bill.

BELONGED TO SAME GROUP

9 I have told about the robber who held up a bishop and after taking everything of value, he noticed the clerical collar. With some consternation he said, "You're a preacher." "I am," the bishop replied. And the robber said, "In what church do you preach?" "I'm a bishop in the Methodist Episcopal Church." The robber passed the pistol over and said, "Shake. That's the church I belong to."

LOOK OUT FOR HIMSELF

10 I recall the old frontiersman coming home from a hunting trip, and a neighbor coasted down the hill and said, "Hurry! Your wife is up there in that cabin and there's a bear in there." He says, "Well, that bear just has to look out for himself."

IS THAT CLEAR?

11 A man filled in an application for an insurance policy. One of the questions he had to answer was: "How old was your father when he died and of what did he die?" Well, his father had been hanged but he did not like to put that on his application. He puzzled over it for quite a while. He finally wrote, "My father was sixty-five when he died. He came to his end while participating in a public function when the platform gave way."

PREPARED

12 An accident witness was put on the stand to testify. After several questions, counsel asked the man, "How close were you when the accident occurred?" Without hesitation, the witness answered, "Twenty-two feet, nine and three-quarter inches." The lawyer was skeptical. "How do you know it was exactly twenty-two feet, nine and three-quarter inches?" "Because," answered the man, "I figured some lawyer would ask that question, so I got a tape measure and measured it."

REVIEW OF THIRTY YEARS' EXPERIENCE IN CONGRESS
(The Executives' Club of Chicago, 1965)

13 Preparing for a discourse on an occasion like this presents a good deal of difficulty. There are so many diverse needs and so much subject matter that could be discussed, but I thought it might be well to fling myself into a reminiscent mood, just because I am back among the home folks.

And in that mood, I wondered how far one would go, and what impression he would make if he tried to crowd thirty years of legislative life into roughly thirty minutes. . . .

I remember holding up my right hand on the ninth day of March,

1933, in the Chamber of the House of Representatives. It's the day I took the oath to become one of the lawmakers of this country.

The conditions, as you well know, were quite untimely—certainly for a Republican. Prices had hit bottom, and likewise the market. The great issue in '32 was bread and butter, and there was a great emotional sentiment in the country.

But strangely enough—and who and what diverse destiny should will it—I was caught up in the vortex and was sent to Congress that year. . . .

I will never forget the first bill. It was the Economy Act of 1933. We threw the word out of the dictionary when we got through with that act because I haven't heard it since that time. The bill was in typewritten form. It reduced the benefits of the veterans, and it reduced the salaries of everybody on the payroll—classified and unclassified.

I voted against it, along with thirty-four others, I think, on my side. Then came the comments: "You one-termer—time cannot go fast enough to take you out of public office." These were mainly from my friends. You can imagine how I felt—that my legislative career almost died a-borning.

But that was thirty years ago, and I am still around the place; and if the Lord is willing and He's got some work for me to do, I apprehend that I'll be around a little while longer, notwithstanding these nine maladies that the *Daily News* reporters ascribe to me; because I think they are all true, but I feel good notwithstanding them.

And so the wheels began to move. The Agricultural Adjustment Act —when we plowed under the little pigs, fifteen million of them, under the skilled hand of Henry Agard Wallace, and we sought birth control for the rest of the hog population of the country.

And frankly, we're still plowed under, thirty years later, only we seem to be doing it with money; and we are paying for things that are not produced.

And then in quick succession came NIRA, the National Industrial Recovery Act. You remember the Blue Eagle. You remember the York, Pennsylvania, factory manufacturer who wouldn't accommodate to the trade association's prices, and they put him in jail.

You remember the New Jersey pants presser, who was pressing for thirty-five cents per pair, but the trade association requirement was fifty cents; and when he refused to charge fifty cents they put him in jail.

And then came the Schecter case, from New York, the two brothers in the chicken business. It is always known as the "sick chicken case." So the sick chicken took the Blue Eagle to the Supreme Court and knocked out the Blue Eagle; and in so doing also went into bankruptcy —one of those rather interesting things in the thirty-year period. And then came the bank closures, and the moratorium.

And then came the Tennessee Valley Authority. Isn't it interesting that I assailed the Tennessee Valley Authority? But today it is entrenched, and I don't believe anybody can untrench it, when you consider how many senators come from those states; how much money is invested; and the fidelity of those devoted to public power—to an institution like the Tennessee Valley Authority.

Then, of course, there was Prohibition. Those were the things that took up the time of the first hundred days, along with a few others, as the wheels began to spin thirty years ago last month, after I held up my hand as a freshman congressman in the Nation's Capitol.

But as the years roll on, why, these patterns somehow continue to spell themselves out. I remember very well the Home Owners Loan Corporation. A gentleman from Boston was called to Washington to run that show. And then came the wave of foreclosures. Before we got through, Uncle Sam was the most opulent mortgagee and forecloser in the country, because he wound up with 250,000 properties.

We're doing pretty well in the foreclosure field today. I looked it up yesterday and it's 108,000. Rather interesting that thirty years later, people in this great free republic are still losing homes under the spectral hand of foreclosure.

And then we passed the Silver Purchase Act in 1934, to buy enough silver so that the ratio to gold in our monetary system would be sixteen to one.

Once I got the Silver Purchase Act repealed in the House of Representatives; but when the senators from the silver states put their profane hands on that poor bill, it was too bad for me.

But I have lived to see the day on the Senate Finance Committee, as a member of that committee, when the Secretary of the Treasury came not only there but before the Banking Committee of the Senate and said, "Please, gentlemen, it is the wish of the Treasury that we now repeal the Silver Purchase Act of 1934."

We also passed the Social Security Act, and I wonder whether you have some appreciation of the monumental dimensions of Social Security.

There are presently, as I recall, 78 million people actively covered by the Social Security System. There are presently 20 million beneficiaries drawing benefits in the Social Security System. There are presently 19 billion 700 million symbolic dollars in the trust funds. And I say "symbolic dollars," because of 19 billion 700 million, 17 billion is in government bonds. That's the interesting way to monetize a public debt of monumental proportions.

So you see, when you talk about Social Security, it expands; it proliferates; and year after year we patch it, and improve the benefits, and expand it, and already there is some concern about the money that is taken out of the economic bloodstream.

And then we got the Reciprocal Trade Act—and I voted for it on occasions, and I voted against it on occasions, as suited my fancy, and as suited the condition of the country.

I presume that's why they've often referred to me as a chameleon, particularly in the foreign field; but I have to intersperse a thought here. When they took me in hand and said, "We need your shoulder to the wheel in order to put over a foreign aid act," and then came around after a while with a record showing that we had sent nineteen tons of bubble gum to Belgium, that's where I jumped off. So I didn't forsake foreign aid. I am afraid that foreign aid forsook me.

We also put a Crop Insurance Act on the books. I got it liquidated once, and then they put it back.

We went on to make work—because we had to provide jobs for the citizenry. They didn't have any very glamorous names. CWA—the Civilian Work Agency; PWA—the Public Works Administration; WPA —the Works Progress Agency; CCC—the Civilian Conservation Corps.

We romanticize it now, and the names are glamorous. They have more appeal.

Why, just think—you can write a poem about Appalachia, and they're going to spend a billion. You could write a poem about the so-called Economic Opportunity Act, or the Domestic Peace Corps. Who couldn't write a paean of praise to the very name itself? But it's an easier way to coax out larger sums of money. And what we shall appropriate, and what we shall spend, will exceed the wildest imagination of anyone who ever sat in either House or Senate in those days thirty years ago. You see, we are learning as time goes on.

So it is interesting—the cycle goes on over a period of years. The same subject matter. The same challenges. The same problems recur over and over again in the whole field of government, and then have to be solved all over again.

In the budget field—and this ought to cheer you some—the first budgets with which I had anything to do in the fiscal year 1934, effective July 1, 1933, were for 4 billion 600 million dollars. That was for all purposes—Army, Navy, Air Corps, the Marines; every agency of government; every administrative expense; every procurement item; everything—4 billion 6. We didn't have trust funds to bother about at the time, and where are we today?

The administrative budget as it was sent up was 700 million short of a 100 billion. Our progress in fiscal degeneracy has been rather rapid, I would say. And if you want to add the trust funds, then just say 127 billion. And I am not sure that that's going to be the top.

You begin to wonder what's going to happen to your country. I think of that lady who went to the governor of Tennessee and said, "Governor, I'd like to get my husband out of the penitentiary."

"Why is he there?"

"For stealing a ham."

"Is he a good husband?"

"No, sir. He drinks; he beats me; he beats the children."

"Well, madam, why do you want him out of prison?"

"We're out of ham again."

So I wonder when we're going to run out of ham, and I wonder when I'm going to run out of time. That isn't very long, is it? . . .

But two or three things disturb me as I think back over this thirty-year trend—first, the deeper and deeper intrusion of federal power into the affairs of the people. The list is as long as your arm, and it continues to grow.

Let no one—no citizen, no governor, no mayor—be so naïve as to think that any money is coming out of the Federal Treasury but what there's a tag on it. Even for myself I wouldn't vote a dollar of the people's money out of the Federal Treasury unless there was some control. So when you get money for urban renewal, and money for schools, and money for Medicare, and ninety-one other items, just remember there's somewhere for you to match. You're going to have to raise state taxes and local taxes, while we beat our breasts and take credit for having reduced taxes on the federal level. But you're not going to be the gainer. Somebody's got to pay the bill. And there is no free money that I have ever seen around any place in the last thirty years. . . .

Today we are indisputably in the welfare state, and you wonder how we got there, notwithstanding that not a jot nor a title in the Constitution has been changed; and the source of authority is still the Congress of the United States.

What bothers me is that in all this development you do jeopardize the sweetest boon that God ever granted to mankind, and that's the boon of freedom and liberty.

You say it's not jeopardy. Oh, is that so, when government is clothed with so much power? And how easy the rest of it seems to erode. I made a speech one time on the subject Frogs and Freedom. And a friend said, "What in the devil would frogs have to do with freedom?"

I said, "You know if you take a frog with his delicate reflexes and drop him in a kettle of boiling water, and the sides are not too high, he'll pop right out of the water. But put that frog in the same kettle and fill it with cold water, then turn on the gas; and that poor, unsuspecting frog will be boiled, because he didn't have sense enough to climb out of that water before it got too hot."

The little erosion, the little precipitation—that's the way freedom is finally lost. And as the son of an immigrant father, who came here to escape tyranny, and an immigrant mother, seventeen years old, who came here to escape tyranny, I wonder whether I've failed sometimes in my responsibility as a public servant. I have a couple of grand-children, and of all the things I want to leave them, as the most sacred of all bequests, is a free system where they'll have a chance to make it just as their grandpappy did.

So, standing on the pinnacle of thirty years of public service, in the House of Representatives and the Senate of the United States, I have seen this civilization unfold. I have seen the challenges and problems recur from time to time. And as I spell it out for myself, and watch its continuing unfoldment, I can only say to you, liberty as we once knew it is really in danger in our own blessed land.

LOST

14 A rather absentminded professor used to come up from Winston-Salem to Washington frequently. He was known by the train people, but he couldn't ever find his ticket. One time, the conductor said, "That's all right, doctor; surely you'll find it and you can turn it in on the next ride." But the professor said, "Mr. Conductor, it isn't all right. I've got to find that ticket because I have to know where I'm going."

NOT PARTICULAR

15 As I think of this spirit of accord and amity and concord, I think of the two deacons, the Republican and Democrat, who were kneeling together in their supplications in a little church in a small village in Illinois. The Republican deacon was praying to the Lord and saying, "O Lord, make us Republicans unlike the Democrats; make us band together in accord; make us hang together in concord." And just then the Democratic deacon said, "Lord, any cord will do."

LUCKY

16 An accident took place at a railroad crossing at night in the course of which the railroad company was sued for damages. Counsel for the company put the crossing watchman on the stand and asked:

"Were you at your post when the accident occurred?"

"I was," said the watchman.

"Did you have your lantern?"

"I did," said the watchman.

A verdict was returned for the company. As the watchman and the railroad counsel left the courtroom, the watchman turned to the company lawyer and said, "I am sure glad they didn't ask whether the lantern was lit."

TAKING NO CHANCES

17 Not to mention the farmer who stopped his son on his way to a date with a young lass up the road. He asked the boy why he was taking a lantern.

"I never needed no light when I went a-sparkin'," the man teased.

"And look what you got," the boy replied.

CIVIL RIGHTS

18 I am no Johnny-come-lately in this field [of civil rights]. Thirty years ago in the House of Representatives, I voted on the anti-poll tax and anti-

lynching measures. Since then, I have sponsored or cosponsored scores of bills dealing with civil rights.

WHEN CRITICIZED FOR HIS ACTION

19 A man is not fit to walk into this chamber as a United States senator if he is to be bilked and influenced by that kind of argument to deter him from his duties under the laws and the Constitution.

DEFENDING PRESIDENT JOHNSON

20 You do not demean the President in the eyes of the people abroad because when you do you demean the prestige of this country.

AS A YOUNG CONGRESSMAN

21 What can a young, inexperienced Republican congressman, divested of all patronage, do for his country and his district in the midst of a three-to-one Democratic majority? . . . It is a stimulus to individual ego and conceit that might easily prompt a recital of good intentions and noble resolves. While this situation has its disadvantages, there is compensation in the fact that it permits much time for study and constructive attention to legislation. The function of the minority party is, after all, in the salutary influence which it can exercise in resolutely opposing things which are fundamentally wrong and supporting those measures which are right. Under such circumstances, opportunities for service are certain to arise. . . .

THE REPUBLICAN PARTY

22 Now, as for the one-party system. It was interesting to contemplate all of the analyses and the comment made after the 1964 campaign.

Was it the end of the Republican Party?

Well, all you have to do is go back and examine the antecedents of the party. There's a lot of vitality in the party. I said to the Republican ladies in Washington that it would probably be there long after the Great Society was gone and forgotten.

To implement this—when Al Smith ran against Hoover in 1928, he got 15 million votes; and the following morning they were ready to hold a wake for the Democratic Party. If you look at the tremendous power and the two-to-one majorities in the House and Senate that my friend Lyndon Johnson enjoys, you can see whether or not it is devoid of vitality. Parties are that way.

As I note now the results of local election returns, where there is a complete about-face, I make so bold as to assert that I look for some big things and wonderful results for my party in 1966 and in the years beyond.

SACRIFICE

23 Our present problems are ethical and moral as well as economic. No one will contend that within this nation we cannot find men with sufficient vision and knowledge to fabricate feasible, practical, and constitutional

measures for the relief of business, agriculture, banking, transportation, and other enterprises. The real problem lies in effecting a subordination of individual and group interests and in ironing out the real and fancied conflict of interests to the point where such measures can be inscribed on the statute books, and that problem is ethical rather than economic. The lush days of prosperity seem to have created within us a total incapacity for sacrifice, yet how can we reach firm ground without it?

THE 1932 ELECTION

24　Too many of the candidates on both state and county tickets were close personal friends and it seemed wholly unfair to say or do anything to injure their candidacies that might be dictated by political differences and considerations, rather than by personal conviction. It was a difficult problem in political strategy and quite often doubts arose as to whether it was a sound and ethical course.

I distinctly recall the occasion when, at an outdoor picnic of one of the ward clubs, I first enunciated this political philosophy and assured the voters that our problems were economic and appealed to citizenship rather than partisanship. I had no stomach for hurling real or fancied charges against the Democrats nor could I convince myself that they were so bad and incompetent as to require a thorough disinfecting before they were prepared to sit in the seats of authority. This seemed eminently acceptable to the Republicans who intended to vote for Roosevelt and to the Democrats who intended to vote for me.

WINNING AN ELECTION

25　I quit Congress in 1949 because of an eye malady. Frankly, they thought I was going to lose my eyesight, and I presume there were people who said, "Well, he's back home and he's washed up."

Then the delegations came and said we'd have to have a candidate for the Senate and "You're the only 'thing' around, and of course you can't win." I had a hundred delegations saying, "You have to run, but of course you can't win." Fancy me being sent from here to the North Pole on a great adventure and then have them say, "Of course you're not going to find it." Well, why start out looking for it in the first place?

I didn't campaign on that theory, and I didn't win on that theory either. So I came back.

INDEPENDENCE DAY
(*Congressional Record,* 1969)

26　Independence Day, Friday, the observance of our 193rd year as a nation, will remind many of us that we are slipping away from our heritage in some respects.

All over the land this weekend our people will be traveling for fun and pleasure—to play golf and to participate in picnics. Generally, they will forget that such a wonderful thing as independence preserved through the centuries is something Americans fought for with a courage and dedication seldom before demonstrated by man.

Independence Day ought to mean more to us than a day off from work, part of a weekend of fun and frolic.

In all the cities and hamlets of our country, in years gone by, the Fourth of July was celebrated with patriotic speeches, parades, and thoughts of both the past and the future. This year, however, as in other recent years, there are many cities that won't even have a parade, that won't officially honor Independence Day.

As a nation, we may be losing some of our concern for the glorious past, a past that should bridge us into the unknown future. This week, then, is the right time to state a few facts of history that will help us to face tomorrow.

The Second Continental Congress, meeting in Philadelphia on July 2, 1776, passed a resolution in favor of independence and, on July 4, that Congress agreed to the Declaration of Independence. The Declaration was signed by fifty-six courageous, farseeing Americans, truly the fathers of our country, on August 2.

Despite the Declaration, the Revolutionary War continued and was not won until the British under Lord Cornwallis surrendered at Yorktown, October 19, 1781.

There was dissent in 1776, as there is today. There was no unanimity for independence. The Tories in the colonial states wanted to dwell under the rule of King George III. Many delegates to the Continental Congress didn't want to sign the Declaration that came alive in the words of Thomas Jefferson. Some of them stayed away from the meeting place in the steepled state house in Philadelphia. But when it came time to be signed, they forgot the dissent and they returned to affix their deathless signatures to the document of freedom.

They decided they were Americans. They stood up for independence. They silenced their dissent. They forged a nation.

Who were those signers of the Declaration of Independence? I mention only two—you can read the other names in a copy of the Declaration in your dictionary or encyclopedia. There was John Hancock, of Massachusetts. He was wealthy for his day, and he had contributed $100,000 to the cause of freedom. Had the revolution failed, his property and business would have been seized by the king. There was Charles Carroll, of Carrolltown, Maryland. He, too, was wealthy, probably the richest of all the signers. He staked his wealth and his very neck on the successful pursuit of the war for freedom. Many others of the fifty-six were men of means and property.

They all risked their every acre of land and farthing of money on an idea that men should be free. They engaged in the dissent of the day and helped to make their views into a dream come true, a dream for a better America where there would be opportunity for all.

They exhibited their devotion to their cause in the highest degree as they signed the document under the last sentence that Jefferson had written into the Declaration: ". . . And for the support of this Declaration, with a firm reliance on the protection of divine Providence, we mutually pledge to each other our Lives, our Fortunes, and our sacred Honor."

How easily we forget that 193 years later we are all of us beneficiaries of the men who signed the Declaration of Independence. They signed for us who live in the turmoil of 1969. They sacrificed for us who may sometimes forget to express our appreciation of their courage and devotion and their willingness to pledge all in the cause of freedom.

A few simple things would do to mark our 1969 observance of Independence Day with reverence for the past and faith in the future. We can display the Flag. We can gather our family and friends about us and read aloud the Declaration and the names of the signers, perhaps putting to shame the commercialized ceremonies where the Declaration will not be recalled to the ears of millions.

We can stop awhile and think about the past that bridges the centuries to come.

CORRECT SO FAR

27 The statements made by the majority leader in the *Record* are quite correct, so far as they go. As I said before, however, it is like the man who fell off the twentieth floor of a building. As he passed the sixth floor, a friend of his shouted to him, "Mike, so far you are all right."

TO BE EXPECTED

28 I remember the man who was on the wrong floor of a hospital in Peoria. He was on the floor where the baby ward was. There were little tykes squalling and bawling. The nurse came out. She had a long, dour countenance. The fellow said, "Nurse, what makes all the little brats squall and bawl the way they do?" The nurse, remembering that the portion of the national debt for the baby was about $1,971, said, "Well, mister, if you were out of work, if you owed $1,971 as your share of the debt, and if your pants were wet, you'd squall too!"

NO NEED TO BE AN OCTOPUS

29 By then the all-embracing arms of Uncle Sam will be found in every business, large and small, in the country. Believe me, those are all-embracing arms.

I never think of arms but that I think of the story of the fellow who called up his best girl and said to her, "Darling, I wish I were an octopus."

She said, "Why would you like to be an octopus?"

He replied, "With all those arms I'd like to embrace you with every one of them."

She said, "What's the matter with the two you've got?"

ON HIS RECORDINGS

30 I have been the target of a certain amount of levity concerning my voice. I believe it was Mr. [Bob] Hope who said I sounded like a duet between Tallulah Bankhead and Wallace Beery. He also challenged the right of a senator to invade the sanctum sanctorum of show business. Well, Mr. Hope, may I make my position clear. I have been speaking for the record for thirty years. I have merely moved from one Capitol to another [Capitol Records].

ON SPEAKING ONLY FROM NOTES

31 I always extemporize. I love the diversions, the detours. Without notes you may digress . . . you may dart . . . and after you've taken on an interrupter, you don't have to flounder around with a piece of paper to find out where in the hell you were.

A GOVERNMENT OFFICIAL AND STATISTICS

32 On one occasion last fall, [a government official] called down a tumbling mass of statistics, which rolled end over end, at express-train speed, to engulf the reporters. It included data ranging from the annual cost of keeping an inmate in the Illinois penitentiary at Menard to the median consumption of fish, classified as to weight and species, by seals in the Seattle zoo.

When the last rush subsided, the shaken questioner was sorry he had asked the little question that started it all, namely: "How much more does it cost to keep a boy in the Job Corps than in Harvard University?"

The question was buried in the statistical snow job. There it will remain forever unless a shift in the political glacier opens a crevasse and exposes it to view.

GOVERNMENT WASTE

33 A phantom statistic which compels even its compilers to smile is that showing "the rising productivity of government employees." There are, of course, many conscientious, hard-working government employees among the myriads, but they are all supported by the work of someone else. What could they produce but statistics?

An old favorite is what might be called the Cheshire Statistic. It is pulled out of the air like a magician producing a bowl of goldfish. Such a statistic was the basis for the charge during the 1960 presidential campaign that "17 million Americans go to bed hungry every night." Not 4 million, or 18.1 million, but 17 million exactly. Unless many of them were reducing, that seemed to indicate a deplorable breakdown in a public relief system which was even then the most gigantic ever conceived. But then, President Johnson raised the figure two years ago to 35 million. It hung on the campaign air awhile like its predecessor and then faded gently from view.

INTRODUCTION TO THE PLATFORM OF THE 1968 REPUBLICAN NATIONAL CONVENTION

34   Mr. Chairman, Delegates and Alternates, and Fellow Americans:

In Philadelphia 181 years ago, farseeing men fashioned us a revolutionary new government—a daring new system reposing all power in the people.

Then, as they prepared to depart for their homes, venerable Benjamin Franklin encountered a concerned citizen.

"Dr. Franklin," he was asked, "what have we got—a monarchy or a republic?"

At once he replied, "A republic—*if* you can keep it."

I repeat those sage words: "A republic—*if* you can keep it."

Seventy-seven years later that challenge still echoed at Gettysburg.

There Abraham Lincoln posed the same deathless question—whether a nation conceived in liberty and dedicated to equality can long endure.

It *did* endure.

Through foreign wars, through depressions, through political storms, through economic tinkering and tampering, it has endured. Through New Deals and Fair Deals, through New Frontiers and Great Societies, it has endured.

Yet today we are challenged anew.

A Soviet leader declaims that ours is a rotten, decadent society. God forbid our having to make the point—but, should he try us, he'll quickly find out what Americans really are!

One hears even here at home that we have a sick society. What nonsense! Only radicals who traffic in trouble—only extremists intolerant of moderation—only celebrating pessimists bemused with a mote in America's eye say it.

No, my friends, we are not sick. We are not even indisposed. But we *are* mismanaged.

Yes, the Great Society may be unwell. But the God-fearing, hardworking, taxpaying, saving, enterprising millions who make this nation tick are clean of mind, strong of heart, and brimming with faith in America.

I repeat, America is *not* ailing. But we *are* indignant. To see why, let's first trace the further unfolding of our nation.

Some two centuries ago, first in a rivulet, then in a torrent, our people thrust out from the colonial seaboard across the mountains and plains to the west, the south, the north, until the frontier closed at the Pacific. Then they swirled together again. Thus grew our teeming urban centers, and our rural economy became enmeshed with vibrant new industry. The vitality and productivity nurtured by this fabulous mix made us prosper as no nation before. So, in time, we matured into the mightiest of nations—the leader, the hope, and the benefactor of the free world.

Twice we rescued the world from tyranny. Not once or twice, but time and time again we uplifted other peoples engulfed in desperation and despair.

Now, today, how strange this world has come to be!

Freedom we continue to succor abroad, but at home we abuse it, we constrict it, we let it erode.

To every disaster, however distant, we swiftly respond with compassion, but all too often ingratitude flows back across the seas.

Boldly we move to save the pound sterling, the franc, the lira, then let our own currency dribble down the drain.

Oh, how cynical, how mocking, that political slogan "The *Great* Society"!

Never has an undeclared war embroiled America so long, never the casualty toll so great, never the outcome so remote.

Never have we been so overextended the world around, never our prestige so low, our alliances so weakened, our image so impaired.

Never has an administration so disregarded the limits of our resources, our patience, our unwillingness—indeed, our inability—to police and sustain a bellicose and insatiable world. Openhearted, yes, openhanded, we long have been—but, my friends, the time to reassess our generosity is now.

Never have we known a time in which foreign financial leaders have been so fearful of America's resolution to overcome fiscal crisis, and never before an administration so ready to justify such concerns.

Not for a century has interest—the price of money—been so high in this land, yet never the drive to pour out public moneys so great.

Never has the nation been so mired in debt—never its budget so bloated, the deficit so huge, the spending so unrestrained, except in all-out war. Once upon a time people talked of the sky as the limit. Now we've been rocketed to fiscal outer space.

Never have work stoppages by public servants been more with us, solutions so uncertain, and prospects for reasoned conduct so unsure.

Never have our farmers been so productive—yet, save in depression, never, for many, profits so low.

Never have consumers seen such an abundance of food and goods, but at prices they flinch to pay.

It is said that the best things in life are free. Well, never has an administration labored so diligently—or so successfully—to prove that nothing at all is free.

Never have our cities writhed in such jeopardy and fear. The President's own Commission depicts our domestic crisis as our most serious since the Civil War. "Great Society" indeed!

Never promises so lavish, performance so dismal, respecting our millions of poor—never their resentment so keen, their protest so violent, and never relations among races so gravely impaired.

Never has obedience to law been so disdained, and never law enforcement so hobbled by unwarranted regulations, strained court decisions, and official solicitude for crime.

Now, let's just "tell it like it is." Must this free people *forever* indulge lawlessness and violence? *Must* law-abiding citizens don bulletproof vests safely to take an evening stroll? *Must* we avoid our great cities by night as if they were hamlets, guerrilla-infested, in Vietnam?

Worse still, never has the sanctity of life been so scorned. Young Marines are brutally murdered in a Washington restaurant. A United States senator is assassinated while campaigning. A Christian crusader is martyred for leading a march. Policemen in our nation's capital are shot down and the killing condoned by a group that should know better. Desperadoes convert the streets of Cleveland to bullet-swept lanes of a frontier town. "Get guns" becomes a battle cry, and homicide a mere statistic. Clamor rises for gun control, but how little is said, how little done, to restrain the finger that pulls the trigger.

Little businesses serving city dwellers face ruin for lack of insurance protection. Yes, there is relief—a pooling of private and public funds—but still no end to the tyranny of the looter, the blackmailer, the robber, the arsonist.

My fellow Americans, let's again "tell it like it is." This lawlessness—this official restraint in meeting lawlessness—this indulged defiance of authority—are the straight road, the very short road, to anarchy and chaos.

But never has the sound of the trumpet been so uncertain, never our leadership so hesitant, in rallying our people to salvage America's inheritance.

How tragic that our America the beautiful has been allowed to become shamed, unhappy, embittered! Patriotism in some quarters seems to be a dirty word. Sacrifice, except for thousands of youths who at this very moment risk death to national cause, is outmoded. This ballyhooed "Great Society"—the fancy of an English socialist six decades ago—is not a new deal—no, not even a fair deal; it's just a straight-out misdeal. Humor it longer, and it will destroy what the Founding Fathers wrought.

Clearly, my friends, the hour is late and our problems legion. It is America's hour of need.

And that need—so urgent, so undeniable—is to depose this fumbling Democratic Party, to depose its inept leadership—that party and those leaders, oh, so long on promise, oh, so short in performance. An outraged, heartbroken, shocked America joins us in this injunction to the

"Great Society"—a sentiment voiced by Oliver Cromwell three centuries ago: "You have sat too long here for any good you have been doing. Depart, I say, and let us have done with you. In the name of God, go!"

And yet, among us still are those few who prefer the alluring political promise, even with its failure, instead of progress that is dependable, orderly, and assured. Let such dreamers heed Lincoln's warning of a century and three years ago: "If destruction be our lot, we must ourselves be its author and finisher. As a nation of free men we must live through all time or die by suicide."

We of the Republican Party believe with Lincoln.

We hold, with him, that the legitimate needs of the people *can* be met without forfeiting freedom.

We hold there *can* be progress without wanton spending, ruinous inflation, and fiscal collapse.

We know there *can* be care for the needy—and *without* the erosion of dignity, *without* the federal domination, *without* the paternalism and waste that demean human endeavor.

We of the Republican Party are eager—and, yes, we are able and determined—to meet those needs.

We really *want* to provide that progress.

We Republicans are literally champing at the bit to *prove* to every citizen, just as we have proved before, that Republicans don't merely promise—Republicans *produce*—and we *really* care.

We call upon all Americans, regardless of party, regardless of section, to join with us in retrieving this nation's birthright of life, liberty, and the pursuit of happiness. When we sing "God Bless America," let us pray that through God's grace we may become a confident, peaceful land again—a land where the larks can once again be heard above the guns and we truly become one nation, under God indivisible, with liberty and justice for all.

It is not merely a political victory that concerns us here, but rather the future of this Republic. Rolling down the years we still hear Ben Franklin's challenge: "A republic—*if* you can keep it."

Inspired with high purpose—resolved that this land of liberty, with its limitless promise for the generations after us, shall not perish from the earth—we now present for the favor of this convention and our countrymen a statement of principles and programs—the 1968 Platform of our party.

In preparing this statement, we have called upon the best minds, the noblest of inspiration, the highest of talents. For this Republic—for one Republican Party—we believe it states the case for a just peace in the world, for dependable progress for all our people, and for a new serenity and unity in this troubled land. . . .

THE MARIGOLD
(*Congressional Record,* 1969)

35 For some years I have been carrying the flag in a cause, and that cause is to have the American marigold officially designated by the Congress as the national floral emblem of the United States.

Incidentally, Mr. President, the American marigold is so rugged that it can resist almost any insect, and it defies air pollution.

I am fully sensible of the fact that all persons, young and old, male and female, rich and poor, have their own preferences when it comes to a flower. But mine is for the marigold for a variety of reasons. It is actually an American native and really not native to any other place on earth. It is grown in great profusion in every one of the fifty states and strangely enough it is not the official flower of any state. Long ago it was acknowledged as a symbol of religious faith and graced altars both at home and abroad.

One of the outstanding characteristics of the marigold is its robustness and rugged character. If there is any flower that can resist the onslaught of the insect world better than the marigold, I would not know what it is. I grow thousands of them every year for my own delight and the delight of my neighbors, and I know what this flower will do.

I class it, therefore, with the American eagle when it comes to a symbol of our country that manifests stamina; and when it comes to beauty, I can think of nothing greater or more inspiring than a field of blooming marigolds tossing their heads in the sunshine and giving a glow to the entire landscape.

Today, therefore, I again introduce this joint resolution, stating very simply that the American marigold shall be designated and shall be adopted as the national floral emblem of the United States, and that the President be requested to declare that fact by proclamation.

THE UNITED STATES AS A LEADER

36 In many areas around the world, it appears that respect for us has vanished. I am not so naïve as to believe that some far-off country will love us particularly and lavish affection on us for what we may do for it. I concluded long ago that probably the only thing we can get is respect; and that respect we will gain through strength. But we must be very sure that we are on good ground; that our facts are straight; and that we either know or do not know whether there was an element of provocation—which can so easily call forth an equivalent expression—to be used as a basis for an interdiction by Congress in a piece of legislation that will have its repercussions in the chancelleries of the world.

But arbitrary, capricious, and precipitate action will not further the cause of the United States as a leader in the free world. That leadership has been thrust upon us, and we could not avoid that responsibility even if we wanted to do so.

CHANGING YOUR MIND

37 I have often thought that the only people who do not change their minds are sleeping peacefully in some cemetery or in an institution—involuntarily—and have lost the capacity of changing their minds. So I hope the time will never come when I can't adjust to new circumstances and new conditions, because it is an accelerated world.

A FREE GOVERNMENT

38 An old waterlogged scow doesn't move very fast, it doesn't move very far at one time, but it never sinks and maybe that is the reason we have a free government today. I was thinking how many free governments are just in so great a hurry that they suddenly flop over and take on a dictatorial and despotic cast because they can't wait for normal forces to undertake the changes that are necessary in the constant climb of people to a better life.

AGE
(Weekly radio-TV report, 1968)

39 How old is old? The question comes about because of a column in one of the recent issues of *Newsweek* magazine. It was written by Kenneth Crawford. He's a fine gentleman. He happens to be sixty-six. And the title was "Old Man Dirksen." Well, it intrigues me a good deal and it was done in a very polished style. So in my mind it did raise the question "How old is old?" because I read it in a context of a number of members who will be retiring from the Senate and also from the House of Representatives for one reason or another. In some cases they are a little older, and in other cases not.

But I began to puzzle a little about it and began to do a little research work. You remember that volume *Life Begins at Forty?* Well, in it is the statement that nine-tenths of the world's significant work is done by older people. You can go back and think of all the people who have done so much of the world's work. Probably one of the greatest in the days of the Roman Empire was Cicero, who did one of his major pieces of work when he was eighty-four. In the days of the Roman Empire, I guess the average age was about twenty-five. I'm speaking of averages now. And then in the days of Charlemagne it was thirty-two. As we got to 1900 it moved up to fifty. Well, at what point does a person lose his capacity for diligence, the acuity of his mind for performing public service? That's a rather interesting question, so we might look at some more examples.

And first, let's take the administrative field. Chiang Kai-shek is doing a phenomenal job for Free China and Formosa, and he is eighty. Mao Tse-tung, who presides over the destinies of Red China with anywhere from 600 to 700 million people, is seventy-four. Ho Chi Minh, who is a thorn in our side if anybody ever was, and who runs the affairs of North Vietnam, is seventy-six. Franco is still going pretty well in ruling over Spain at age seventy-five. De Gaulle, who is another one of our real headaches, is seventy-seven. Adenauer was still doing great work as the chancellor of Germany when he was eighty. We have a troubleshooter, Averell Harriman, one-time governor of New York, who does a lot of work, and at the present time he is seventy-five. J. Edgar Hoover, head of the FBI, is seventy-three; George Meany, who is the president of the American Federation of Labor and the CIO, is seventy-three; and then I think of Eisenhower; he's now seventy-five, but the President consults with him freely and very frequently. So look at the people in that range in the administrative field.

Well, let's go on a little bit further and think about those in judicial positions. Let's think about the Supreme Court, for example. They have the last word in the field of law. The Congress can make law, the President can sign what we do, it can go on the lawbooks, but the interpretation that will hold water finally comes from the Supreme Court if a matter is litigated and it raises either a real question or a constitutional question. Some of the most rugged opinions that emanate from the Supreme Court have been written by Hugo Black, one-time senator, who is now eighty-one and still on the Court. The Chief Justice, one-time governor of California, Earl Warren, is seventy-five. Justice Douglas is sixty-eight; Justice Clark, when he retired last year, was sixty-eight; Justice Harlan is presently sixty-eight; Justice Brennan is sixty-one; Justice Stewart is fifty-two; Justice White is fifty; Justice Fortas is fifty-seven; and then there is Stanley Reid, who retired ten years ago at age seventy-three, but is available for duty and often called into duty. A majority of the justices of the Supreme Court are therefore over sixty-five.

So we get back to the question "How old is old?" Well, nothing like looking at the legislative branch, but particularly the United States Senate. There are two members of the Senate today who are over eighty. Senator Hayden of Arizona and Senator Gruening of Alaska. And then there are thirteen who are over age seventy. There are thirty-one who are over age sixty and there are twenty-one who are over age fifty. And also twenty-one who are under age fifty. Well, agewise, it would appear to me that that makes a pretty good balance, because that way you retain a reservoir of experience while the younger members are beginning to earn their spurs in the legislative branch. I say that makes for a balance and I think history bears that out pretty well.

DANGER SIGNS ON CIGARETTE PACKAGES

40 Next somebody will suggest that a skull and crossbones be put on corn juice. . . . Two shots of that stuff (before the fusel oil is removed) and you're on a Kentucky binge. You know what that is? You fall to the ground and hang on so you won't fall off.

HIS HEALTH

41   I guess I've got everything any seventy-three-year-old man has—except floating kidneys and housemaid's knee.

HIS DEBT
(*Congressional Record,* 1966)

42   My mother came from the old country when she was only seventeen years of age. She came here on a sailing vessel, buffeted by the tumultuous North Atlantic, when even the crew caught scurvy. She knew nothing about this new land except from letters of those who had gone before and who said that this was the land of freedom and opportunity, where only one's diligence, one's perseverance, one's willingness to achieve, one's willingness to engage in the great virtues of thrift and frugality could put a limit on what a person could accomplish. My father came here at a young age only a few years after the Civil War. He brought here a craft. He died when I was a youngster of five years of age. Let no man stand in his place in the Senate and say that the Dirksen family did not come up the hard way. Here was a widowed mother with a brood of orphan children and we had to strike out and make it as best we could.

A thousand times I have said to people in all parts of the country: There is one debt greater than the public debt itself and that is the debt Everett Dirksen owes to this country and to all that it represents, to the freedoms that are here, because it affords an opportunity that is well within the grasp of every citizen, young and old, if he will undertake to apply himself to it.

AT GETTYSBURG
(Speech at Gettysburg, 1961)

43   ... What strange doubts assail this timid generation of today as it beholds the challenges to both liberty and equality. We seem beset with fear not faith, with doubt not confidence, with compromise not conviction, with dismay not dedication. We are drenched with the literature of fear and doubt. Survival has become the main theme. The fallout shelter from which the stars of hope and courage cannot be seen has become the symbol of our fears and misgivings.

Are we to become fearful, unworthy legatees in a blessed, united land where the earth is fertile to our every need, where the skills and ingenuity of men are boundless, where the burdens are bearable, where decent living is within the reach of all, and where the genius to produce is unlimited?

Perhaps we have lost our sense of continuity. Perhaps we have forgotten that we move in that same endless stream which began with our forefathers and which will flow on and on to embrace our children and our children's children. If we have, there will have gone with it that sense of individual responsibility which is the last best hope on which a nation conceived in liberty and dedicated to equality can long endure.

Comes then the reminder from the man from Illinois. Men died here and men are sleeping here who fought under a July sun that the nation might endure, united, free, tolerant, and devoted to equality. The task was unfinished. It is never quite finished.

ABRAHAM LINCOLN
(Speech at Springfield, Illinois, 1968)

44　On the night of Good Friday, 1865, he left us to join a blessed procession, in neither doubt nor fear, but his soul does indeed go marching on. For this was the Bible-reading lad come out of the wilderness, following a prairie star, filled with wonder at the world and its Maker, who all his life, boy and man, not only knew the Twenty-third Psalm but, more importantly, knew the Shepherd. Now, in 1968, it seems possible that we shall never see his like again. This is a sobering thought, but it should be a kindling one, for upon us now, as a people and a party, has been laid perhaps the greatest responsibility any nation was ever asked to shoulder, yet certainly not greater than we can bear. Our days are no longer than were Lincoln's, our nights are no darker, and if there is any difference between his time and this it lies in the tremendous advantage that is ours: that he stood so tall before us. In such a time and at such a moment we surely can say, then, from hopeful, brimful hearts:

We are standing, Father Abraham, devoted millions strong, firm in the faith that was yours and is ours, secure in the conviction bequeathed by you to us that right *does* make might and that if we but dare to do our duty as we understand it, we shall not only survive—we shall prevail.

SPEAKING TO THE DAUGHTERS OF THE AMERICAN REVOLUTION
(Washington, D.C., 1952)

45　Your organization is a far-flung group with an impressive membership. The communities whence you come are the true frontier of the Republic. As you return to your homes, it is there at the grass-roots level that the salvation of the Republic will be accomplished. For it is there in the hearts of the people that the Republic will live or die. It is there that the American dream will fade or be fulfilled.

TAKE IT STRAIGHT

46　I take my freedom straight. I am like little Johnny. His teacher asked him, "How do you spell 'straight'?" He said, "S-t-r-a-i-g-h-t." The teacher then asked, "What does it mean?" He said, "Without ginger ale." That is the way I take my freedom. I take it without ginger ale. I take it straight.

THE FLOWERS OF SPRING
(*Congressional Record,* 1969)

47 Long ago, the poet Shelley wrote, "O Wind,/If Winter comes, can Spring be far behind?"

It takes a careless spirit to write that, and today, in all the turmoil of our world, we would do well to take some moments to dream of careless things—like spring and marigolds and the other flowers that soon will come.

It is March. I look out the window and it is snowing, a wet kind of snow that clings to the branches like cotton and magnifies the appearance of winter. But I don't care, because on the desk before me is a chart of my garden and beside it are some seed catalogs—a feast for the eyes and the soul, too.

I wouldn't care at all about the bluster and cold of winter if I could only get results in my garden that would be something like the beauties painted by the seed-catalog artist.

Now I begin to think about my garden to come as I turn the pages of the catalog. First, I look out to a shady spot that gets little sun. It's a place for blue ageratum and impatiens because they do so well in full shade, and what a color combination they will be.

The humble nasturtium grows almost anywhere with half a chance—not a showy creation, but as cut flowers nasturtiums are a comfort indeed.

Now to the tulips, those dark-red, stately soldiers of the garden who defy the elements and come nosing out of the soil almost as soon as nature relents with the balmy breezes and the warm sun. How good it is that tulips come so early.

The daffodil and narcissus are not far behind. They can pop their gorgeous yellows before I expect it, and they are a joyous note in early spring.

Now I must leave the catalogs for a few moments to think of some other things in the garden. It's time to prune back the tea roses, cut away the dead wood and make ready for the grandeur of the roses in all their colors. Is there anything more beautiful than the rose?

Where do we put the snapdragons, which will stand like gorgeous sentinels against the roughest of weather and the bugs? The garden closest to the roadway is best, where every passerby can enjoy them. And snapdragons are exquisite as cut flowers for all occasions.

The zinnias must have full sun. Somehow, more than any other flower, the zinnias seem to drink in the bright sunlight and the heat and then are transformed into deep, majestic colors—peach, salmon, deep red, yellow, ivory—with huge many-petaled heads. But the zinnias should have some edging. The petunia is just the dish—singles and doubles, plain blue, white, crimson, peppermint-stick, candy-stripe in vast variety. How hardy they are and how determined not to be outdone.

Now a momentary detour to look at the climbing roses. They wintered well, but they must be tied up. What a rare diversion that will be after a day that has tried the soul and tired the mind.

Now here are the clematis, both regular and hybrid. How dead they seem. But wait a little while and suddenly they'll be there in the warming days in their red, white, and blue. All this and much more with the resurrection of spring.

Could the Resurrection have come in any season but spring? It makes me think of the question that Job in all his misery propounded to his friends: "If a man die, shall he live again?" He will, surely, for the earth becomes vital all over again with spring.

Most important of all, I must not forget the marigold. For ten years I have sought to persuade the Congress to adopt the marigold as our national floral emblem. Some prefer the rose (a shrub) or the carnation or the petunia, violet, daffodil, or some other bloom. But the marigold is native to this hemisphere and grows in every one of the fifty states, evidence of a robustness against the elements and insects that is unequaled in performance by any other flower.

Let kings and emperors, presidents and senators suffer highly important matters to furrow their brows. There must be a little time to draw back and just think about the noblest creations from the hand of a generous Creator—the endless variety of flowers.

Was it not the Galilean who said, "Consider the lilies of the field, how they grow; they toil not, neither do they spin: And yet I say unto you, That even Solomon in all his glory was not arrayed like one of these"?

And the flowers are there—for every man, woman, and child—for the asking.

ON FEDERAL SPENDING
48 Your representatives called on me and made very strong statements about federal spending and what I should do about it. . . . Now, I know there are eighty-five projects in the state of Illinois being supported by federal funds. I feel it would be most helpful if you would circularize your representatives and let them decide which ones they would like to have eliminated in order to carry out their express desire to cut federal spending.

THE INDIVIDUAL STATE
49 The Constitution guarantees every state a republican form of government. We have a republican form of government in this country, because it is representative. . . . That is the issue. It will not die. I do not propose to let it die.

I love this country. My parents came from the old country. I went to school in overalls. I lost my father at the age of five. Drew Pearson was right this morning when he referred to me as the driver of a bakery truck. Yes, I was.

Show me the country that will give any humble person the opportunity that this country does. I do not want it eroded; I do not want it soiled; I do not want it impaired. I want no court to destroy this great inheritance that has come from men who signed the Declaration of Independence, who vouchsafed to us the greatest government on the face of the earth, and for which, and because we hope to maintain its perpetuity, we have boys twelve thousand miles from home.

I say to senators—mark it well—"You have not heard the last of this." It will be tragic indeed when we have to campaign and say, "We are sorry; we tried to make you understand, but we could not," and so we can only say, "You do not love the people. You do not trust them."

May it never be said of me that I quailed in the endeavor to keep my trust in the people and keep intact the power which the people reserved to themselves in 1787, until they are prepared to forfeit it to the central government in Washington.

MORAL PRINCIPLES

50   There are some things you get with your mother's milk, and among them is the recognition of moral principles. . . . I come of immigrant stock. My mother stood on Ellis Island as a child of seventeen, with a tag around her neck directing that she be sent to Pekin, Illinois. My saintly mother helped build a church and then took her brood there. We had to walk two miles, and that is a long way for a youngster of three or four to toddle. You knew nothing about automobiles or conveyances, but there you learned prayer, and you learned it at your mother's knee and you learned it in school.

ABOUT SENATORS OUT CAMPAIGNING

51   What about those empty saddles in the New Frontier?

LEISURE TIME

52   If and when I find a little leisure time I will try to tell you how I deal with leisure time.

SPEAKING AT THE 1964 REPUBLICAN NATIONAL CONVENTION

53   Consider the moral courage of this humble peddler's grandson, Barry Goldwater. When a poll was taken some years ago to select five former senators whose portraits might adorn the unfilled ovals in the Senate reception room, those who participated selected Henry Clay and John C. Calhoun, Daniel Webster and Robert Marion La Follette and Robert A. Taft. Their common attribute was courage in facing the challenges of their day and time. Each took to heart the thunderous admonition of the Lord to Joshua as he took command of the ancient host: "Have I not commanded thee? Be strong and of good courage; be not afraid, neither be thou dismayed."

Already in twelve short years in the United States Senate, Barry Goldwater has repeatedly cast votes that won him no applause, that gained him nothing politically, that did nothing more than show the man's blazing courage in refusing to take the easy paths already so heavily trafficked by some of his colleagues. . . .

THE "TEXAS TWIST"
(*Congressional Record,* 1964)

54 We Republicans are very literal and, frequently, literate people. When we read perfectly plain English we are invariably led into taking it at face value. If we read that capital investment should be encouraged, that consumer purchasing power should be stimulated, that consumers should be protected, or, for example, that higher education should be encouraged, who can censure us—except possibly for our innocence—for believing that any proposals we might make to hasten these ends would not receive White House approval, even active support?

So perhaps you can imagine my bedridden amazement, my pajama-ruffled consternation, yes, my pill-laden astonishment, this week, to learn that three Republican-sponsored proposals to assist in achieving these laudable goals had been defeated by very narrow margins, victims of that new White House telephonic half nelson known as the "Texas twist."

To those of you on the Democratic side of the aisle who are still rubbing your bruised arms, I can only extend my sympathy and hope that you who must face the electorate this fall won't need them. To you on the Republican side of the aisle I happily extend my admiration and gratitude for the unanimous support you gave each of the three proposals. When Republicans stand together, without a single defector, on three crucial Senate votes, then the entire nation must know we were right.

THE BRAVE AND COURAGEOUS ASTRONAUTS
(*Congressional Record,* 1969)

55 Yesterday I had a chance to read Wordsworth's very gentle poem:

> The world is too much with us; late and soon,
> Getting and spending, we lay waste our powers . . .

When frustrations overwhelm me, then, of course, I have to turn elsewhere for a little comfort. I received inspiration for a little comfort this morning as that rocket started lunar bound, and I wondered what they would find.

Then I thought, well, it is all put down here somewhere, because in the very first chapter of Genesis it is recorded that:

> In the beginning God created the heaven and the earth.

Fortunately, Mr. President, the long arm of the Supreme Court has not yet reached into this chamber to interdict prayer, or to prevent one from reading from this majestic book:

And the earth was without form, and void; and darkness was upon the face of the deep. And the Spirit of God moved upon the face of the waters. . . .

And God said, Let the waters under the heaven be gathered together unto one place, and let the dry land appear: and it was so.

And God called the dry land Earth; and the gathering together of the waters called he Seas; and God saw that it was good.

And God said, Let the earth bring forth grass, the herb yielding seed, and the fruit tree yielding fruit after his kind, whose seed is in itself, upon the earth: and it was so. . . .

And God said, Let there be lights in the firmament—

This was what I was getting around to—

of the heaven to divide the day from the night; and let them be for signs, and for seasons, and for days, and years:

I do not know how long ago that was written, but you cannot improve on it, and no scientist has ever been able to improve on it.

And let them be for lights in the firmament of the heaven to give light upon the earth: and it was so.

And God made two great lights; the greater light to rule the day, and the lesser light to rule the night: he made the stars also.

And God set them in the firmament of the heaven to give light upon the earth,

And to rule over the day and over the night, and to divide the light from the darkness: and God saw that it was good.

They are proceeding on this missile program way out there, more than 214,000 miles. It is something whose creation was recorded when this book was compiled.

The thing that I was thinking about, Mr. President, as these brave and courageous astronauts left this globe, was just what they will find among other things? I had hoped that maybe out of it all there could come some truth about space and the interrelationships between all of these planets, even if they are inferior planets: Mars, Mercury, Venus, Jupiter, Saturn, Uranus, Pluto. They are all up there and they all have a strange relationship that the astronomers have pointed out. However, these men are going to the moon. They started this morning. Oh, what a body that really is! Is it all dust? Who knows? It may be impregnated with gold. We cannot tell.

They are going to bring back 180 pounds of material and distribute it to these laboratories. Maybe the rocks they bring back, Senator Byrd [of West Virginia], will somehow be loaded with diamonds. We cannot say, I do not know. However, I do know that that moon up there is a moving force that holds the water up against the earth when we have an ebb tide, and when it gets around and turns loose its attractive power, we get a flood tide.

If one wants to call up the Coast and Geodetic Survey, they can tell when the tide is coming in at Capetown, South Africa, ten years from now or longer, or when it is coming into Chesapeake Bay. It has all been worked out, and it works. That is the important thing.

If that moon were any closer, I expect those tides would engulf all of the land surface of the earth. And if it were farther away, we might be wanting for water.

If that sun were any closer, we would burn to a crisp. It would burn everything we grow, the flowers I raise, and the vegetables. And if it were much farther away, they would all freeze. So would we.

There is an amazing calibration in the whole universe. And so this morning as I watched—and I watched for as long as I could see it—I hoped that out of all this vast expenditure we could at long last develop some truths about these interplanetary relationships, the impact on our weather, the impact on our lives, and our impact on the moon.

TO SENATOR GEORGE MURPHY
(Conversation during the 1965 civil rights filibuster in the U.S. Senate)

56   Dirksen: "I want your vote and I need your vote."
Murphy: "No."
Dirksen: "You pray over it, George, and I'll pray over you."

GETTING RESULTS

57   I get a lot of mail from all over the nation, complaining that I'm too close and nice to the President. Well, when I'm called in by Mr. Johnson, what am I supposed to do? Carry a ball bat? I'm asking for something for my party when I go, and I seem to be getting results.

CRITICAL
(Press conference, 1966)

58   The . . . Administration has a remarkable collection of hummingbird economists who can reverse themselves without first stopping. They stand in midair while making motions in an attempt to confuse everyone that the government can spend for vast new domestic programs while at the same time supporting a war costing 25 billion dollars a year.

CONFUSION
(*Congressional Record,* 1951)

59   I remember some years ago a colleague of mine in the House of Representatives introduced a bill to amend the Constitution of the U.S. to provide for three vice-presidents. I used to josh him a good deal about it. In his proposal and in an explanatory note he set forth what the duties of the three vice-presidents should be. I said, "John, you ought to have made it four. I am more persuaded to that point of view today than ever before, because it has occurred to me that, as never before, we need a vice-president in charge of confusion. . . ."

Quite recently the distinguished senator from Minnesota said, "It is becoming clear to me that today the Democratic Party is becoming the peace party and unfortunately, under its present leadership, the Republican Party, the war party."

That represents such a confused state of mind—and I say this with the utmost charity in my heart—that probably confusion ought to be put under direction.

CHINA SHOP OF DIPLOMACY
(Radio-TV program, 1961)

60 We know that ——— was recently scheduled to be fired, but was not. We suggest that he be either completely muzzled or removed from the china shop of diplomacy lest he break something really costly.

TO HIS OWN PARTY
(Philadelphia, Pa., 1952)

61 I need but briefly sketch the forces which menace and threaten our Republic today. There is a fading faith in the moral integrity of the trustees who are now in power. We are threatened by the economic cancer of insolvency. There is the strange delusion of prosperity built on young blood and on the production of things with which to kill. New doctrines of power have arisen to flaunt the very document which Franklin helped prepare. There is the menace of back-door socialism in the form of controls. There are those sappers in the citadel who would subvert liberty from within. There are those commitments which hold forth promise of a kind of permanent war everywhere all of the time so long as a single aggressive force exists in the world. These are but some of the forces, subtle as autumn smoke, which are making inroads upon the Republic that has been entrusted to us.

In 1952, therefore, we raise our voices to ask, "Whence cometh salvation." We can drift as we have done in other days and go about saying that victory is in the bag. We can succumb to defeatism as so many have done. We can follow a line of expediency and seek to outlure and outpromise with political blandishments even as we have done in other days. On the other hand, we can do the noble thing. We can do the American thing. We can fight.

THE REPUBLICAN PARTY
(Washington, D.C., 1965)

62 Let me tell you about Nehemiah. He was a slave and he went to the king and said, "King, I've got a Western Union message that the walls around my home town of Jerusalem have fallen down. I would like to go back and, as a matter of pride, rebuild the wall." Why, the king gave him Cadillacs, gave him everything he wanted, gave him a guard. And so Nehemiah went off to Jerusalem. There were the hostile Samaritans trying to kill them off. He brought all the people together and said, "You work on the west wall; you work on the south wall; you work on the west

gate; you work on the north gate," organized them, and got the wall around that ancient city built. And when he got all through, he left a very short sentence on the parchments of history. He said, "So built we the wall, for the people had a mind to work."

You are the workers, and with you we will rebuild the wall in the tradition of the Republican Party and to the glory of this great Republic.

THE DEATH OF DWIGHT D. EISENHOWER
(*Congressional Record,* 1969)

63 To all that is mortal comes the day of dissolution. What comfort there is is in the fact that to the moment when the shadow of death hovered over him, he was lucid, peaceful, and ready. What counts now is the lesson of his life.

We refer to Washington as the Father of Our Country. Eisenhower was a father to the country. He came at a time when concern and ferment were everywhere. He came when an uneasy Nation needed him. In his touch was that magic balm to dissipate fear, to restore confidence, and to set the Nation on the high road again.

What words or what phrase best describes his impact on the people? I would have to say from my friendship with him that it was the "wholesome touch." Perhaps there are times when a nation needs brilliance in diplomacy, skill in administration, in-depth background on legislative needs. But there are also times when a nation needs an abiding father with the wholesome approach of a national leader, and this is precisely what he brought when it was needed.

Years ago, a senator said to me: "If there were no third-term limit, Eisenhower could be elected and reelected as long as he lived, because people believe in him."

To that I replied: "And because he believes in people."

Prior to World War II, he might have been considered just another among many officers in the U.S. Army. But there was a difference. He did his homework and he did it well. And when the time came to find a grand captain for the vast and serious task which confronted the world, he was ready. The military hierarchy, whose task it was to find an outstanding planner and tactician, made no mistake.

First he became the commander in chief of the U.S. forces in Europe. Later he became commander in chief of the Allied Forces in Africa. Later he became supreme commander of the Allied Expeditionary Forces.

It was all done with so little personal publicity. It was done without propaganda. It was not glory but victory that he sought.

How comparatively little we heard about his rescue of Africa from British disaster. How little we heard about his healing touch in dissipating the fear and gloom in Britain after the tragic retreat to Dunkirk. Only when he mounted the grand assault from the beaches of Normandy did we hear much of him. Eleven months later the enemy surrendered.

I was privileged to be present at the Thanksgiving service in Rheims, France. It was the day after victory. I saw him there. But I also saw something else—humble people, kneeling in church, expressing their gratitude for victory and their appreciation for his services and leadership.

It was not so strange that a grateful people in this land should turn to him in time of peace for guidance and leadership. . . . So from supreme commander he became President and Commander in Chief of the Armed Forces of the United States. It was not so much some vast, undisclosed administrative talent which endeared him to the people, but the rightness of his outlook, his humane views, his compassionate heart, and his dedication to the cause of peace. . . .

This—all this—is a monument to the universality of mind and heart and spirit of one who in our time achieved greatness without losing his humility, who was loyally served because he was esteemed, and who found a place deep in the throbbing hearts of Americans and the world because they loved him.

TO THE WOMEN

64 . . . an ancient lawgiver in Greece once observed: "Greece rules the world, Athens rules Greece, I rule Athens, and my mother rules me."

ADDRESSING A WOMEN'S GROUP

65 Girls . . . I'm a little breathless this morning . . . who wouldn't be with all this loveliness and all this grace.

FILIBUSTERS

66 Extended periods of expression which somehow made it difficult to secure action on a bill . . .

A METAPHOR

67 That idea has as much effect as a snowflake on the bosom of the Potomac.

CRITICAL

68 . . . the Administration goes its higgledy-piggledy way, its high priests no longer the flower of American culture who pursue domestic social progress with the pop-eyed ardor of a Harpo Marx chasing blondes.

BRIEF OBSERVATIONS

69 The senator is the victim of a fortuity. I shall invoke upon him every condign imprecation.

Never pound on the desk too hard; you may hurt yourself.

BROKEN THIGHBONE

70 If I have to, I can use the crutches for weapons. . . . The Bible says Samson slew the Philistines with a jawbone of an ass. . . . I may have to slay an ass with the jawbone of a crutch.

TRADITION

71 A great part of me has gone into that record [Gallant Men]. I think I would die unhappy unless I made some contribution to putting America, particularly young America, back into the stream of tradition.

A MINORITY LEADER

72 I've only got thirty-three soldiers, the Democrats have sixty-seven. That's why this Administration has legislative indigestion.

THE DIRKSEN PHILOSOPHY
(Printed material in the Senator's office)

73 He [Dirksen] believes in private enterprise as the keystone of our economic system and is steadfastly committed to fighting for sound fiscal policies which will ensure and preserve the solvency of the nation. He is a dedicated foe of paternalistic "big brother" type of government, believing—as did Lincoln—that it is the function of government to do for the individual only what he cannot do for himself.

SENATOR DIRKSEN ON DOUGLAS

74 First, indulge me for a moment while I throw a little salute to my distinguished colleague, Paul Douglas. Probably nobody campaigned any harder for my defeat than Paul Douglas but he did so honorably and he did so fairly, and so, while we have differences of opinion, I do salute him as a great statesman and as a forthright American citizen. . . .

AMERICAN WOMEN

75 American women, by and large, have every lovely and charming attribute that a mother, wife, and lady should have. They are the best looking, best dressed, best mannered, most efficient and businesslike women in the world. What's more, they have the best taste in hats.

COMPROMISE

76 There are times when the middle of the road is the proper course to pursue and especially so in view of the extreme thinking with which one must contend both left and right. I am afraid some of my friends forget that my job as party leader is to bring about a maximum of agreement between the extremes in the party. Has it ever occurred to you how far apart Senator Goldwater on the one hand and Senator Javits on the other really are, yet both are voting Republicans in the Senate?

PERSPECTIVE

77 With regard to the editorial in *The New York Times*, I determined long ago that those who would serve their country and their constituents to the best of their ability cannot afford the luxury of undue sensitivity to attacks of this nature, but must content themselves with the knowledge that Father Time and the history books will be the best and ultimate judges of their motives and ability.

EXPECTATIONS

78 I don't just want him here. I want him here in a good frame of mind, prepared to do a good job on the machine.

THE POVERTY PROGRAM
(*Congressional Record,* 1965)

79 . . . I am ready, as the great Bard has said, to accept all the slings and arrows of outrageous fortune. I am ready to accept the criticism. I am ready to have people say, "You are against the poor." The only answer I shall have is: I am not against the poor. I was impoverished once, without a father, and the best that I could do was to go to school in overalls, and to work, peddling milk, berries, fruit, and honey from the bees I kept, in order to keep the family going. I will vote it, but I will never vote it for this kind of program.

FIFTY-FIFTY

80 I attended some meetings here this morning, and they left the question with me: "Couldn't we get a little more money out of the Federal Treasury?" even though the matching basis was ninety versus ten —ninety U.S.; ten percent local.

That's the old story of one-horse rabbit sandwiches. You remember that fellow making rabbit sandwiches, and when the Pure Food collared him he said, "That's easy—one horse, one rabbit: fifty-fifty."

CIVIL RIGHTS
(*Congressional Record,* 1957)

81 There has to be a force behind all these developments. What is the force? There has to be a pervading conscience. If I did not believe history was the unfolding of a divine history, I would resign at once from the Senate; and that remark is no pleasantry. But I have a deep conviction that the whole unfolding is according to the great design and plan of the Great Architect. That is the way I interpret the history of our times. If that is a firm conviction and conclusion—and it is—then there has to be a great force behind that development. William James, the philosopher, once used the term "stubborn and irreducible facts." One can never escape them.

So, regardless of the speeches, what we are dealing with here today will continue to roll into law, because a moral and ethical consideration is involved; and all the speeches, all the obstruction, all the efforts to stop it, will not prevail, because we are dealing with human beings. Though their color may be black, I cannot imagine for a moment that they were not endowed with a spirit and a soul, just as is every other human being under the canopy of God's blue heaven. So you see we are dealing with something that is probably a divine force. It is not going to be stopped. It may be stopped now, but it will roll because we are dealing with people, all the people of this country.

BLINDNESS
(Comments on his visit to Johns Hopkins Hospital, 1948)

82   I got down on my knees in the aisle and asked God if blindness was to be my lot. If so, I intended to ask Him for the strength to bear it. But the answer came back unmistakably "No." Later that day when doctors urged that I submit to surgery, I told them, "I guess not. Another doctor advises against it." The Big Doctor upstairs—and the answer is no.

ASKING FOR SUPPORT OF A BILL
(U.S. Senate, 1960)

83   Was it not Solomon who pleaded with the Lord for understanding? The Lord said, "Ask and I shall give thee." Solomon said, "Give therefore thy servant an understanding heart."

Have an understanding heart.

TRADITIONS
(Washington, D.C., 1965)

84   And one thing that we ought to remember, I believe, as members identified with a common party, is our traditions. I hope he puts that in the paper, whoever wrote that [newspaper article], because I'm quite satisfied with what that greatest of all salesmen who ever lived, the Apostle Paul, wrote in one of his letters to the Thessalonians, the people living in Thessalonica long, long ago. He said: ". . . stand fast, and hold the traditions which ye have been taught. . . ." If you want to put it down and read it, Second Thessalonians, chapter 2, verse 15. Hold fast to the traditions ye have been taught.

CHERISHED SCRIPTURE

85   One of my most cherished verses comes from the Epistle of James, fifth chapter, sixteenth verse and reads as follows: "Confess your faults one to another, and pray one for another, that ye may be healed. The effectual fervent prayer of a righteous man availeth much."

SPOKEN AT A MEMORIAL SERVICE
(Washington, D.C., 1965)

86   The work of the Great Designer cannot be destroyed by fire, for that but transmutes what man put together into other forms such as light, heat, energy, and gases. Not by earthquakes, which but tumble man's work, but do not destroy the elemental substance. Not by storms and tidal waves, which only rearrange what the Great Designer placed here. In autumn the gaily colored leaves fall gently on earth, not to be destroyed but to be embraced by nature for future use. From the hand of the Great Designer comes the inevitable caress of spring to bring life and color and fragrance and beauty to the eager earth.

It is the resurrection of spring. It is an answer to the ageless question of Job. "If a man die, shall he live again? Surely he shall, as surely as day follows night, as surely as the stars follow their courses, as surely as the crest of every wave brings its trough."

GOD CREATED MAN
(Congressional Record, 1965)

87   Then came the only creature that was created with intelligence, a soul, a personality, the prospect of divinity. There he was, this lonely creature. He had a beautiful home, if a garden can be called a home. God made it without the aid of the Housing Administration. They were not even around then.

THE COUNTRYSIDE
(Radio-TV program, 1967)

88   Have you noticed how lovely the countryside really is in this autumn season? There's a lot of color in the trees, particularly the hardwoods, and the farmsteads look so nice, so comfortable, and so clean. Sheds are usually painted, so is the farmhouse. Cattle are grazing, either milk cows or beef cattle, some sheep perhaps and certainly hogs out in our area, and then chickens and a vegetable garden and a flower garden, which, of course, is that lovely final note of beauty. But the countryside is as lovely as it can be and it's something of a tonic to just drive around and muse a little about things that are particularly rural.

I've said to myself on occasion, this is the life. After all, you want a chicken for the table, you go out and grab one of your own chickens. You want meat, well, butcher a calf and you've got all the veal you want, some that you can store in the refrigerator or deep freeze. You want a hog, well, it's there to be butchered. And then, of course, those succulent hams and juicy pork chops and pork loins. Makes your mouth water, doesn't it? Then you've got a vegetable garden and there's everything, carrots, red beets, cabbage, just anything you can name. Well, isn't that the life? What more do you want?

MEMORIES

89   Mr. President, I suppose about five or six weeks from now the delicate color of the bluebells will be manifest in the timber again; and I suppose that I live in memory of the days when, as a youngster, I used to go into the woods and dig up devil-in-the-bandbox and jack-in-the-pulpit. It will be that season of the year when we shall be observing the sixth anniversary of V-Day. . . .

UNDER POLICE GUARD AFTER A THREAT

90   I didn't want anybody to blow my head off, because the flowers were in bloom and they needed me. I told the sheriff that whoever this creature was, I hoped he would wait till the frost came and the barn swallows had gone.

FLOWERS

91 Let us consider the gentle, multicolored pansies. They can be planted in the winter; and when spring comes, after the winter has ended, we find them with their beautiful dainty heads, helping to beautify the world. Then there is the daffodil, a hardy flower. I remember the little ode by Wordsworth: "Ten thousand saw I at a glance/Tossing their heads in sprightly dance." The dahlias always entrance the eye; but one must be careful lest the tiny shoots of the dahlias come up before the frost ends, in which case it is necessary to do the work all over again. . . .

COMMENCEMENT ADDRESS
(Hanover College, 1965)

92 I had only one graduation while I did my undergraduate work at the University of Minnesota. I was not allowed to finish and I never did participate in commencement. [He received a law degree in Washington.] There was a fellow named Uncle Sam who was operating an involuntary institution called the army and he thought I would look awfully good in an olive-drab Easter suit, and as a result I came out of school, so that the only commencement that I had was high school. I was the salutatorian. I do not know what kind of world-shaking speech I made that day, I've forgotten it. Our commencement speaker was a local judge. One other fact I remember about it: it was the first time I ever wore a tailored suit. I also had on a boiled shirt and we held our commencement in the opera house. Those were the days when we still had opera houses. I have forgotten what the judge said on that occasion, but I do remember the title and the only reason I remember the title is that it contained a word that I could not pronounce. The title was "The Vicissitudes of Life" and I could not say "vicissitude." I'm not sure that I can say it today, but that's all that I remember and so I suppose that today I ought to be heavy and bring you an urgent message. Perhaps I ought to talk about the age of reason or enthusiasm for humanity or a crisis in my mental history. Wouldn't you love to hear me talk for an hour and fifteen minutes on that subject? But frankly, I am not going to do so, nor is this going to be too long because I want you to enjoy it. So after a search, I picked out a very intriguing title: "The Next Twenty Thousand Days." That has abundant latitude and I like subjects with latitude.

JOHN F. KENNEDY
(Congressional Record, 1963)

93 . . . In this moment when death has triumphed, when hearts are chastened, when the spirit reels in sheer bewilderment, what do we say, now that the book of life has been closed?

Let me say what we have always said when he was alive, gay, happy, friendly, ambitious, and ready to listen.

He had vision that went beyond our own. His determination to effectuate a test-ban treaty is a living example.

He was his own profile in courage. His unrelenting devotion to equality and civil rights attests that fact. He was devoted to our system of constitutional government. His attitude toward the separation of church and state looms like a shining example. He had the great virtue of spiritual grace. If at any moment he may have seemed frustrated over a proposition, it was so transitory. If he showed any sign of petulance, it was so fleeting. There were no souring acids in his spirit. If, at any moment, he may have seemed overeager, it was but the reflection of a zealous crusader and missioner who knew where he was going. If, at any moment, he seemed to depart from the covenant which he and his party made with the people, it was only because he believed that accelerated events and circumstances did not always heed the clock and the calendar. If his course sometimes seemed at variance with his own party leaders or with the opposition, it was only because a deep conviction dictated his course. . . .

HARRY S. TRUMAN'S EIGHTY-FIFTH BIRTHDAY
(*Congressional Record,* 1969)

94 Yesterday I dispatched a telegram to the Honorable Harry S. Truman at Independence, Missouri. I wished him well on his eighty-fifth birthday anniversary, which is today, and also expressed my good wishes to his beloved wife, Bess.

I have always felt that Mr. Truman was one of those incredibly colorful Americans who became something of an institution in public life.

When I decided to quit the House of Representatives because of eye difficulties, I determined that I was not going to leave Washington until I had gone to the White House and said good-bye to President Truman. The White House told me that he was busy. I said, "Yes, I know." His secretary, Matt Connelly, said, "I can only give you a minute or two to see him."

"Well," I said, "I'll wait, Matt. I'll stay a month, if necessary, to see him."

He said, "Could you come next Tuesday?"

I said, "Yes, I'll be here."

I went to the White House on Tuesday, and President Truman and I spent a most delightful hour. He was not too busy, and I was not too busy. Thus, we leisurely enjoyed ourselves.

He said, "You should not have quit. We need you around here."

"Well," I said, "Mr. President, I have got to do those things which are conducive to a recovery of my vision."

We left it at that. I went home to convalesce and see what the fates had in store for me.

At long last, as a result of a good deal of urging, I found myself in the middle of a senatorial race. Just before the campaign wound up, President Truman came to St. Louis, Missouri. He had a network hookup to speak, and that night he paid his respects to me, but not quite in the way I wanted it, because I was running against his majority leader. I think at one point he referred to me as "that thing over in Illinois."

I saw him about three weeks later in Chicago, Illinois, because he had accepted Mayor Daley's invitation to come to a party at the Edgewater Beach Hotel. I must say for the distinguished mayor of Chicago that he always invites me, too, and I always go—although my opposite number in the Senate at that time did not show up. But I went.

While we were making merry and having some fun, through the back door came President Truman. I was the first one he encountered. He said, "Well, Dirksen, how are you?" "Oh," I said, "Mr. Truman, I am fine." He said, "What have you got in your hand?" I said, "That's an old-fashioned." He said, "I'll have one." So before he got through shaking hands with everyone else, we began to visit a little.

I said, "Mr. President, you not only interest me, you also intrigue me. You are a most colorful human being, the peppery way in which you always address yourself to the business in hand. Remember, I said good-bye to you at the White House a few years ago, and you said we need you around here and I should not quit, and now when I find myself confronting your own majority leader from my state, you put me in a slightly different cast."

He said to me, "Well, now, Dirksen, what do you think I should have done under the circumstances?"

"Well," I said, "Mr. President, you should have done exactly what you did do, because I am in the enemy camp, so to speak, and you would have no business giving me any quarter."

As Shakespeare wrote in the tragedy of *Macbeth:* "Lay on, Macduff,/ And damned be him that first cries 'Hold, enough!' "

"Mr. President," I said further, "you are worthy of any foeman's steel. I salute you."

So, Mr. Truman, I wish you long years of health and of felicity, as well as your family, because you are, indeed, a colorful figure in the contemporary scene.

CLOSING A SPEECH

95 I think we ought to come to a termination here on a gently high and felicitous note.

FIGURES

96 . . . hallucinatory estimates for masquerade and mirage in an extravaganza of political chicanery . . .

WASHINGTON

97   Let me welcome you to your Capital, let me bid you welcome to the Federal City, let me bid you welcome to the Capital of the World . . . and to the financial center of the world . . . because it's to this city that all the countries of the world repair with their tin cups. This is the home of planned deficit. Deficits used to occur, but they were never planned . . . today they're planned. This is presently the home of confusion of the calculated type, this is the land of a hundred billion budgets, this is the laboratory where all things happen.

PRAYER

98   Is there anything more ennobling than prayer? A New York court forbade two young children to say in school: "God is great, God is good, and we thank Him for this food." What are we coming to?

GIVE GOD A LITTLE ALSO

99   Now, already, problems are developing with respect to the treatment of Christmas, Santa Claus, Christmas decorations, Christmas carols, the Nativity scene and everything pertinent to Christmas.

In a suburban school district just outside Pittsburgh, where they planned to use the Nativity scene in a public school, they went down to see an attorney to get an opinion. Finally, his opinion was, "Well, it will be all right if you present it in a cultural vein."

How in God's name do we present the manger in a cultural vein and have any significance left?

How ludicrous, how stupid, how silly are they getting, those destroyers who want to destroy the religious traditions of this country?

Interest is mounting in this matter of prayer in the public schools, and it will continue to mount. If I have anything to do with it, it will escalate and mount even faster. . . . It will not be stopped by the social engineers, by the world-savers, by the cynics, or by some professor—that strange kind of liberal who is bemused by the idea of prayer in public schools, where pupils and students spend more of their waking hours than they do at home or in the church combined.

In various parts of the country, teachers are now asserting the right to eliminate from the Pledge of Allegiance the words "under God." . . .

The question has been raised concerning the propriety of having prayer aboard United States vessels.

One school board felt that to have an invocation or a benediction at a graduation exercise came within the ban.

Pupils in one Long Island school have refused to join in the Pledge of Allegiance on the ground that it has become meaningless by repetition.

Flying a pennant containing the words "One Nation Under God" over a municipal building in New Jersey has been regarded as open to legal attack.

I think of the children, the millions whose souls need the spiritual rehearsal of prayer.

Right now we are in the football season. . . . Imagine the Chicago Bears football team, made up of green, inexperienced, unpracticed, and unrehearsed players, undertaking a game against the Cleveland Browns. It would be unthinkable because they have not been disciplined by practice. The soul needs practice too. It needs rehearsal. . . .

Prayer is a road map to God. It should become the greatest adventure for young minds. Each must find the way for himself. This takes some doing . . . the development of right habits, the building of spiritual muscle. This can come only from practice and rehearsal day after day when young minds are alert.

How strange that we spend hundreds of millions in public funds every year to develop physical fitness and harden the muscles of American youth, but when it comes to hardening the spiritual muscles through the practice and rehearsal of prayer, it becomes enshrouded in quaint legalism and the jargon of "church and state."

Mr. President, I finish by saying: Give Caesar what he requires, but give God a little also.

NAME CALLING
(Congressional Record, 1966)

100   Mr. President, I like George Meany. He is a nice fellow. I also like Mrs. Meany. She is a charming person. Mrs. Dirksen likes her also. We meet often at dinner. We met at the Touchdown Club recently. He was on the program, but for reasons unknown to me we were not introduced. We did not have to be, of course. But I am always glad to acknowledge him, to acknowledge what he has done for labor and labor organizations in the country. But Mr. Meany, like many other people, can be fallible; he can be wrong.

I remember from my college days what Sir Richard Steele said about the Church of England and the Church of Rome in one of his essays: "The one is infallible and the other is never wrong." One cannot quite claim that for an individual, and so he can be wrong. I tried to make it plain that this was a matter of principle and that I thought we had the people on our side. But people are being called names. Anybody can call one a name, but that does not make him what he is called. Mr. Meany called me a windbag. He called me other things too. It does not make me a windbag.

I am reminded of a story that Mr. Lincoln used to tell about two men who were arguing and fussing. Finally one of the men said, "If you call a sheep's tail a leg, how many legs does that sheep have?" He said, "Five." The friend said, "Oh, no. Calling a sheep's tail a leg does not make it a leg." And calling me a name does not make me that.

PUBLIC SPEAKING

101 I was compelled to school myself over the years to speak without manuscript and without notes. The books that have had a durable impact on my career include the Bible, the essays of Ralph Waldo Emerson, the essays of Henry David Thoreau, a good many biographies of American enterprisers and statesmen, and then, of course, the many things which have been written on the life of Abraham Lincoln since he practiced law and initiated his campaign from Springfield, Illinois, about sixty miles from where I live.

Techniques of effective speech are not remote, mysterious, or complicated. A speaker should behave not only as if he enjoyed making a speech, but as if he had a conviction with respect to the subject which he is discussing. His material should be well organized and drive directly to the central aim or point in view. This means that diversions and digressions should be eliminated unless they take the form of a surefire anecdote if he is beginning to lose his audience.

SPEECH NOTES

102 I've scribbled a few notes on this and out of it will come thousands of words. I wonder what they will be.

TO STRIVE AFTER AN IDEAL

103 Man's nobility, his success if you will, comes, I think, with his determination to try, his willingness to strive after an ideal. Resolve, young man, early in life what you want your purpose to be, then walk steadfastly toward that goal. Most men do not accomplish all that they would like to have in life. Had they been able to, their aims would not have been high enough. Remember the line by Robert Browning: "The aim, if reached or not, makes great the life."

WHEN CIVIL RIGHTS LEGISLATION WAS MOVING SLOWLY
(U.S. Senate, 1962)

104 I remember the old ditty, "The King of France with twenty thousand men/Went up the hill, and then came down again." I have marched up the hill many times; I have marched down. God willing, if I am alive long enough, I suppose I will march up the hill again and march back down again. But when I reach the bottom of the hill, I will still be looking at the summit to see where I rightfully belong.

LONG HOURS IN THE SENATE

105 The flesh rides herd on the spirit. Sooner or later I'm going to have to lie down and let Morpheus embrace me.

TO SENATOR MANSFIELD

106 Give us some comfort and solace in this Easter season, when the joys of spring are everywhere and the delights of the cherry blossoms

somehow tantalize the eye as the swelling buds burst forth into life and the jonquils, the tulips, and the hyacinths spring forth in all their glory.

THE OBJECTIVE

107 When you speak, you're striving for an end. It may be persuasion for a vote. Sometimes a flight of Shakespearean fancy helps to nurse it along. Then you move in for the kill.

LYNDON BAINES JOHNSON
(*Congressional Record,* 1969)

108 When Lyndon Baines Johnson leaves the nation's capital we shall miss him. He will also miss us. He will miss the familiar scenes. He will miss the legislative battlefield. He will miss the give and take of everyday life where government is involved.

Probably no President had so good a combination of physical drive and conviction on big matters as Lyndon Johnson. I have known him for thirty-four years.

I remember when this lanky man from Texas, perhaps hardly a man but a stripling boy, was a doorkeeper on the third floor of the House of Representatives. I had been elected to Congress.

He became a secretary to a congressman. When a vacancy developed, he became a candidate for Congress, and he won. Then, through the years, by a very narrow margin, he won the senatorship, then the vice-presidency, and finally the presidency.

There was an amazing consistency in his course, always with that relentless drive to get things done, but in all the give and take, all the caterwauling, and all the fussing, fretting, and stewing, he never lost sight of the fact that the Senate had to be a viable working institution and that it was our duty, as officeholders, to make it that way; and we tried to do so.

Sometimes we had some rather heavy words over the issues that confronted us from time to time. Those were not just manifestations of an unhealthy spleen; they reflected, after all, a deep conviction in the matter that was before us and how it might affect the welfare of this great, free country.

He had going with him one circumstance that probably was not true of any other President. Having served in the House and in the Senate, when the leadership of his party went to consult with him he probably had served with everybody in that leadership. When the joint leadership was asked to come and consult he had served with everybody in the joint leadership.

I recall on one occasion at the White House when the joint leadership was present, starting with that great patriarch from Arizona, Carl Hayden. I took account of everybody who was there and I think every one of them had served with the President either in the House of Representatives or in the Senate. That imparted a kind of camaraderie in those meetings and it had this blessed effect: Everybody and anybody could and did speak freely on any subject that developed. That was a wholesome situation and it was in the interest of our country.

No matter where he may roam, whether it be in academic and professorial halls, or whether it be out on the ranch, or any other place, he will doubtless keenly miss this center of the universe, Washington, D.C., where he spent so much of his life. I can only say hail and farewell, and God speed.

WELCOMING THE NEW VICE-PRESIDENT
(*Congressional Record*, 1965)

109 Only a few days ago it was my privilege to present the distinguished Vice-President-elect to a national convention at the Statler Hotel. I was advised that I might begin my speech, and that I would be interrupted when he arrived. The signal was to be that the chairman would pull my coattails to announce the fact that the Vice-President-elect had arrived.

When he appeared, I looked at his audience and said, "Ladies and gentlemen, permit me to split an infinitive and let a participle hang from the air for a moment while I present the distinguished Vice-President-elect of the United States."

His good fortune has been our good fortune. By electing him to office, we have now shorn him of a good deal of authority. His principal function now will be to break a tie—if ever there is a tie in a body having a ratio of 2 to 1.

AS CONGRESS ADJOURNED
(*Congressional Record*, 1960)

110 Old faces go and new faces come, but somehow, like Tennyson's brook, the free Republic continues to go on with vitality, vigor, and an energized faith, as it moves to newer heights and newer achievements for its people in the great moral climate of freedom. As I think of the word "friend," I recall that all the really great things in life and all the great impelling forces are expressed in the simplest words—"God," "love," "child," "friend." Those are words of one syllable, but they are the great words. Those are the great compelling symbols that somehow move us on, and the word "friend" stands out majestically as we think of ourselves in this chamber dedicated to great and common purposes, and how easily we adjust because the friendship is deeper and it is greater than any other force that we encounter.

Notwithstanding that friendship, in due course I shall go back to the hustings, and in the nature of things I shall have to recite all of the sins of those on the other side of the aisle. I shall recite the sins of omission and the sins of commission. Tomorrow I shall examine the *Record* fervently and earnestly to see what my distinguished friend Lyndon did not say and what he did say. The result of that study must necessarily then become the basis for some of the utterances that I am expected to make on the platform.

But I wish to say to the majority leader and all senators that whatever our utterances may be, they shall not be tainted with malice. They will be fair. But I assure the Senate they will be vigorous. They will be equitable, but I can assure the Senate they will be aggressive.

I wish our distinguished compatriots who seek higher political estate everything good—up to a point. I have always been amazed to see what a difference sixteen blocks can make. I extend the senators who are candidates the warm hand of fellowship. We want to keep them here. I want to keep them here. It would be lonesome without my distinguished friend the majority leader, and my distinguished friend from Massachusetts, with whom it has been my honor and pleasure to work on the Senate Labor Committee. My affection is as high as the sky and it is as deep as the sea—and I do not want sixteen blocks to intervene. We shall be charitable and gracious, there will be no malice; but we will pursue our responsibilities as an opposition party and do our best. . . .

To my distinguished friend the majority leader, I say it has been a great pleasure to serve with him. When it has become my disagreeable duty to take him to task, I have always warned him in advance. I would go to his office and drink Sanka with him. Certainly I do not intend a TV plug, but even at the risk of being commercial, I must say I have never found too much inspiration in Sanka. On those occasions I would tell him that it had become my duty and responsibility to take him to task, and even though the voice might reach an upper register, and I might brandish my arms and make it appear that I was fairly suffused with ire and anger, he knew better. Then if, peradventure, the scene appeared on the front page of a newspaper and his beloved wife, Lady Bird, would say, "I thought Everett Dirksen was your friend?" he always had the right answer. He said, "Oh, that was prearranged." . . .

I shall see some of you in your respective states. When I come, I shall be kind. I shall call you up on the telephone when I arrive. I shall say, "I am in town." You will say, "Yes, I saw it in the newspapers." I shall say, "I am delighted to see you and I hope we can have a chance to visit." You will say, "I wish you well in everything except the mission that brings you here."

That is another part of the greatness of this country. So, *au revoir*. We shall see you on the home diamond somewhere; and when it is all over, on the morning of November 9, all the healing waters will somehow close over our dissidence, and we shall go forward as a solid phalanx once more.

RESPECT

111   I make it a point never to demean any man, no matter what kind of bloke he is.

STAND UP AND BE COUNTED

112   This is not a financial question. This is a moral question. We must stand up and be counted in our generation. It does not make any difference what the mail from back home says.

FAITH IN THE PRESIDENT

113   We had some faith in Dwight Eisenhower. And I have not forfeited my faith in John Fitzgerald Kennedy. I am willing always to trust the President because I think he has a sense of responsibility.

ON A SENATOR'S CRITICISM OF THE PRESIDENT
(*Congressional Record,* 1957)

114   I hope that we can be a little more circumspect in the way in which we talk about one another. We can speak and still maintain the intensity of our political disagreements. But to do so does not call for personal castigation or reflection upon character. I can only hope, out of a sense of pain and distress, rather than anger, that we can watch our tongues and make certain that false impressions are not created abroad, impressions which can do no good to the esteem of this country, its people, or its noble and beloved leader.

LEADERSHIP
(*Congressional Record,* 1963)

115   At the outset, let me say that I shall support the treaty. It is no easy vote. In my office are probably forty thousand letters, and on my Capitol desk are petitions containing ten thousand names in opposition to the treaty. But I must equate those against the whole number of electors in my state. Moreover, I have admonished them over and over again that, regardless of the entreaties and presentations that have been made to me, I feel that I must follow a type of formula laid down by Edmund Burke, the great parliamentarian . . . , when he said it was his business to consult with his people, but it would be a betrayal of his conscience and a disservice to them if he failed to exercise his independent judgment.

So today my statement that I shall support the treaty is an exercise of my independent judgment based upon what I think is best for my country. . . .

WHAT IS BEST

116   I believe perhaps Shakespeare was essentially correct when he said in *Hamlet:* "There's a divinity that shapes our ends,/Rough-hew them how we will."

He might well have used the word "destiny." This could be, conceivably, a time of destiny for the country and for the world. Who am I to judge? Time and history will have to render that judgment. But this is an important matter that engrosses our attention. I pray that I may be on the right side. I accept this assignment, and I accept the responsibility for my vote with a sense of gravity and concern. . . .

I said to my people, I said to the country publicly, and I said in the press gallery that I would take a hard look at the treaty. I said I would be diligent in examining its every implication, and that there would be only one standard by which to come to a vote, and that would be: what is best for the present and for the future of the United States of America, which has been so good to me as a citizen.

ON THE NUCLEAR TEST-BAN TREATY
(U.S. Senate, 1963)

117 Late the other night I went back to refresh myself on a little history. One of the classic reports made in our generation was the one made by John Hersey, to *The New Yorker*, on what happened at Hiroshima. It makes one think. It came as an account from a Japanese preacher who long ago was educated at Emory University in Atlanta, Georgia. He did his undergraduate work there and developed great fluency in English. He was one of the principal witnesses when John Hersey went to Hiroshima to write that almost deathless account.

The B-29s had bombed nearly every Japanese town except Kyoto and Hiroshima. The Japanese called the B-29 "Mr. B," out of respect for the might and the power of that great wartime bomber. As he relates the story, it was 8:15 in the morning of a bright, sunny day. The weather was a little humid and warm. At 8:15, things happened. Out of the 20th Air Wing, Colonel Paul W. Tibbetts, Jr., flying that B-29, and with two escort observation planes, flew over the center of Hiroshima, a town of probably 375,000 persons. Then, for the first time, the whole bosom of God's earth was ruptured by a man-made contrivance that we called a nuclear weapon.

Oh, the tragedy. Oh, the dismay. Oh, the blood. Oh, the anguish. When the statisticians came to put the cold figures on paper, they were as follows: As a result of one bomb—66,000 killed; 69,000 injured; 62,000 structures destroyed. That was the result of that one bomb, made by man in the hope of stopping that war. Little did he realize what this thermonuclear weapon would do, and the anguish that would be brought into the hearts of men, women, and children. At Hiroshima it caused a mass incineration such as never before had been witnessed in the history of the whole world. The result was almost too catastrophic to contemplate. In the accelerated march of history, how quickly we forget. But there is the account, for all to read; and it all happened at 8:15, on a bright and shining morning, when God's day began, and when, I suppose, hundreds of thousands of people were thinking that, despite the war, they had been privileged to live another day.

Mr. President, that happened eighteen years ago last month. Since then, what have we done? What steps have we taken? How far have we moved? The President calls this treaty a first step. What sort of steps have we taken, except steps to make the bombs that fell on Hiroshima and Nagasaki look like veritable toys when compared to the heavy-duty, heavy-yield weapons of today?

I want to take a first step, Mr. President. I am not a young man; I am almost as old as the oldest member of the Senate, certainly I am older than a great many senators. One of my age thinks about his destiny a little. I should not like to have written on my tombstone, "He knew what happened at Hiroshima, but he did not take a first step." . . . "The longest journey begins with a single step." This is a first, single step. It is for destiny to write the answer. It is for history to render judgment. But with consummate faith and some determination, this may be the step that can spell a grander destiny for our country and for the world. If there be risks, Mr. President, I am willing to assume them for my country. So I support the treaty; and I will vote for approval of the treaty with no reservations whatsoever.

THE WPA
(U.S. Senate, 1965)

118 It is too bad that one has a memory of things in this town. I was in the House of Representatives when we approved the Works Progress Administration—WPA. They had everything. Finally, they decided something had to be done for unemployed actors and actresses and singers and people in the performing arts, and that got them started. They did it in tents throughout the country. I remember when they came to Peoria, in my country. There they were putting on popular plays. Guess what was the really popular play then? In the University of Michigan there was a playwright by the name of Avery Hopwood, I believe. The really popular play at that time was entitled *Getting Gertie's Garter*. So they played it all over the country. The second most popular one was *Up in Mabel's Room*. That was entrancing for rural audiences. They did not know what to make of this business. I do not know how much money we spent on it, but they had to be employed, and that is how we wasted our money.

Then, for good measure, we decided to employ all the artists in the country—good, bad, and indifferent. I am not much of an artist, but I know art when I see it. I remember the little sticker someone put across a work of art in a London museum: "Don't touch with a cane." Some wag added the words: "Use an ax." He had a better appreciation of art than probably some of the other people did.

WHY POLITICIANS HEDGE

119 A man might say, "I apprehend from a certain feeling in my bones that there is a possibility of rain tomorrow." If it doesn't rain, you can't say to him, "That just shows what a bum forecaster you are!"

HIS SECOND RECORD
(Weekly radio-TV report, 1967)

120 Almost immediately thereafter there came a request for another record and this was the one on which I had set my heart in the first place. It was a religious record. I thought at a time like this it would be a good idea if it were possible to reorient a good many people. I remember Henry David Thoreau the philosopher wrote that most men lead lives of quiet desperation, they sort of lose their anchorage, and it could be that I could say something that was comforting and probably could dispel some of that desperation; but I thought also of the shut-ins, and then I thought of another group: having once been menaced with blindness, which caused me to quit the House of Representatives, I thought of those who couldn't see; but they could hear, and maybe such a record would be of extraordinary comfort to them.

So at long last I got it together and it was made. It will be on the market, as a matter of fact, very shortly. It begins with the story of the Creation, and then it picks up Moses in Sinai receiving the Tablets, and it includes the Beatitudes and the Lord's Prayer. It includes the Twenty-third Psalm, Paul speaking to the Corinthians, and a few other things; and then it includes a very short one-sentence prayer, and the reason that's included is because in all the visits I had with the late President John Fitzgerald Kennedy, on his desk was this little inscription, this little one-line prayer, and that's included also. I included one other thing because it has been reproduced in millions of copies, the prayer of St. Francis of Assisi, and you see it on Christmas cards and you see it everywhere; but that is the substance of the second record and when I heard it with all the music put in, it really entranced me no end.

TRADITION
(Washington, D.C., 1967)

121 There are those who put no great store on the value of tradition. But I like the idea very much and often the further back we go, the better I like it. I think frequently of the man who went into the restaurant and ordered a meal. He said to the waiter, "What kind of soup do you have?" And the waiter said, "Oxtail." He said, "Well, why go back that far?" But I like to go back.

FROM A SPEECH IN BOSTON
(1962)

122 One of history's most exciting exploits happened here, and to my imagination as a schoolboy it was a fascinating adventure. I refer to

Paul Revere's ride from Charlestown to Lexington in 1775. It will soon be 187 years. To be sure, the poets have added a quality of fantasy, including the incident of one lantern by land and two if by sea in the old North Church tower. If that happened today, according to certain young men in this general area, it might impel the belief that Ev and Charlie were coming. But the symbolism of the real story was that of a rugged citizen riding into the night to warn his fellow countrymen of the danger. That is a historic fact.

It is still a necessary duty to give a warning, for in every generation a free republic is exposed to danger from without and within. The battle for freedom is never entirely won at any given time.

In 1775 it was a struggle of a distant king posed against a people who had long been forbearing and restrained and then struggled to be free and independent.

In 1812 it was the struggle of that same people, then free, as they protested the British practice of impressing free Americans into an alien navy.

In 1861 it was a sectional struggle with the Union at issue, but freedom also became an incandescent part of the struggle. Incidentally, in this year we shall observe the hundredth anniversary of the Emancipation Proclamation, which struck the shackles of enslavement from millions of people.

JUSTICE

123 The task of giving an adequate description of the essence of justice has occupied philosophers since Plato first penned the *Republic* and indicated that justice consisted of each man doing what he was best suited for and refraining from infringing on someone else's work. I do not believe it can be adequately discussed until a consensus is reached that every human being has unique capacities and is in the fullest sense an individual. Justice is simply the condition of free men living harmoniously in society, with each individual having the opportunity of the fullest expression for his fellows. It cannot exist without freedom and it is the precondition for peace.

...2...
Epigrams and Wit of Distinguished Persons

FRANKLIN P. ADAMS

124 If a man keeps his trap shut, the world will beat a path to his door.

125 Middle age occurs when you are too young to take up golf and too old to rush up to the net.

HENRY ADAMS

126 They also serve who only stand and cheer.

JOEY ADAMS

127 If you want to feel important, go on a diet.

JOSEPH ADDISON

128 Nothing is capable of being well set to music that is not nonsense.

GEORGE ADE

129 The music teacher came twice each week to bridge the awful gap between Dorothy and Chopin.

AESCHYLUS

130 A prosperous fool is a grievous burden.

FRED ALLEN

131 A conference is a gathering of important people who singly can do nothing, but together can decide that nothing can be done.

132 Her hat is a creation that will never go out of style; it will just look ridiculous year after year.

133 If a circus is half as good as it smells, it's a great show.

134 What's on your mind?—if you'll forgive the overstatement.

135 I like long walks, especially when they are taken by people who annoy me.

RUSSELL PETTIS ASKUE

136 A minor operation is one that was performed on the other fellow.

LOUIS AUCHINCLOSS

137 Most fathers would rather see their sons dead than either cultivated or devout.

PHILIP JAMES BAILEY

138 The worst men often give the best advice.

W. T. BALLARD

139 The guy is so smooth he could slide on sandpaper.

HONORÉ DE BALZAC

140 Friendships last when each friend thinks he has a slight superiority over the other.

141 One of the first conditions of learning in a woman is to keep the fact a profound secret.

JOHN KENDRICK BANGS

142 Pandemonium did not reign; it poured.

ALBEN W. BARKLEY

143 Economist: a guy with a Phi Beta Kappa key on one end of his watch chain and no watch on the other end.

PHINEAS T. BARNUM

144 Every crowd has a silver lining.

JAMES M. BARRIE

145 Every man who is high up loves to think that he has done it all himself; and the wife smiles, and lets it go at that.

146 I am not young enough to know everything.

JOHN BARRYMORE

147 One of my chief regrets during my years in the theater is that I couldn't sit in the audience and watch me.

BERNARD M. BARUCH

148 I have not had my hearing aid open to that man for years.

HENRY WARD BEECHER

149 Next to ingratitude, the most painful thing to bear is gratitude.

150 Selfishness is that detestable vice no one will forgive in others and no one is without in himself.

MAX BEERBOHM

151 To give an accurate and exhaustive account of that period would need a far less brilliant pen than mine.

APHRA BEHN

152   He that will live in this world must be endowed with the three rare qualities of dissimulation, equivocation, and mental reservation.

ROBERT BENCHLEY

153   Drawing on my fine command of language, I said nothing.

154   It took me fifteen years to discover I had no talent for writing, but I couldn't give it up because by that time I was too famous.

155   It was one of those plays in which all the actors unfortunately enunciated very clearly.

AMBROSE BIERCE

156   Positive: being mistaken at the top of one's voice.

JOSH BILLINGS

157   As long as we are lucky we attribute it to our smartness; our bad luck we give the gods credit for.

158   The best way to convince a fool that he is wrong is to let him have his own way.

159   The choicest compliment that can be paid to virtue is that the best lies we have are those which most resemble the truth.

160   A dog is the only thing on this earth that loves you more than he loves himself.

161   If the world despises a hypocrite, what must they think of him in heaven?

162   Live within your income, even if you have to borrow money to do so.

163   Man was created a little lower than the angels, and has been getting a little lower ever since.

JIM BISHOP

164   The mayor was a man you had to know to dislike.

HAL BOYLE

165   Some husbands are born optimists. They go through life believing that somehow, somewhere, they eventually will arrive someplace on time —with their wife. It never happens.

166   The reason everybody loves a fat man is that everyone feels superior to him; if you give a fellow a reason to feel superior to you he can't help liking you.

GAMALIEL BRADFORD

167   Until harsh experience taught him the folly of it, he was always willing to endorse a friend's note, and surely greater love hath no man than this: laying down one's life is nothing in comparison.

OMAR BRADLEY

168 The world has achieved brilliance without conscience.

169 Ours is a world of nuclear giants and ethical infants.

SHELLAND BRADLEY

170 I always did think that cleverness was the art of hiding ignorance.

KINGMAN BREWSTER, JR.

171 You and I know that there is a correlation between the creative and the screwball. So we must suffer the screwball gladly.

JOHN MASON BROWN

172 His life was what the marquees describe as a "continuous performance."

THOMAS BROWNE

173 He who discommendeth others obliquely commendeth himself.

GIORDANO BRUNO

174 With luck on your side you can do without brains.

EDMUND BURKE

175 It is a general popular error to suppose the loudest complainers for the public to be the most anxious for its welfare.

176 They defend their errors as if they were defending their inheritance.

SAMUEL BUTLER

177 She went up the Nile as far as the first crocodile.

EDDIE CANTOR

178 Two dollars will buy all the happiness or all the misery in the world. At least that used to be the price of a marriage license.

ANDREW CARNEGIE

179 They [industrial promoters] throw cats and dogs together and call them elephants.

LEWIS CARROLL

180 "One *can't* believe impossible things." "I daresay you haven't had much practice," said the Queen. "When I was your age, I always did it for half-an-hour a day. Why, sometimes I've believed as many as six impossible things before breakfast."

WYNN CATLIN

181 Diplomacy: the art of saying "Nice doggie" till you can find a rock.

MARCUS PORCIUS CATO

182 I had rather men should ask why no statue has been erected in my honor, than why one has.

JAKOB CATS

183 A fool is like other men as long as he is silent.

LORD CHESTERFIELD

184 Most people enjoy the inferiority of their best friends.

185 He adorned whatever subject he either wrote or spoke upon, by the most splendid eloquence.

GILBERT KEITH CHESTERTON

186 Christianity has not been tried and found wanting; it has been found difficult and not tried.

187 I hate a quarrel because it interrupts an argument.

188 Merely having an open mind is nothing; the object of opening the mind, as of opening the mouth, is to shut it again on something solid.

JOHN CIARDI

189 Gentility is what is left over from rich ancestors after the money is gone.

JAMES FREEMAN CLARKE

190 A politician thinks of the next election; a statesman, of the next generation.

LUCAS CLEEVE

191 A woman must never let a man get accustomed to her absence.

GEORGES CLEMENCEAU

192 Everything I know I learned after I was thirty.

193 War is much too important a matter to be left to the generals.

WILLIAM CONGREVE

194 In my conscience I believe the baggage loves me, for she never speaks well of me herself nor suffers anybody else to rail at me.

JOSEPH CONRAD

195 I can't imagine a human being so hard up for something to do as to quarrel with me.

ANTHONY COPLEY

196 Poor men want meat for their stomachs, rich men stomachs for their meat.

EDGAR COWAN

197 History is but little more than a graveyard in which one reads the epitaphs of buried states.

NOEL COWARD

198 Alfred Lunt has his head in the clouds and his feet in the box office.

ABRAHAM COWLEY

199   God the first garden made, and the first city Cain.

A. CRAIG

200   A man is known by the company he keeps out of.

OLIVER CROMWELL

201   No one rises so high as he who knows not whither he is going.

GEORGE WILLIAM CURTIS

202   Anger is an expensive luxury in which only men of a certain income can indulge.

CARDINAL RICHARD CUSHING

203   When I see a bird that walks like a duck and swims like a duck and quacks like a duck, I call that bird a duck.

GEORGE WARWICK DEEPING

204   I spent a year in that town, one Sunday.

ANTOINETTE DESHOULIÈRES

205   No one is satisfied with his fortune, nor dissatisfied with his intellect.

DIOGENES

206   Man is the most intelligent of animals—and the most silly.

BENJAMIN DISRAELI

207   Little things affect little minds.

JOHN DONNE

208   Who are a little wise the best fools be.

JOHN DRYDEN

209   We are glad to have God on our side to maul our enemies, when we cannot do the work ourselves.

FINLEY PETER DUNNE

210   The wise people are in New York because the foolish went there first; that's the way the wise men make a living.

WILL DURANT

211   No man who is in a hurry is quite civilized.

GEORGE ELIOT

212   Blessed is the man who, having nothing to say, abstains from giving wordy evidence of the fact.

213   He was like a cock who thought the sun had risen to hear him crow.

T. S. ELIOT

214   To say I always look my best can only mean the worst.

RALPH WALDO EMERSON

215　Conversation is an art in which a man has all mankind for competitors.

216　The louder he talked of his honour, the faster we counted our spoons.

GEORGE ETHEREGE

217　Men are seldom in the right when they guess at a woman's mind.

CLIFTON FADIMAN

218　Gertrude [Stein] has always done justice to Gertrude, but this book sets a high-water mark in the delicate art of self-appreciation.

219　Do not feel bad when you hear the broadcaster say he feels badly. Just remember that all men are created equally.

FRANÇOIS FÉNELON

220　The more you say, the less people remember.

B. C. FORBES

221　A big head and a big bank account don't keep company very long.

222　Acting without thinking is like shooting without aiming.

223　The fellow who gets too big for his shoes is apt to finish up barefooted.

✓ 224　Diamonds are chunks of coal that stuck to their job.

ANATOLE FRANCE

225　Never lend books, for no one ever returns them; the only books I have in my library are books that other folk have lent me.

BENJAMIN FRANKLIN

226　All would live long, but none would be old.

✓ 227　He that falls in love with himself will have no rivals.

228　Keep your eyes wide open before marriage, and half-shut afterwards.

BEATRICE AND IRA FREEMAN

229　The bagel: an unsweetened doughnut with rigor mortis.

JULIAN GEROW

✓ 230　Ours seems to be the only nation on earth that asks its teen-agers what to do about world affairs, and tells its golden-agers to go out and play.

WILLIAM SCHWENCK GILBERT

231　He did nothing in particular, and did it very well.

JOHANN WOLFGANG VON GOETHE

232　Once you have missed the first buttonhole you'll never manage to button up.

ARTHUR GOLDBERG

✓ 233　Modern diplomats approach every problem with an open mouth.

ISAAC GOLDBERG

234 Grammar school never taught me anything about grammar.

BARRY M. GOLDWATER

235 The only summit meeting that can succeed is one that does not take place.

H. GORDON-BROWNE

236 It is better to be a has-been than one of the never-wases.

BILLY GRAHAM

237 A real Christian is a person who can give his pet parrot to the town gossip.

WHITNEY GRISWOLD

238 The world is always upside down to a baccalaureate speaker.... Things have got to be wrong in order that they may be deplored.

PHILIP GUEDALLA

239 History repeats itself; historians repeat each other.

JOHN GUNTHER

240 The famous politician was trying to save both his faces.

THOMAS CHANDLER HALIBURTON

241 A college education shows a man how little other people know.

MARGARET HALSEY

242 His handshake ought not to be used except as a tourniquet.

OSCAR HAMMERSTEIN II

243 The trouble with Howard is that he won't take yes for an answer.

J. C. AND A. W. HARE

244 Half the failures in life arise from pulling in one's horse as he is leaping.

HENRY S. HASKINS

245 The greatest masterpieces were once only pigments on a palette.

WILLIAM HAZLITT

246 Silence is one great art of conversation.

247 There are names written in her immortal scroll at which Fame blushes.

LILLIAN HELLMAN

248 Cynicism is an unpleasant way of saying the truth.

DON HEROLD

249 I wish I were either rich enough or poor enough to do a lot of things that are impossible in my present comfortable circumstances.

250 There is little use to talk about your child to anyone; other people either have one or haven't.

THEODORE HESBURGH
251 The most important thing a father can do for his children is to love their mother.

THOMAS W. HIGGINSON
252 The truth is that Mr. [Henry] James's cosmopolitanism is, after all, limited; to be really cosmopolitan, a man must be at home even in his own country.

ALFRED HITCHCOCK
253 I deny I ever said that actors are cattle. What I said was "actors should be treated like cattle."

ERIC HOFFER
254 It is well to treasure the memories of past misfortunes; they constitute our bank of fortitude.

HEDDA HOPPER
255 At one time I thought he wanted to be an actor. He had certain qualifications, including no money and a total lack of responsibility.

WILLIAM DEAN HOWELLS
256 The Bostonian who leaves Boston ought to be condemned to perpetual exile.

CHARLES EVANS HUGHES
257 Clarity the greatest of legislative and judicial virtues, like the sunshine, revealing and curative.

VICTOR HUGO
258 Waterloo was a battle of the first rank won by a captain of the second.

HUBERT HUMPHREY
259 The first quality of a good education is good manners—and some people flunk the course.

260 I learned more about economics from one South Dakota dust storm than I did in all my years in college.

ALDOUS HUXLEY
261 We are geniuses up to the age of ten.

ANDREW JACKSON
262 A man [Sam Houston] made by God and not by a tailor.

WILLIAM JAMES
263 An unlearned carpenter of my acquaintance once said in my hearing: "There is very little difference between one man and another; but what little there is *is very important*."

LYNDON B. JOHNSON

264 I wish there were some giant-economy-size aspirin tablet that would work on international headaches. But there isn't. The only cure is patience with reason mixed in.

HARRY KARNS

265 A wise man puts aside 10 percent of the money he gets—and 90 percent of the free advice.

JEAN KERR

266 Fred Allen used to talk about a man who was so thin he could be dropped through a piccolo without striking a single note. Well, I'm glad I never met *him;* I'd hate to have to hear about *his* diet.

267 Marrying a man is like buying something you've been admiring for a long time in a shop window. You may love it when you get home, but it doesn't always go with everything else in the house.

ORPHEUS C. KERR

268 Flattery very seldom changes a woman's character, though it may sway her judgment. She accepts it as her right, but seldom believes it.

ALEXANDER KING

269 He spoke beautiful French and had a warm, sympathetic heart despite his good manners.

FLETCHER KNEBEL

270 Never give up. For fifty years they said the horse was through. Now look at him—a status symbol.

ALFRED A. KNOPF

271 Economist: a man who states the obvious in terms of the incomprehensible.

F. M. KNOWLES

272 There's no place like home, and many a man is glad of it.

HENRY LABOUCHÈRE

273 I don't object to Gladstone always having the ace of trumps up his sleeve, but merely to his belief that the Almighty put it there.

CHARLES LAMB

274 The human species is composed of two distinct races: the men who borrow, and the men who lend.

MELVILLE D. LANDON

275 A bore is a man who spends so much time talking about himself that you can't talk about yourself.

PAUL LARMER

276 I'm still waiting for some college to come up with a march protesting student ignorance.

FRANÇOIS DE LA ROCHEFOUCAULD

277 Everyone complains of memory, no one of his judgment.

278 There are bad people who would be less dangerous if they had no good in them.

EVA LATHBURY

279 I can't help it—that's what we all say when we don't want to exert ourselves.

STANISLAW J. LEC

280 We looked into each other's eyes. I saw myself, she saw herself.

OSCAR LEVANT

281 I have given up reading books; I find it takes my mind off myself.

SAM LEVENSON

282 Insanity is hereditary. You can get it from your children.

ABRAHAM LINCOLN

283 It's a good rule never to send a mouse to catch a skunk or a polliwog to tackle a whale.

JOSEPH LINCOLN

284 It's always the feller that's lookin' on that gits hit.

LING PO

285 He who neglects to drink of the spring of experience is apt to die of thirst in the desert of ignorance.

MARY WILSON LITTLE

286 There is no pleasure in having nothing to do; the fun is in having lots to do and not doing it.

HENRY CABOT LODGE, JR.

287 This organization [United Nations] is created to prevent you from going to hell. It isn't created to take you to heaven.

ANITA LOOS

288 So this gentleman said a girl with brains ought to do something else with them besides think.

289 I always say that a girl never really looks as well as she does on board a steamship, or even a yacht.

DR. CHARLES D. McIVER

290 When you educate a man you educate an individual; when you educate a woman you educate a whole family.

SEUMAS MacMANUS

291 He's no-way covetous, but he'd fain have what is yours.

NORMAN MAILER

292 And she gave me a sisterly kiss. Older sister.

DON MARQUIS

293 Thrift cannot be too highly commended. Teach all those with whom you come in contact to be saving. You never know when you may need their savings to finance one of your ventures.

TOM MASSON

294 "Be yourself!" is about the worst advice you can give some people.

295 To feel themselves in the presence of true greatness many men find it necessary only to be alone.

ANDRÉ MAUROIS

296 The only thing experience teaches us is that experience teaches us nothing.

DR. WILLIAM J. MAYO

297 Specialist: a man who knows more and more about less and less.

ADDISON MIZNER

298 Never call a man a fool; borrow from him.

FRANKFORT MOORE

299 There is no stronger bond of friendship than a mutual enemy.

J. P. MORGAN

300 You can do business with anyone, but you can only sail a boat with a gentleman.

ROBERT MORLEY

301 Show me the man who has enjoyed his school days, and I will show you a bully and a bore.

LEWIS MUMFORD

302 Let us confess it: the human situation is always desperate.

OGDEN NASH

303 Marriage is the alliance of two people, one of whom never remembers birthdays and the other never forgets them.

GEORGE JEAN NATHAN

304 Bad officials are elected by good citizens who do not vote.

JOHN HENRY NEWMAN

305 A great memory does not make a philosopher, any more than a diction-ary can be called a grammar.

EDGAR WILSON NYE

306 Kind words will never die—neither will they buy groceries.

307 I do not believe that it will always be popular to wear mourning for our friends, unless we feel a little doubtful about where they went.

308 Winter lingered so long in the lap of Spring that it occasioned a great deal of talk.

HARRY OLIVER

309 Legend: a lie that has attained the dignity of age.

BLAISE PASCAL

310 Had Cleopatra's nose been shorter, the whole face of the world would have been different.

PRINCE PHILIP

311 The trouble with senior management to an outsider is that there are too many one-ulcer men holding down two-ulcer jobs.

WILLIAM PITT

312 Don't tell me of a man's being able to talk sense; everyone can talk sense—can he talk nonsense?

MATTHEW PRIOR

313 Be to her virtues very kind,
Be to her faults a little blind.

NATHAN M. PUSEY

314 The true business of liberal education is greatness.

WALTER RALEIGH

315 Passions are likened to floods and streams:
The shallow murmur, but the deep are dumb.

MARJORIE KINNAN RAWLINGS

316 You can't change a man, no-ways. By the time his mummy turns him loose and he takes up with some innocent woman and marries her, he's what he is.

JAMES RESTON

317 Nations talk about what they lack; America is talking about peace, Germany about unity, France about glory, Russia about freedom, and India about food.

CARDINAL RICHELIEU

318 Give me six lines written by the most honorable of men, and I will find an excuse in them to hang him.

DAVID RIESMAN

319 The students would be much better off if they could take a stand against taking a stand.

RAINER MARIA RILKE

320   Fame: the aggregate of all the misunderstandings that collect around a new name.

NED ROREM

321   What is bad cannot endure; it must grow worse.

GIOACCHINO ROSSINI

322   Give me a laundry list and I'll set it to music.

ANNA RUSSELL

323   The reason that there are so few women comics is that so few women can bear being laughed at.

GEORGE SANTAYANA

324   Fanaticism consists in redoubling your effort when you have forgotten your aim.

JEAN PAUL SARTRE

325   I depended on him for everything; what he worshiped in me was his generosity.

HYMAN JUDAH SCHACHTEL

326   Happiness is not having what you want, but wanting what you have.

WILLIAM SHAKESPEARE

327   Everyone can master a grief but he that has it.

BISHOP FULTON SHEEN

328   An atheist is a man who has no invisible means of support.

PERCY BYSSHE SHELLEY

329   As a bankrupt thief turns thief-taker, so an unsuccessful author turns critic.

GEORGE SHUSTER

330   You ought not to educate a woman as if she were a man, or to educate her as if she were not.

ALGERNON SIDNEY

331   Liars ought to have good memories.

WALTER SLEZAK

332   Not many Americans have been around the world but their money sure has.

JOHN SLOAN

333   Since we have to speak well of the dead, let's knock them while they're alive. (Quoted by Allen Churchill)

LOGAN PEARSALL SMITH

334   What music is more enchanting than the voices of young people when you can't hear what they say.

SYDNEY SMITH

335   He is remarkably well, considering that he has been remarkably well for so many years.

336   I am just going to pray for you at St. Paul's but with no very lively hope of success.

CARDINAL FRANCIS SPELLMAN

337   You've heard of the three ages of man—youth, age, and "You are looking wonderful."

HERBERT SPENCER

338   A jury is a group of twelve people of average ignorance.

CASEY STENGEL

339   Ability: the art of getting credit for all the home runs somebody else hits.

ABEL STEVENS

340   Politeness is the art of choosing among one's real thoughts.

ADLAI STEVENSON

341   Do you know the difference between a beautiful woman and a charming one? A beauty is a woman you notice; a charmer is one who notices you.

ROBERT LOUIS STEVENSON

342   Politics is perhaps the only profession for which no preparation is thought necessary.

LORD STOWELL

343   A dinner lubricates business.

JONATHAN SWIFT

344   Censure is the tax a man pays to the public for being eminent.

HERBERT BAYARD SWOPE

345   I cannot give you the formula for success, but I can give you the formula for failure—which is: Try to please everybody.

SEMYON TSARAPKIN

346   I am not a gentleman. I am representative of the Soviet Union here [United Nations].

LOUIS UNTERMEYER

347   A metaphor is a thing you shout through.

348 A diplomat these days is nothing but a headwaiter who's allowed to sit down occasionally.

349 Middle age is when a man figures he has enough financial security to wear the flashy sports coats he didn't have the courage to wear when he was young.

350 When a government project is described as "imaginative" you know it is going to be almost as expensive as those that are called "bold."

351 . . . in its idiot way our system, though it usually keeps us from having the very best man as President, does protect us from the worst.

352 When he who hears doesn't know what he who speaks means, and when he who speaks doesn't know what he himself means—that is philosophy.

353 My advice to the women's clubs of America is to raise more hell and fewer dahlias.

354 He [President McKinley] walked among men a bronze statue, for thirty years determinedly looking for his pedestal.

355 The modern idea of home has been well expressed as the place one goes from the garage.

356 They say that we are better educated than our parents' generation. What they mean is that we go to school longer. They are not the same thing.

...3...

Great Passages from Great Minds

357 There is something in the contemplation of the mode in which America has been settled that, in a noble breast, should forever extinguish the prejudices of national dislikes.

Settled by the people of all nations, all nations may claim her for their own. You can not spill a drop of American blood without spilling the blood of the whole world. Be he Englishman, German, Dane, or Scot; the European who scoffs at an American, calls his own brother *Raca,* and stands in danger of the judgment.

We are not a narrow tribe of men. . . . No; our blood is as the flood of the Amazon, made up of a thousand noble currents all pouring into one.

We are not a nation so much as a world. *Herman Melville*

358 Abandon your animosities and make your sons Americans. *Robert E. Lee*

359 On July 20 we were removing the accumulation of more than fifteen centuries of debris from the floor of a Roman bath that had been built on the eastern shore of the Mediterranean in a good natural harbor between Tyre and Sidon. Sailors and travelers had relaxed there in a steaming room, and plied their bodies generously with perfumed oil from bottles, many of which were still lying about. They had become in fact sufficiently relaxed—broken wine jars were also in evidence—to have lost from their purses some money—coins that supplied the date for the use of the building. From the evidence available we were beginning to feel reasonably at home in the culture of the fourth–fifth centuries.

On the very morning when we had succeeded in projecting our-

19824

selves backward in time far beyond the memory of any one of our team by digging only a few feet below the surface of earth, two men had opened up a future by flying a quarter of a million miles and setting foot on the moon. We talked of that achievement of twentieth century technology. Yet I could not but think also of the segment of man's experience on this planet we had just that day discovered. Although it was only a fraction of the long life-span of man, it was a part of man's past, the increment of time from which even the astronauts, as far from home as the moon, could not free themselves.

Consider the Roman traveler who enjoyed the comforts of his marble-lined bath after crossing from Italy to the Phoenician coast. It would be a grave mistake to underestimate his achievements: he knew how to use the wind to bring his ship over sea; he could build with stones weighing 750 tons and hoist them, as he did at Baalbek, to a height of 20 feet. He read law, literature, poetry. He enjoyed plays and races, as well as baths. He was knowledgeable and sophisticated.

How surprised the Roman would have been to have heard the news that electrified our staff and Lebanese workmen on July 20. I am sure that, had he somehow survived to our day by a kind of science-fiction deep freeze, he would have believed firmly that the gods had made the trip through the heavens. Certainly not men.

Although he knew about the Greeks, of Herodotus, "the father of history," he knew nothing of the story of man's life on this planet beyond a short thousand years of his immediate past. Beyond that span he believed in a vague shadowy world of legends, of myths about gods and men. How could he have known? For this story of man's achievements over a span of about one million years of his life is one which has been dug from the earth only in the past century. *Dr. James B. Pritchard, Professor of Religious Thought, and Associate Director of the University Museum, University of Pennsylvania*

THE BIVOUAC OF THE DEAD

360   The muffled drum's sad roll has beat
The soldier's last tattoo;
No more on Life's parade shall meet
The brave and fallen few.
On Fame's eternal camping-ground
Their silent tents are spread,
And Glory guards, with solemn round,
The bivouac of the dead. *Theodore O'Hara*

COMPROMISE

361   Compromise makes a good umbrella, but a poor roof; it is a temporary expedient, often wise in party politics, almost sure to be unwise in statesmanship. *James Russell Lowell*

CONSERVATIVE

362 We are reformers in spring and summer; in autumn and winter we stand by the old; reformers in the morning, conservers at night. *Ralph Waldo Emerson*

CONSISTENCY

363 A foolish consistency is the hobgoblin of little minds, adored by little statesmen and philosophers and divines. With consistency a great soul has simply nothing to do. He may as well concern himself with his shadow on the wall. Speak what you think now in hard words and tomorrow speak what tomorrow thinks in hard words again, though it contradict everything you said today.—"Ah, so you shall be sure to be misunderstood." It is so bad then to be misunderstood? Pythagoras was misunderstood, and Socrates, and Jesus, and Luther, and Copernicus, and Galileo, and Newton, and every pure and wise spirit that ever took flesh. To be great is to be misunderstood. *Ibid.*

CONSTITUTION

364 I wish the Constitution which is offered, had been made more perfect; but I sincerely believe it is the best that could be obtained at this time. And, as a constitutional door is opened for amendment hereafter, the adoption of it, under the present circumstances of the Union, is in my opinion desirable. *George Washington*

365 The Constitution is either a superior, paramount law, unchangeable by ordinary means, or it is on a level with ordinary legislative acts, and like other acts, is alterable when the legislature shall please to alter it. . . . Certainly all those who have framed written constitutions contemplate them as forming the fundamental and paramount law of the nation, and consequently the theory of every such government must be that an act of the legislature, repugnant to the constitution, is void. *John Marshall*

CONTENTMENT

366 One should be either sad or joyful. Contentment is a warm sty for eaters and sleepers. *Eugene O'Neill*

CONTROVERSY

367 No great advance has ever been made in science, politics, or religion, without controversy. *Lyman Beecher*

COUNSEL

368 Once in Persia reigned a king
Who upon his signet ring
Graved a maxim true and wise,
Which if held before the eyes
Gave him counsel at a glance
Fit for every change and chance.

Solemn words, and these are they:
"Even this shall pass away." *Theodore Tilton*

CROWD

369   If it had to choose who is to be crucified, the crowd will always save
Barabbas. *Jean Cocteau*

CURIOSITY

370   The important thing is not to stop questioning. Curiosity had its own
reason for existing. One cannot help but be in awe when he contem-
plates the mysteries of eternity, of life, of the marvelous structure of
reality. It is enough if one tries merely to comprehend a little of this
mystery every day. Never lose a holy curiosity. *Albert Einstein*

DEATH

371   Whoever has lived long enough to find out what life is, knows how
deep a debt of gratitude we owe to Adam, the first great benefactor
of our race. He brought death into the world. *Mark Twain*

DEBT

372   Goethe said there would be little left of him if he were to discard what
he owed to others. *Charlotte Cushman*

DEMAGOGUE

373   The insolence of demagogues is generally the cause of ruin in democracies. First they calumniate the wealthy and rouse them against a
common danger. Next, they produce the same result by stirring up the
populace and creating a sense of insecurity. Nearly all the tyrants of
old began with being demagogues. *Aristotle*

DEMOCRACY

374   While democracy must have its organization and controls, its vital
breath is individual liberty. *Charles Evans Hughes*

375   If our democracy is to flourish, it must have criticism; if our government is to function, it must have dissent. *Henry Steele Commager*

376   The French Revolution of 150 years ago gradually ushered in an age
of political equality, but the times have changed, and that by itself is
not enough today. The boundaries of democracy have to be widened
now so as to include economic equality also. This is the great revolution
through which we are all passing. *Jawaharlal Nehru*

377   I have not the slightest doubt that, if we had a purely democratic
government here, the effect would be the same. Either the poor would
plunder the rich and civilization would perish, or order and property
would be saved by a strong military government, and liberty would
perish. *Thomas Babington Macaulay*

378   I have long been convinced that institutions purely democratic must,
sooner or later, destroy liberty, or civilization, or both. *Ibid.*

379   Either some Caesar or Napoleon will seize the reins of government with a strong hand; or your republic will be as fearfully plundered and laid waste by barbarians in the twentieth century as the Roman Empire was in the fifty—with this difference . . . that your Huns and Vandals will have been engendered within your own country by your own institutions. *Ibid.*

DEMOCRACY OF DEATH

380   It comes equally to us all equally when it comes. The ashes of an oak in the Chimney are no Epitaph of that Oak to tell me how high or large that was; it tells me not what flocks it sheltered, while it stood, nor what men it hurt when it fell. The dust of great persons' graves is speechless too, it says nothing. It distinguishes nothing; as soon the dust of a wretch whom thou wouldest not, as of a Prince thou couldest not look upon, will trouble thine eyes, if the wind blows it thither; and when a whirlwind hath blown the dust of the Churchyard into the Church, and the man sweeps out the dust of the Church into the Churchyard, who will undertake to sift those dusts again, and to pronounce, This is the Patrician, this is the noble flower, and this the yeomanly, this the Plebeian bran. *John Donne*

DIFFICULTY

381   All great and honorable actions are accompanied with great difficulties, and must be both enterprised and overcome with answerable courages. The dangers were great, but not desperate; the difficulties were many, but not invincible. For though there were many of them likely, yet they were not certain; it might be sundry of the things feared might never befall; others by provident care and the use of good means might in great measure be prevented; and all of them, through the help of God, by fortitude and patience, might either be borne or overcome. *William Bradford* (History of the Plymouth Plantation)

DISPUTE

382   How many a dispute could have been deflated into a single paragraph if the disputants had dared to define their terms. *Aristotle*

DISSENT

383   Protection, therefore, against the tyranny of the magistrate is not enough; there needs protection also against the tyranny of the prevailing opinion and feeling; against the tendency of society to impose, by other means than civil penalties, its own ideas and practices as rules of conduct on those who dissent from them. *John Stuart Mill*

DOGMA

384   Jesus no doubt fits his teaching into the late-Jewish messianic dogma. But he does not think dogmatically. He formulates no doctrine. He is

far from judging any man's belief by reference to any standard of dogmatic correctness. Nowhere does he demand of his hearers that they shall sacrifice thinking to believing. *Albert Schweitzer*

DOUBT

385   The majority of mankind is lazy-minded, incurious, absorbed in vanities, and tepid in emotion, and is therefore incapable of either much doubt or much faith. *T. S. Eliot*

EARTH

386   After I had addressed myself to this very difficult and almost insoluble problem, the suggestion at length came to me how it could be solved with fewer and much simpler constructions than were formerly used if my assumptions (which are called axioms) were granted me. They follow in this order.
　　1. There is no center of all the celestial circles of spheres.
　　2. The center of the earth is not the center of the universe, but only of gravity and of the lunar sphere.
　　3. All the spheres revolve about the sun as their midpoint, and therefore the sun is the center of the universe. *Nicolaus Copernicus*

EDUCATION

387   The prosperity of a country depends, not on the abundance of its revenues, nor on the strength of its fortifications, nor on the beauty of its public buildings, but it consists in the number of its cultivated citizens, in its men of education, enlightenment, and character. *Martin Luther*

388   A liberal education is the education which gives a man a clear, conscious view of his own opinions and judgments, a truth in developing them, an eloquence in expressing them, and a force in urging them. It teaches him to see things as they are, to go right to the point, to disentangle a skein of thought, to detect what is sophistical, and to discard what is irrelevant. . . .
　　He is at home in any society, he has common ground with every class; he knows when to speak and when to be silent. *John Henry Newman*

389   Only the educated are free. *Epictetus*

390   On the diffusion of education among the people rest the preservation and perpetuation of our free institutions. *Daniel Webster*

EQUALITY

391   All men are by nature equal, made, all, of the same earth by the same Creator, and however we deceive ourselves, as dear to God is the poor peasant as the mighty prince. *Plato*

ERROR

392   It is much easier to recognize error than to find truth; error is superficial and may be corrected; truth lies hidden in the depths. *Johann Wolfgang von Goethe*

ETERNITY

393   The prophet and the martyr do not see the hooting throng. Their eyes are fixed on the eternities. *Benjamin N. Cardozo*

EVIL

394   He that is good is free, though he is a slave; he that is evil is a slave, though he be a king. *St. Augustine*

395   The only thing necessary for the triumph of evil is for good men to do nothing. *Edmund Burke*

EXISTENCE

396   All essential knowledge relates to existence, or only such knowledge as has an essential relationship to existence is essential knowledge. *Sören Kierkegaard*

FACTS

397   Facts do not cease to exist because they are ignored. *Aldous Huxley*

398   I am a firm believer in the people. If given the truth, they can be depended upon to meet any national crisis. The great point is to bring them the real facts. *Abraham Lincoln*

FAITH

399   If the work of God could be comprehended by reason, it would be no longer wonderful, and faith would have no merit if reason provided proof. *Gregory I*

FALSEHOOD

400   The united voice of millions cannot lend the smallest foundation to falsehood. *Oliver Goldsmith*

401   You never need think you can turn over any old falsehoods without a terrible squirming of the horrid little population that dwells under it. *Oliver Wendell Holmes*

FOUR FREEDOMS

402   In the future days which we seek to make secure, we look forward to a world founded upon four essential human freedoms.

The first is freedom of speech and expression—everywhere in the world.

The second is freedom of every person to worship God in his own way—everywhere in the world.

The third is freedom from want, which, translated into world terms, means economic understanding which will secure to every nation a healthy peacetime life for its inhabitants—everywhere in the world.

The fourth is freedom from fear, which, translated into world terms, means a worldwide reduction of armaments to such a point and in such a thorough fashion that no nation will be in a position to commit an act of physical aggression against any neighbor—anywhere in the world.

That is no vision of a distant millennium. It is a definite basis for the kind of world attainable in our own time and generation. *Franklin D. Roosevelt*

FREEDOM

403   England tried for two hundred years to restrain the right of discussion. She utterly failed. She is now the freest country in speech and the press under the sun—and it has more than once been her salvation. Every enlightened Englishman appreciates the value of Trafalgar Square and Hyde Park. When you drive men from the public arena, where debate is free, you send them to the cellar, where revolutions are born. "Better an uproar than a whisper." *William E. Borah*

404   It is our task not to produce "safe" men, in whom our safety can never in any case lie, but to keep alive in young people the courage to dare to seek the truth, to be free, to establish in them a compelling desire to live greatly and magnanimously, and to give them the knowledge and awareness, the faith and the trained facility to get on with the job. Especially the faith. *Nathan M. Pusey*

405   If a nation values anything more than freedom, it will lose its freedom; and the irony of it is that if it is comfort or money that it values more, it will lose that too. *W. Somerset Maugham*

406   A man can be himself only so long as he is alone; and, if he does not love solitude, he will not love freedom; for it is only when he is alone that he is really free. *Arthur Schopenhauer*

407   Yes! To this thought I hold with firm persistence;
The last result of wisdom stamps it true:
He only earns his freedom and existence
Who daily conquers them anew. *Johann Wolfgang von Goethe*

408   The greater the importance of safeguarding the community from incitements to the overthrow of our institutions by force and violence, the more imperative is the need to preserve inviolate the constitutional rights of free speech, free press, and free assembly in order to maintain the opportunity for free political discussion, to the end that government may be responsible to the will of the people and that changes, if desired, may be obtained by graceful means. Therein lies the security of the Republic, and the very foundation of constitutional government. *Charles Evans Hughes*

FREEDOM OF THE PRESS

409   If a nation expects to be ignorant and free, in a state of civilization, it expects what never was and never will be. The functionaries of every

government have propensities to command at will the liberty and property of their constituents. There is no safe deposit for these but with the people themselves; nor can they be safe with them without information. Where the press is free, and every man able to read, all is safe. *Thomas Jefferson*

FREE SPEECH

410 You say that freedom of utterance is not for time of stress, and I reply with the sad truth that only in time of stress is freedom of utterance in danger. . . . Only when free utterance is suppressed is it needed, and when it is needed it is most vital to justice. *William Allen White*

GOALS

411 Perfection of means and confusion of goals seem—in my opinion—to characterize our age. *Albert Einstein*

GOD

412 The liberty enjoyed by the people of these states of worshiping Almighty God, agreeably to their consciences, is not only among the choicest of their *blessings,* but also of their rights. *George Washington*

GOOD NAME

413 Good name in man and woman, dear my lord,
Is the immediate jewel of their souls;
Who steals my purse steals trash; 'tis something, nothing;
'Twas mine, 'tis his, and has been slave to thousands;
But he that filches from me my good name
Robs me of that which not enriches him,
And makes me poor indeed. *William Shakespeare*

GOVERNMENT

414 For he that thinks absolute power purifies men's blood and corrects the baseness of human nature need read but the history of this, or any, age to be convinced to the contrary. *John Locke*

GRATITUDE

415 You pray in your distress and in your need; would that you might pray also in the fullness of your joy and in your days of abundance. *Kahlil Gibran*

HATE

416 I shall never permit myself to stoop so low as to hate any man. *Booker T. Washington*

HEAVEN

417 The mind is its own place, and in itself
Can make a heaven of Hell, a hell of Heaven. *John Milton*

HISTORY

418 Anybody can make history; only a great man can write it. *Oscar Wilde*

IDEA

419 There is one thing stronger than all the armies in the world: and that is an idea whose time has come. *Victor Hugo*

IGNORANCE

420 There is nothing more frightful than ignorance in action. *Johann Wolfgang von Goethe*

421 Ignorance is the night of the mind, a night without moon or star. *Confucius*

IMPROVEMENT OF THE SOUL

422 Men of Athens, I honor and love you; but I shall obey God rather than you, and while I have life and strength I shall never cease from the practice and teaching of philosophy, exhorting anyone whom I meet after my manner, and convincing him, saying: O my friend, why do you, who are a citizen of the great and mighty and wise city of Athens, care so much about laying up the greatest amount of money and honor and reputation, and so little about wisdom and truth and the greatest improvement of the soul, which you never regard or heed at all? Are you not ashamed of this? And if the person with whom I am arguing says: Yes, but I do care, I do not depart or let him go at once; I interrogate and examine and cross-examine him, and if I think that he has no virtue, but only says that he has, I reproach him with undervaluing the greater, and overvaluing the less. And this I should say to everyone whom I meet, young and old, citizen and alien, but especially to the citizens, inasmuch as they are my brethren. For this is the command of God, as I would have you know; and I believe that to this day no greater good has ever happened in the State than my service to the God. For I do nothing but go about persuading you all, old and young alike, not to take thought for your persons and your properties, but first and chiefly to care about the greatest improvement of the soul. I tell you that virtue is not given by money, but that from virtue come money and every other good of man, public as well as private. This is my teaching, and if this is the doctrine which corrupts the youth, my influence is ruinous indeed. But if anyone says that this is not my teaching, he is speaking an untruth. Wherefore, O men of Athens, I say to you, do as Anytus bids or not as Anytus bids, and either acquit me or not; but whatever you do, know that I shall never alter my ways, not even if I have to die many times. *Socrates*

INDIVIDUAL

423 I believe in the supreme worth of the individual and in his right to life, liberty, and the pursuit of happiness. *John D. Rockefeller, Jr.*

424 The first panacea for a mismanaged nation is inflation of the currency; the second is war. Both bring a temporary prosperity; both bring a permanent ruin. But both are the refuse of political and economic opportunists. *Ernest Hemingway*

INGRATITUDE
425 I have learned silence from the talkative, toleration from the intolerant, and kindness from the unkind; yet strange, I am ungrateful to these teachers. *Kahlil Gibran*

JUDGMENT
426 If you can take upon yourself the crime of the criminal your heart is judging, take it at once, suffer for him yourself, and let him go without reproach. And even if the law itself makes you his judge, act in the same spirit so far as possible, for he will go away and condemn himself more bitterly than you have done. *Fyodor Dostoyevsky*

JUSTICE
427 The administration of justice is the firmest pillar of government. *George Washington*

428 Justice is the earnest and constant will to render to every man his due. The precepts of the law are these: to live honorably, to injure no other man, to render to every man his due. *Justinian*

KILLING
429 Yet each man kills the thing he loves,
By each let this be heard,
Some do it with a bitter look,
Some with a flattering word.
The coward does it with a kiss,
The brave man with a sword! *Oscar Wilde*

430 Theft, incest, infanticide, patricide, have all had a place among virtuous actions. Can anything be more ridiculous than that a man should have the right to kill me because he lives on the other side of the water, and because his ruler has a quarrel with mine, though I have none with him? *Blaise Pascal*

KNOWLEDGE
431 As the Spanish proverb says, "He who would bring home the wealth of the Indies must carry the wealth of the Indies with him." So it is in traveling: a man must carry knowledge with him, if he would bring knowledge home. *Samuel Johnson*

432 By academic freedom I understand the right to search for truth and to publish and teach what one holds to be true. This right implies also a duty: one must not conceal any part of what one has recognized to

be true. It is evident that any restriction of academic freedom acts in such a way as to hamper the dissemination of knowledge among the people and thereby impedes national judgment and action. *Albert Einstein*

KNOW THYSELF

433 But self-examination, if it is thorough enough, is nearly always the first step toward change. I was to discover that no one who learns to know himself remains just what he was before. *Thomas Mann*

434 Know then thyself, presume not God to scan;
The proper study of mankind is man. *Alexander Pope*

LAW

435 The most learned men have determined to begin with Law, and it would seem that they are right, if according to their definition Law is the highest reason, implanted in Nature, which commands what ought to be done and forbids the opposite. This reason, when firmly fixed and fully developed in the human mind, is Law. *Marcus Tullius Cicero*

436 Law is the security for the enjoyment of the high rank which we enjoy in the Republic; this is the foundation of liberty, this is the fountainhead of all justice; in the laws are found the will, the spirit, the prudence, and the decision of the state. *Ibid.*

437 There are two, and only two, foundations of law . . . equity and utility. *Edmund Burke*

438 Where law ends, tyranny begins. *William Pitt*

LEARNING

439 We see then how far the monuments of wit and learning are more durable than the monuments of power, or of the hands. For have not the verses of Homer continued twenty-five hundred years, or more, without the loss of a syllable or letter; during which time infinite palaces, temples, castles, cities have been decayed and demolished? *Francis Bacon*

LEISURE

440 They talk of the dignity of work. Bosh. The dignity is in leisure. *Herman Melville*

LIBERTY

441 Experience should teach us to be most on our guard to protect liberty when the government's purposes are beneficent. Men born to freedom are naturally alert to repel invasion of their liberty by evil-minded rulers. The greatest dangers to liberty lurk in insidious encroachment by men of zeal, well-meaning but without understanding. *Louis D. Brandeis*

442 When liberty becomes license, dictatorship is near. *Will Durant*

443 It behooves every man who values liberty of conscience for himself to resist invasions of it in the case of others. *Thomas Jefferson*

444 Despotism can no more exist in a nation until the liberty of the press be destroyed than night can happen before the sun is set. *Charles Caleb Colton*

445 The spirit of liberty is the spirit which is not too sure that it is right; the spirit of liberty is the spirit which seeks to understand the minds of other men and women; the spirit of liberty is the spirit which weighs their interests alongside its own without bias; the spirit of liberty remembers that not even a sparrow falls to earth unheeded; the spirit of liberty is the spirit of Him who, near two thousand years ago, taught mankind that lesson it has never learned, but has never quite forgotten: that there is a kingdom where the least shall be heard and considered side by side with the greatest. *Learned Hand*

LIFE

446 The mass of men lead lives of quiet desperation. *Henry David Thoreau*

LONELINESS

447 The whole conviction of my life now rests upon the belief that loneliness, far from being a rare and curious phenomenon, peculiar to myself and to a few other solitary men, is the central and inevitable fact of human existence. *Thomas Wolfe*

LUST OF POWER

448 Lust of power is the most flagrant of all the passions. *Cornelius Tacitus*

LUXURY

449 Avarice and luxury, those pests which have ever been the ruin of every great state. . . . *Titus Livius Livy*

450 How much there is in the world I do not want. *Socrates*

MAN

451 One man with courage makes a majority. *Andrew Jackson*

452 No man is an island, entire of itself; every man is a piece of the continent, a part of the main; if a clod be washed away by the sea, Europe is the less, as well as if a promontory were, as well as if a manor of thy friends or of thine own were; any man's death diminishes me, because I am involved in mankind; and therefore never send to know for whom the bell tolls; it tolls for thee. *John Donne*

453 I beg of you to remember that wherever our life touches yours we help or hinder . . . wherever your life touches ours, you make us stronger or weaker. . . . There is no escape—man drags man down, or man lifts man up. *Booker T. Washington*

454 Man is not made for defeat. *Ernest Hemingway*

THE MASS

455 The mass never comes up to the standard of its best member, but on the contrary degrades itself to the level with the lowest. *Henry David Thoreau*

THE MOB

456 The mob is the mother of tyrants. *Diogenes Laertius*

457 It is proof of a bad cause when it is applauded by the mob. *Lucius Annaeus Seneca*

MONUMENTS

458 Monuments! what are they? the very pyramids have forgotten their builders, or to whom they were dedicated. Deeds, not stones, are the true monuments of the great. *John L. Motley*

MORTALITY

459 Oh! Why should the spirit of mortal be proud?
Like a swift-fleeting meteor, a fast-flying cloud,
A flash of the lightning, a break of the wave,
Man passes from life to his rest in the grave. *William Knox*

MUSIC

460 Beethoven can write music, thank God—but he can do nothing else on earth. *Ludwig van Beethoven*

NATIONAL DECAY

461 There is no greater sign of a general decay of virtue in a nation than a want of zeal in its inhabitants for the good of their country. *Joseph Addison*

NEWSPAPERS

462 Our citizens may be deceived for a while, and have been deceived; but as long as the presses can be protected, we may trust them for light. *Thomas Jefferson*

463 To the press alone, checkered as it is with abuses, the world is indebted for all the triumphs which have been gained by reason and humanity over error and oppression. *Ibid.*

OPINION

464 Free government is government by public opinion. Upon the soundness and integrity of public opinion depends the destiny of our democracy. *Robert M. La Follette*

465 Our institutions were not devised to bring about uniformity of opinion; if they had been we might well abandon hope. It is important to remember, as has well been said, "the essential characteristic of true liberty is that under its shelter many different types of life and character and opinion and belief can develop unmolested and unobstructed." *Charles Evans Hughes*

466   How poor are they that have not patience!
       What wound did ever heal but by degrees? *William Shakespeare*

467   I join with you most cordially in rejoicing at the return of peace. I hope
       it will be lasting, and that mankind will at length, as they call them-
       selves reasonable creatures, have reason to settle their differences
       without cutting throats; for, in my opinion, there never was a good war
       or a bad peace. *Benjamin Franklin*

468   Pity is the feeling which arrests the mind in the presence of whatso-
       ever is grave and constant in human sufferings and unites it with the
       human sufferer. *James Joyce*

469   The good of man must be the end of the science of politics. *Aristotle*

470   Experience constantly proves that every man who has power is im-
       pelled to abuse it. *Montesquieu*

471   So that in the first place, I put for a general inclination of all mankind,
       a perpetual and restless desire of power after power, that ceaseth only
       in death. *Thomas Hobbes*

472   In men of the highest character and noblest genius there generally
       exists insatiable desire of honor, command, power, and glory. *Marcus
       Tullius Cicero*

473   There is nothing, absolutely nothing which needs to be more carefully
       guarded against than that one man should be allowed to become more
       powerful than the people. *Demosthenes*

474   That kings should become philosophers, and philosophers kings, can
       scarcely be expected, nor is it to be wished, since the enjoyment of
       power inevitably corrupts the judgment of reason, and perverts its
       liberty. *Immanuel Kant*

475   The great question which, in all ages, has disturbed mankind, and
       brought on them the greatest part of these mischiefs which have
       ruined cities, depopulated countries, and disordered the peace of the
       world, has been, not whether there be power in the world, nor whence
       it came, but who should have it. *Ibid.*

476   The truth is that all men having power ought to be mistrusted. *James
       Madison*

477   Power, like a desolating pestilence,
       Pollutes whate'er it touches; and obedience,

Bane of all genius, virtue, freedom, truth,
Makes slaves of men, and of the human frame. *Percy Bysshe Shelley*

PREJUDICE

478 The prejudices of ignorance are more easily removed than the prejudices of interest; the first are all blindly adopted, the second willfully preferred. *George Bancroft*

REASON

479 Let us not dream that reason can ever be popular. Passions, emotions, may be made popular, but reason remains ever the property of the few. *Johann Wolfgang von Goethe*

RELIGION

480 The humble, meek, merciful, just, pious, and devout souls everywhere are of one religion, and when death has taken off the mask, they will know one another, though the diverse liveries they wore here make them strangers. *William Penn*

RESPONSIBILITY

481 I believe that every right implies a responsibility; every opportunity, an obligation; every possession, a duty. *John D. Rockefeller*

SCHOOL

482 The Common School is the greatest discovery ever made by man. *Horace Mann*

SCRIPTURE

483 We search the world for truth; we cull
The good, the pure, the beautiful,
From all old flower fields of the soul;
And, weary seekers of the best,
We come back laden from our quest,
To find that all the sages said
Is in the Book our mothers read. *John Greenleaf Whittier*

SILENCE

484 Men fear silence as they fear solitude, because both give them a glimpse of the terror of life's nothingness. *André Maurois*

SPIRIT

485 Because I have confidence in the power of truth and of the spirit, I believe in the future of mankind. *Albert Schweitzer*

STATESMAN

486 The great ends for a statesman are, security to possessors, facility to acquirers, and liberty and hope to the people. *Samuel Taylor Coleridge*

STRIKE

487 Show me the country in which there are no strikes and I'll show you that country in which there is no liberty. *Samuel Gompers*

488 The right of the police of Boston to affiliate, which has always been questioned, never granted, is now prohibited. There is no right to strike against the public safety by anybody, anywhere, anytime. *Calvin Coolidge, in letter to Samuel Gompers*

STUPIDITY

489 The good Lord set definite limits on man's wisdom, but set no limits on his stupidity—and that's just not fair! *Konrad Adenauer*

SUCCESS

490 Success is the brand on the brow of the man who has aimed too low. *John Masefield*

TAXES

491 An unlimited power to tax involves, necessarily, the power to destroy. *Daniel Webster*

492 Taxes are not to be laid on the people but by their consent in person or by deputation. *James Otis*

THEORY

493 I never once made a discovery. . . . I speak without exaggeration when I say that I have constructed *three thousand* different theories in connection with the electric light. . . . Yet in only two cases did my experiments prove the truth of my theory. *Thomas Alva Edison*

THOUGHT

494 Less than 15 percent of the people do any original thinking on any subject. . . . The greatest torture in the world for most people is to think. *Luther Burbank*

495 If there is any principle of the Constitution that more imperatively calls for attachment than any other it is the principle of free thoughts —not free for those who agree with us but freedom for the thought we hate. *Oliver Wendell Holmes, Jr.*

TRUTH

496 But when men have realized that time has upset many fighting faiths, they may come to believe even more than they believe the very foundations of their own conduct that the ultimate good desire is better reached by free trade in ideas—that the best test of truth is the power of the thought to get itself accepted in the competition of the market, and that truth is the only ground upon which their wishes safely can be carried out. That at any rate is the theory of our Constitution. *Ibid.*

497   The greatest friend of truth is Time, her greatest enemy is prejudice, and her constant companion is humility. *Charles Caleb Colton*

498   I seem to have been only like a boy playing on the seashore and diverting myself in now and then finding the smoother pebble or a prettier shell than ordinary whilst the great ocean of truth lay all undiscovered before me. *Isaac Newton*

499   A man who seeks truth and loves it must be reckoned precious to any human society. *Frederick the Great*

500   Our minds possess by nature an insatiable desire to know the truth. *Marcus Tullius Cicero*

501   Honesty of thought and speech and written word is a jewel, and they who curb prejudice and seek honorably to know and speak the truth are the only builders of a better life. *John Galsworthy*

502   Once to every man and nation comes the moment to decide,
In the strife of Truth with Falsehood, for the good or evil side;
Some great cause, God's new bloom or blight,
Parts the goats upon the left hand, and the sheep upon the right;
And the choice goes by forever 'twixt that darkness and that light.
James Russell Lowell

UP THROUGH THE RANKS

503   There is not of necessity any such thing as the free hired laborer being fixed to that condition for life. Many independent men everywhere in these States a few years back in their lives were hired laborers. The prudent, penniless beginner in the world labors for wages awhile, saves a surplus with which to buy tools or land for himself, then labors on his own account another while, and at length hires another new beginner to help him. This is the just and generous and prosperous system which opens the way to all, gives hope to all, and consequent energy and progress and improvement of condition to all. No men living are more worthy to be trusted than those who toil up from poverty; none less inclined to take or touch aught which they have not honestly earned. Let them beware of surrendering a political power which they already possess, and which if surrendered will surely be used to close the door of advancement against such as they and fix new disabilities and burdens upon them till all of liberty shall be lost. *Abraham Lincoln*

VICTORY

504   Another such victory and we are undone. *Pyrrhus*

WEALTH

505   Ill fares the land, to hastening ills a prey,
Where wealth accumulates, and men decay. *Oliver Goldsmith*

506   Do not talk to me of Archimedes' lever. He was an absentminded
       person with a mathematical imagination. Mathematics command my
       respect, but I have no use for engines. Give me the right word and the
       right accent and I will move the world. *Joseph Conrad*

WORK

507   I never did anything worth doing by accident; nor did any of my
       inventions come by accident; they came by work. *Thomas Alva Edison*

508   All work, even cotton-spinning, is noble; work is alone noble. *Thomas
       Carlyle*

...4...

Selections from Speeches and Writings of Notables

ABILITY

509 With my own ability, I cannot succeed without the sustenance of Divine Providence, and of the great free, happy, and intelligent people. Without these I cannot hope to succeed; with them, I cannot fail. *Abraham Lincoln*

ABUNDANCE

510 Some see America's vast wealth and protest that this has made us "materialistic." But we should not be apologetic about our abundance. We should not fall into the easy trap of confusing the production of things with the worship of things. We produce abundantly; but our values turn not on what we have but on what we believe.

We believe in liberty, and decency, and the process of freedom. On these beliefs we rest our pride as a nation; in these beliefs we rest our hopes for the future; and by our fidelity to the process of freedom, we can assure to ourselves and our posterity the blessings of freedom. *Richard M. Nixon*

ADVICE

511 Be careful that victories do not carry the seed of future defeats. *Ralph W. Sockman*

ALLIANCE

512 It is our true policy to steer clear of permanent alliances with any portion of the foreign world. *George Washington*

AMBITION

513 It will not be amiss to distinguish the three kinds and as it were three grades of ambition in mankind. The first is of those who desire to extend their own power in their native country; which kind is vulgar and degenerated. The second is of those who labor to extend the power of their country and its dominion among men. This certainly has more

dignity, though not less covetousness. But if a man endeavor to establish and extend the power and dominion of the human race itself over
the universe, his ambition (if ambition it can be called) is without doubt
both a more wholesome thing and a more noble than the other two.
Now the empire of man over things depends wholly on the arts and
sciences. For we cannot command nature except by obeying her. *Francis Bacon*

AMERICA

514   Grateful to Almighty God for the blessings which, through Jesus Christ
our Lord, he has conferred on my beloved country in her emancipation, and on myself in permitting me under circumstances of mercy to
live to the age of eighty-nine years, and to survive the fiftieth year of
American Independence adopted by Congress on the fourth of July,
1776, which I originally subscribed on the second of August of the same
year, and of which I am now the last surviving signer, I do now here
recommend to the present and future generations the principles of
that important document as the best earthly inheritance their ancestors could bequeath to them, and pray that the civil and religious
liberties they have secured to my country may be perpetuated to the
remotest posterity and extend to the whole family of man! *Charles
Carroll*

515   Here in America we are descended in blood and in spirit from revolutionists and rebels—men and women who dared to dissent from accepted doctrine. As their heirs, we may never confuse honest dissent
with disloyal subversion. *Dwight D. Eisenhower*

516   Our way of living together in America is a strong but delicate fabric.
It is made up of many threads. It has been woven over many centuries
by the patience and sacrifice of countless liberty-loving men and
women. It serves as a cloak for the protection of poor and rich, of black
and white, of Jew and Gentile, of foreign and native born. Let us not
tear it asunder. For no man knows, once it is destroyed, where or when
man will find its protective warmth again. *Wendell L. Willkie*

517   America is not a mere body of traders; it is a body of free men. Our
greatness is built upon our freedom—is moral, not material. We have
a great ardor for gain; but we have a deep passion for the rights of man.
Woodrow Wilson

518   Your diffusion of literacy and average comfort and well-being among
the masses, in my opinion is one of the major achievements in human
history. With all its limitations, life in America is better and kinder
than anywhere on earth that I have ever heard of. *Alfred North Whitehead*

519   We are now a mighty nation: We are thirty, or about thirty, millions
of people. . . . We have, besides these men—descended by blood from

our ancestors—among us, perhaps half our people who are not descendants at all of these men; they are men who have come from Europe—German, Irish, French, and Scandinavian—men who have come from Europe themselves, or whose ancestors have come hither and settled here, finding themselves our equal in all things. If they look back through this history, to trace their connection with those days of blood, they find they have none; they cannot carry themselves back into that glorious epoch and make themselves feel that they are part of us; but when they look through that old Declaration of Independence, they find that those old men say that "we hold these truths to be self-evident, that all men are created equal," and then they feel that that moral sentiment taught in that day evidences their relation to those men, that it is the father of all moral principle in them, and that they have a right to claim it as though they were blood of the blood, and flesh of the flesh, of the men who wrote that Declaration; and so they are. *Abraham Lincoln*

520 Go, seeker, if you will, throughout the land and you will find us burning in the night. . . . To every man his chance, to every man, regardless of his birth, his shining golden opportunity—to every man the right to live, to work, to be himself, and to become whatever thing his manhood and his vision can combine to make him—this, seeker, is the promise of America. *Thomas Wolfe*

521 From this day forward, the millions of our schoolchildren will daily proclaim in every city and town, every village and rural schoolhouse, the dedication of our nation and our people to the Almighty. *Dwight D. Eisenhower, signing law including the words "under God" in the pledge of allegiance to the flag, June 14, 1954*

522 If our history teaches us anything, it is this lesson: So far as the economic potential of our nation is concerned, the believers in the future of America have always been the realists. I count myself as one of this company. *Ibid.*

523 I have found out in later years we were very poor, but the glory of America is that we didn't know it then. *Ibid.*

524 I can only say tonight to you that I believe in the American dream because I have seen it come true in my own life. *Richard M. Nixon*

525 When an American says he loves his country, he means not only that he loves the New England hills, the prairies glistening in the sun or the wide rising plains, the mountains and the seas. He means that he loves an inner air, an inner light in which freedom lives and in which a man can draw the breath of self-respect. *Adlai Stevenson*

526 With the supermarket as our temple and the singing commercial as our litany, are we likely to fire the world with an irresistible vision of America's exalted purposes and inspiring way of life? *Ibid.*

527 The face which we present to the world . . . is the face of the individual
or the family as a high-consumption unit with minimal social links or
responsibilities—father happily drinking his beer, mother dreamily
fondling soft garments newly rinsed in a wonderful new detergent, the
children gaily calling from the new barbecue pit for a famous sauce for
their steak. *Ibid.*

528 I was born an American; I will live an American; I shall die an American; and I intend to perform the duties incumbent upon me in that
character to the end of my career. I mean to do this with absolute
disregard of personal consequences. What are the personal consequences? What is the individual man, with all the good or evil that may
betide him, in comparison with the good or evil which may befall a
great country, and in the midst of great transactions which concern
that country's fate? Let the consequences be what they will, I am
careless. No man can suffer too much, and no man can fall too soon,
if he suffer, or if he fall, in the defense of the liberties and constitution
of his country. *Daniel Webster*

529 Let it be understood in my parting words to you that I am no pessimist
as to this republic. I always bet on sunshine in America. *Henry W.
Grady*

530 God did not make the American people the mightiest human force of
all time simply to feed and die. He did not give our race the brain or
organization and heart of domain to no purpose and no end. No; he has
given us a task equal to our talents. He has appointed for us a destiny
equal to our endowments. *Albert J. Beveridge*

531 When honored and decrepit age shall lean against the base of this
monument, and troops of ingenuous youth shall be gathered round it,
and when the one shall speak to the other of its objects, the purposes
of its construction, and the great and glorious events with which it is
connected, there shall rise from every youthful breast the ejaculation,
"Thank God, I—I also—*am an American!*" *Daniel Webster*

532 What constitutes an American? Not color, nor race, nor religion. Not
the pedigree of his family nor the place of his birth. Not the coinci-
dence of his citizenship. Not his social status nor his bank account. Not
his trade nor his profession. An American is one who loves justice and
believes in the dignity of man. An American is one who will fight for
his freedom and that of his neighbor. An American is one who will
sacrifice property, ease, and security in order that he and his children
may retain the rights of free men. An American is one in whose heart
is engraved the immortal second sentence of the Declaration of Independence.

Americans have always known how to fight for their rights and their way of life. Americans are not afraid to fight. They fight joyously in a just cause. *Harold L. Ickes*

533 I am a free man, an American, a United States Senator, and a Democrat in that order. I am also a liberal, a conservative, a Texan, a taxpayer, a rancher, a businessman, a consumer, a parent, a voter, and not as young as I used to be nor as old as I expect to be—and I am all these things in no fixed order. *Lyndon B. Johnson*

THE AMERICAN'S CREED

534 I believe in the United States of America as a government of the people, by the people, for the people; whose just powers are derived from the consent of the governed; a democracy in a republic, a sovereign Nation of many sovereign States; a perfect Union one and inseparable; established upon those principles of freedom, equality, justice, and humanity for which American patriots sacrificed their lives and fortunes. I therefore believe it is my duty to my country to love it, to support its Constitution, to obey its laws, to respect its flag, and to defend it against all enemies. *William Tyler Page*

ARCHBISHOP OF CANTERBURY

535 What does it take to be an Archbishop of Canterbury? The strength of a horse—the ability to be a cart horse one day and a race horse the next. *Geoffrey Fisher*

ARISTOCRACY

536 There is a natural aristocracy among men. The grounds of this are virtue and talents. . . . There is also an artificial aristocracy founded on wealth and birth, without either virtue or talents; for with these it would belong to the first class. The natural aristocracy I consider as the most precious gift of nature, for the instruction, the trusts, and government of society. . . .

May we not even say that that form of government is best which provides the most effectually for a pure selection of these natural aristoi into the offices of government? The artificial aristocracy is a mischievous ingredient in government, and provision should be made to prevent its ascendancy. *Thomas Jefferson*

BERLIN

537 There are many people in the world who really don't understand—or say they don't—what is the great issue between the free world and the Communist world. . . . There are some who say that Communism is the wave of the future. . . . And there are some who say in Europe and elsewhere "we can work with the Communists." . . . And there are even a few who say that it's true that Communism is an evil system but it permits us to make economic progress. Let them come to Berlin! *John F. Kennedy*

BOOKS

538   And yet, on the other hand, unless wariness be used, as good almost kill a man as kill a good book: who kills a man kills a reasonable creature, God's image; but he who destroys a good book kills reason itself, kills the image of God, as it were, in the eye. *John Milton*

THE BRAVE

539   We are not weak if we make a proper use of those means which the God of Nature has placed in our power . . . the battle, sir, is not to the strong alone; it is to the vigilant, the active, the brave. *Patrick Henry*

CANADA

540   Geography has made us neighbors. History has made us friends. Economics has made us partners; and necessity has made us allies. *John F. Kennedy*

CHANCE

541   Those who trust to chance must abide by the results of chance. They have no legitimate complaint against anyone but themselves. *Calvin Coolidge*

CHANGE

542   Any change in men's views as to what is good and right in human life makes its way but tardily at the best. Especially is this true of any change in the direction of what is called progress; that is to say, in the direction of divergence from the archaic position; from the position which may be accounted the point of departure at any step in the social evolution of the community. *Thorstein Veblen*

WINSTON CHURCHILL

543   In the dark days and darker nights when England stood alone—and most men save Englishmen despaired of England's life—he mobilized the English language and sent it into battle. The incandescent quality of his words illuminated the courage of his countrymen. *John F. Kennedy*

544   His stately ship of life, having weathered the severest storms of a troubled century, is anchored in tranquil waters, proof that courage and faith and zest for freedom are truly indestructible. The record of his triumphant passage will inspire free hearts all over the globe. *Ibid.*

THE CITIES

545   A strong America depends on its cities—America's glory and sometimes America's shame. *Ibid.*

CIVILIZATION

546   Civilization begins with order, grows with liberty, and dies with chaos. *Will Durant*

CIVIL LIBERTIES

547   In respect of civil rights, common to all citizens, the Constitution of the United States does not, I think, permit any authority to know the race of those entitled to be protected in the enjoyment of such rights. *John Marshall*

548   The sure guarantee of the peace and security of each race is the clear, distinct, unconditional recognition by our governments, national and state, of every right that inheres in civil freedom, and of the equality before the law of all the citizens of the United States without regard to race. *Ibid.*

549   Law enforcement is a protecting arm of civil liberties. Civil liberties cannot exist without law enforcement; law enforcement without civil liberties is a hollow mockery. They are parts of the same whole—one without the other becomes a dead letter. *J. Edgar Hoover*

CIVIL RIGHTS

550   We are confronted primarily with a moral issue. It is as old as the Scriptures and is as clear as the American Constitution. *John F. Kennedy*

551   No one has been barred on account of his race from fighting or dying for America—there are no "white" or "colored" signs on the foxholes or graveyards of battle. *Ibid.*

552   Unfortunately many Americans live on the outskirts of hope—some because of their poverty, some because of their color, and all too many because of both. Our task is to help replace their despair with opportunity. *Lyndon B. Johnson*

CLOSE OF THE STATE OF THE UNION MESSAGE

553   President-elect Nixon in the days ahead is going to need your understanding, just as I did. He is entitled to have it. I hope every member will remember that the burdens he will bear as our President will be borne for all of us. Each of us should try not to increase these burdens for the sake of narrow personal or partisan advantage.

And now it is time to leave.

I hope it may be said, a hundred years from now, that by working together we helped to make our country more just, more just for all of its people—as well as to insure and guarantee the blessings of liberty for all of our posterity. That is what I hope, but I believe that it will be said that we tried. *Lyndon B. Johnson*

COLONIZATION

554   ... that the American continents, by the free and independent conditions which they have assumed and maintained, are henceforth not to be considered as subjects for future colonization by any European powers. *James Monroe*

COMMITMENT

555 This nation will keep its commitments from South Vietnam to West Berlin. We will be unceasing in the search for peace, resourceful in our pursuit of areas of agreement even with those with whom we differ, and generous and loyal to those who join with us in common cause. *Lyndon B. Johnson*

COMMUNISM

556 Communism is based on the belief that man is so weak and inadequate that he is unable to govern himself, and therefore requires the rule of strong masters. *Harry S. Truman*

CONGRESS

557 It is all so solemn. Somebody will get up and say: "I thank the gentleman for his contribution," when all the guy did was belch or garble. Now I'm all for back-scratching, but I'd like to see a wink once in a while. *James Tumulty*

CONQUEST

558 I came, I saw, I conquered. *Julius Caesar*

CRITICISM

559 To speak ill of others is a dishonest way of praising ourselves; let us be above such transparent egotism.... If you can't say good and encouraging things, say nothing. Nothing is often a good thing to say, and always a clever thing to say. *Will Durant*

CONSERVATIVE

560 By "radical" I understand one who goes too far; by "conservative" one who does not go far enough; by "reactionary" one who won't go at all. *Woodrow Wilson*

561 The true conservative seeks to protect the system of private property and free enterprise by correcting such injustices and inequalities as arise from it. The most serious threat to our institutions comes from those who refuse to face the need for change. Liberalism becomes the protection for the farsighted conservative. *Franklin D. Roosevelt*

CONSTITUTION

562 As the patriots of seventy-six did to the support of the Declaration of Independence, so to the support of the Constitution and Laws let every American pledge his life, his property, and his sacred honor; let every man remember that to violate the law is to trample on the blood of his father, and to tear the charter of his own and his children's liberty. *Abraham Lincoln*

COSTLIEST GENERATION

563 In the past generation, since 1941, this nation has paid for fourteen years of peace with fourteen years of war. The American war dead of

this generation has been far greater than all of the preceding generations of Americans combined. In terms of human suffering, this has been the costliest generation in the two centuries of our history.

Perhaps this is why my generation is so fiercely determined to pass on a different legacy. We want to redeem that sacrifice. We want to be remembered, not as the generation that suffered, but as the generation that was tempered in its fire for a great purpose: to make the kind of peace that the next generation will be able to keep. *Richard M. Nixon*

COUNTRY

564   Our country, right or wrong. When right, to be kept right; when wrong, to be put right. *Carl Schurz*

565   And so, my fellow Americans: ask not what your country can do for you —ask what you can do for your country. *John F. Kennedy*

CRISES

566   In times of grave crises, there are always some who fall a prey to doubt and unreasoning fear; some who seek refuge in cynicism and narrow self-interest; some who wrap themselves in the treacherous cloak of complacency. All these are dangers that lie within us. All these impair the faith and weaken the determination without which freedom cannot prevail.

A responsibility seldom equaled in gravity and danger rests upon each and every one of us. Neglect or delay in assuming it, willingly and fully, would place in mortal danger our way of life and the sacred cause of human freedom. Were we to fail in that responsibility, we would fail ourselves; we would fail the generations that went before us; we would fail the generations that are to come after us; we would fail mankind; we would fail God.

I am completely confident that we shall not fail. I am certain that in the minds and hearts of our people still—still—lie welling springs— inexhaustible and indestructible—of faith in the things we cherish, of courage and determination to defend them, of sacrificial devotion, or unbreakable unity of purpose. I am certain that, however great the hardships and the trials which loom ahead, our America will endure and the cause of human freedom will triumph. *Cordell Hull*

DANGERS

567   If I were asked to name the three influences which I thought were most dangerous to the perpetuity of American institutions, I should name corruption, in business and politics alike; lawless violence; and mendacity, especially used in connection with slander.

We Americans are children of the crucible.

Americanism means the virtues of courage, honor, justice, truth, sincerity, and hardihood—the virtues that make America. The things that will destroy America are prosperity-at-any-price, peace-at-any-price, safety-first instead of duty-first, the love of soft living and the get-rich-quick theory of life. *Theodore Roosevelt*

DECIMAL POINTS

568 I never could make out what those damned dots meant. *Lord Randolph Churchill*

DEDICATION

569 The only worthy response to danger and failure is a renewed dedication to success; and I trust it will be written of the American people in our time, not that we refused to soil our hands with the imperfections of ourselves and of the world, but that we grew stronger, striving to overcome them. *Adlai Stevenson*

A DEEPLY TROUBLED TIME

570 We live in a deeply troubled and profoundly unsettled time. Drugs, crime, campus revolts, racial discord, draft resistance—on every hand we find old standards violated, old values discarded, old precepts ignored. A vocal minority of the young are opting out of the process by which a civilization maintains its continuity: the passing on of values from one generation to the next. Old and young shout across a chasm of misunderstanding—and the more loudly they shout, the wider the chasm grows.

As a result, our institutions are undergoing what may be their severest challenge yet. I speak not of the physical challenge: the forces and threats of force that have racked our cities, and now our colleges. Force can be contained.

We have the power to strike back if need be, and to prevail. The nation has survived other attempts at this. It has not been a lack of civil power, but the reluctance of a free people to employ it, that so often has stayed the hand of authorities faced with confrontation. *Richard M. Nixon*

DEFENSE

571 Let no one think that the expenditure of vast sums for weapons and systems of defense can guarantee absolute safety for the cities and citizens of any nation. The awful arithmetic of the atomic bomb does not permit of any such easy solution. *Dwight D. Eisenhower*

DESCRIPTION

572 Well, I'm about as tall as a shotgun, and just as noisy. *Truman Capote*

DESTINY

573 This generation of Americans has a rendezvous with destiny. *Franklin D. Roosevelt*

574 Our destiny offers not the cup of despair, but the chalice of opportunity. So let us seize it, not in fear, but in gladness—and "riders on the earth together," let us go forward, firm in our faith, steadfast in our purpose, cautious of the dangers; but sustained by our confidence in the will of God and the promise of man. *Richard M. Nixon*

DISCONTENT

575 Restlessness is discontent—and discontent is the first necessity of progress. Show me a thoroughly satisfied man—and I will show you a failure. *Thomas Alva Edison*

DUTY

576 I preach to you, then, my countrymen, that our country calls not for the life of ease, but for the life of strenuous endeavor. The twentieth century looms before us big with the fate of many nations. If we stand idly by, if we seek merely swollen, slothful ease, and ignoble peace, if we shrink from the hard contests where men must win at hazard of their lives and at the risk of all they hold dear, then the bolder and stronger peoples will pass us by and will win for themselves the domination of the world. Let us therefore boldly face the life of strife, resolute to do our duty well and manfully; resolute to uphold righteousness by deed and by word; resolute to be both honest and brave, to serve high ideals, yet to use practical methods. Above all, let us shrink from no strife, moral or physical, within or without the nation, provided we are certain that the strife is justified; for it is only through strife, through hard and dangerous endeavor, that we shall ultimately win the goal of true national greatness. *Theodore Roosevelt*

577 The nation which indulges towards another an habitual hatred, or an habitual fondness, is in some degree a slave. It is a slave to its animosity or to its affection, either of which is sufficient to lead it astray from its duty and its interest. *George Washington*

EDUCATION

578 We have entered an age in which education is not just a luxury permitting some men an advantage over others. It has become a necessity without which a person is defenseless in this complex, industrialized society. . . . We have truly entered the century of the educated man. *Lyndon B. Johnson*

579 The human mind is our fundamental resource. *John F. Kennedy*

580 If, almost on the day of their landings, our ancestors founded schools and endowed colleges, what obligations do not rest upon us, living under circumstances so much more favorable both for providing and for using the means of education? *Daniel Webster*

581   But it was in making education not only common to all, but in some sense compulsory on all, that the destiny of the free republics of America was practically settled. *James Russell Lowell*

ELECTION

582   Someone asked me . . . how I felt and I was reminded of a story that a fellow townsman of ours used to tell—Abraham Lincoln. They asked him how he felt once after an unsuccessful election. He said he felt like a little boy who has stubbed his toe in the dark. He said that he was too old to cry, but it hurt too much to laugh. *Adlai Stevenson*

EMPIRE

583   Let me, however, make this clear, in case there should be any mistake about it in any quarter. We mean to hold our own. I have not become the King's First Minister in order to preside over the liquidation of the British Empire. *Winston Churchill*

EPITAPH

584   In presenting this scroll . . . I am rewarding "a good public servant." I hope that will be my epitaph. *Harry S. Truman*

EXPERIENCE

585   I have but one lamp by which my feet are guided, and that is the lamp of experience. I know of no way of judging of the future but by the past. *Patrick Henry*

FAREWELL TO HIS ARMY

586   After four years of arduous service, marked by unsurpassed courage and fortitude, the Army of Northern Virginia has been compelled to yield to overwhelming numbers and resources. I need not tell the survivors of many hard-fought battles, who have remained steadfast to the last, that I have consented to this result from no distrust of them: but, feeling that valor and devotion could accomplish nothing that could compensate for the loss that would have attended the continuation of the contest, I have determined to avoid the useless sacrifice of those whose past services have endeared them to their countrymen. By the terms of the agreement, officers and men can return to their homes and remain there until exchanged. You will take with you the satisfaction that proceeds from the consciousness of duty faithfully performed; and I earnestly pray that a merciful God will extend to you His blessing and protection. With an increasing admiration of your constancy and devotion to your country, and a grateful remembrance of your kind and generous consideration of myself, I bid you an affectionate farewell. *Robert E. Lee*

FEAR

587   This is preeminently the time to speak the truth, the whole truth, frankly and boldly. Nor need we shrink from honestly facing conditions

in our country today. This great nation will endure as it has endured, will revive and will prosper.

So first of all let me assert my firm belief that the only thing we have to fear is fear itself—nameless, unreasoning, unjustified terror which paralyzes needed efforts to convert retreat into advance. *Franklin D. Roosevelt*

THE FLAG

588   The things that the flag stands for were created by the experience of a great people. Everything that it stands for was written by their lives. The flag is the embodiment, not of sentiment, but of history. *Woodrow Wilson*

FORCE

589   The use of force alone is but *temporary*. It may subdue for a moment; but it does not remove the necessity of subduing again: and a nation is not governed, which is perpetually to be conquered. *Edmund Burke*

FOREIGN POLICY

590   Our policy in regard to Europe . . . remains the same, which is, not to interfere in the internal concerns of any of its Powers; to consider the government de facto as the legitimate government for us; to cultivate friendly relations with it, and to preserve those relations by a frank, firm, and manly policy, meeting in all instances the just claims of every Power, submitting to injuries from none. *James Monroe*

591   We Americans have no commission from God to police the world. *Benjamin Harrison*

FRANCE

592   The whole world recognizes that order and progress have once again got a chance in our country. What to do with it? Ah, to do a great deal. For we have to transform our old France into a new country and martyr it to its time. France must find prosperity in this way. This must be our great national ambition. *Charles de Gaulle*

593   Old Earth, eaten away by the ages, buffeted by rains and winds, exhausted, but ever ready to produce again what life needs to go on. Old France, weighted down by History, racked by wars and revolutions, rising and falling from grandeur to decline, yet ever renewed, from century to century, with its genius for renewal. Old man, perennial recruit of crisis, not detached from enterprise, feeling the approach of the eternal cold, but never weary of staring into the shadows watchful for the gleam of hope. *Ibid.*

FREEDOM

594   The American idea . . . a democracy—that is, a government of all the people, by all the people, for all the people; of course, a govern-

ment of the principles, of eternal justice, the unchanging law of God: for shortness sake, I will call it the idea of Freedom. *Theodore Parker*

595   It [freedom] is a thing of the spirit. Men must be free to worship, to think, to hold opinions, to speak without fear. They must be free to challenge wrong and oppression with surety of justice. Freedom conceives that the mind and spirit of man can be free only if he be free to pattern his own life, to develop his own talents, free to earn, to spend, to save, to acquire property as the security of his old age and his family. *Herbert Hoover*

596   The time is now near at hand which must probably determine whether Americans are to be freemen or slaves; whether they are to have any property they can call their own; whether their houses and farms are to be pillaged and destroyed, and themselves consigned to a state of wretchedness from which no human efforts will deliver them. The fate of unborn millions will now depend, under God, on the courage and conduct of this army. . . . We have, therefore, to resolve to conquer or to die. *George Washington*

597   There are more instances of the abridgment of the freedom of the people by gradual and silent encroachments of those in power than by violent and sudden usurpation. *James Madison*

598   Freedom is an indivisible word. If we want to enjoy it, and fight for it, we must be prepared to extend it to everyone, whether they are rich or poor, whether they agree with us or not, no matter what their race or the color of their skin. *Wendell L. Willkie*

599   If we in America choose to live in Lincoln's tradition, we will keep our freedom because we have earned it. We will inspire others to do likewise. I have no doubt as to the outcome. America will always choose the path of freedom. We will make that choice because brave men and women, fearing God, can make no other. Ours is an abiding faith in the cause of human freedom. We know it is God's cause. *Thomas E. Dewey*

600   We must be ready to dare all for our country. For history does not long entrust the care of freedom to the weak or the timid. *Dwight D. Eisenhower*

601   May the light of freedom, coming to all darkened lands, flame brightly —until at last the darkness is no more. *Ibid.*

FRENCH

602   The American arrives in Paris with a few French phrases he has culled from a conversational guide or picked up from a friend who owns a beret. He speaks the sort of French that is really understood by another American who also has just arrived in Paris. *Fred Allen*

GENIUS

603 In every work of genius we recognize our own rejected thoughts; they come back to us with a certain alienated majesty. Great works of art have no more affecting lesson for us than this. They teach us to abide by our spontaneous impression with good-humored inflexibility the most when the whole cry of voices is on the other side. *Ralph Waldo Emerson*

A GIANT OF OUR TIME

604 For a quarter of a century, to the very end of his life, Dwight Eisenhower exercised a moral authority without parallel in America and in the world.

And America and the world is better because of him.

And so, today, we render our final salute. It is a fond salute to a man we loved and cherished. It is a grateful salute to a man whose whole extraordinary life was consecrated to service.

It is a profoundly respectful salute to a man larger than life who by any standard was one of the giants of our time.

Each of us here will have a special memory of Dwight Eisenhower.

I can see him now standing erect, straight, proud and tall eleven years ago as he took the oath of office as the thirty-fourth President of the United States of America.

We salute Dwight David Eisenhower standing there in our memories—first in war, first in peace, and, wherever freedom is cherished, first in the hearts of his fellowmen. *Richard M. Nixon*

GOD

605 Nor will that day dawn at a human nod,
When, bursting through the network superposed
By selfish occupation—plot and plan,
Lust, avarice, envy—liberated man,
All difference with his fellow mortal closed,
Shall be left standing face to face with God. *Matthew Arnold*

606 No people can be bound to acknowledge and adore the invisible hand which conducts the affairs of men, more than the people of the United States. Every step by which they have advanced to the character of an independent nation, seems to have been distinguished by some token of providential agency. *George Washington*

607 Before all else, we seek, upon our common labor as a nation, the favor of Almighty God. And the hopes in our hearts fashion the deepest prayers of our people:

May we pursue the right—without self-righteousness.

May we know unity—without conformity.

May we grow in strength—without pride of self.

May we, in our dealings with all people of the earth, ever speak truth and serve justice. *Dwight D. Eisenhower*

608   Finally, whether you are citizens of America or citizens of the world, ask of us here the same high standards of strength and sacrifice which we ask of you. With a good conscience our only sure reward, with history the final judge of our deeds, let us go forth to lead the land we love, asking His blessing and His help, but knowing that here on earth God's work must truly be our own. *John F. Kennedy*

609   The supreme reality of our time is our indivisibility as children of God and the common vulnerability of this planet. *Ibid.*

GOOD

610   Ring out false pride in place and blood,
The civic slander and the spite;
Ring in the love of truth and light,
Ring in the common love of good. *Lord Tennyson*

GOVERNMENT

611   The government of the United States is a device for maintaining in perpetuity the rights of the people, with the ultimate extinction of all privileged classes. *Calvin Coolidge*

612   Free government is the political expression of a deeply felt religious faith. *Dwight D. Eisenhower*

613   We admit of no government by divine right . . . the only legitimate right to govern is an express grant of power from the governed. *William Henry Harrison*

614   There are no necessary evils in government. Its evils exist only in its abuses. If it would confine itself to equal protection, and, as heaven does its rain, shower its favors alike on the high and on the low, the rich and the poor, it would be an unqualified blessing. *Andrew Jackson*

615   Government is a trust, and the officers of the government are trustees; and both the trust and the trustees are created for the benefit of the people. *Henry Clay*

616   But there never yet has been devised a scheme of emptying the pockets of one portion of the community into those of the other, however unjust or oppressive, for which plausible reasons could be found. *John C. Calhoun*

617   The very essence of a free government consists in considering offices as public trusts, bestowed for the good of a country, and not for the benefit of an individual or a party. *Ibid.*

618   I believe this government cannot endure permanently half slave and half free. *Abraham Lincoln*

619   Every citizen owes to the country a vigilant watch and close scrutiny of its public servants and a fair and reasonable estimate of their fidelity

and usefulness. Thus is the people's will impressed upon the whole framework of our civil policy—municipal, state, and federal. *Grover Cleveland*

620   If the chosen representative does not represent the citizen, his voice is stifled; is denied any part in government. If majority decision as determined by the law of the land is ignored and reversed, if the expressed will of the people is scorned and scorned again—then the popular government fails, then government of the people, by the people, and for the people is at an end. Its forms may be observed— you may have the mockery of "elections," and the force of "representation"—but a government based upon the will of the people has perished from the earth. *Robert M. La Follette*

621   As I get older . . . I become more convinced that good government is not a substitute for self-government. *Dwight Morrow*

GREAT BRITAIN

622   Let us therefore brace ourselves to our duties, and so bear ourselves that, if the British Empire and its Commonwealth last for a thousand years, men will say, "This was their finest hour." *Winston Churchill*

GREATNESS

623   If blood be shed, let it be our blood. Cultivate the quiet courage of dying without killing. For man lives freely only by his readiness to die, if need be, at the hands of his brother, never by killing him. *Mahatma Gandhi*

624   I did not know the dignity of their birth, but I do know the glory of their death. *Douglas MacArthur*

THE GREATNESS OF A PEOPLE

625   Whether our values are maintained depends ultimately not on the government, but on the people.

A nation can only be as great as its people want it to be.

A nation can be only as free as its people insist that it be.

A nation's laws are only as strong as its people's will to see them enforced.

A nation's freedoms are only as secure as its people's determination to see them maintained.

A nation's values are only as lasting as the ability of each generation to pass them on to the next. *Richard M. Nixon*

GRIEVANCE

626   There is no grievance that is a fit object of redress by mob rule. *Abraham Lincoln*

THE HIGHEST REALISM

627   My friends of the United Church of Christ, ever since Moses, probably long before, man has been dreaming of the Promised Land. Even in

Moses' time it was possible for small groups of men, inspired by faith, endowed with courage and enterprise, to make deserts bloom and to offer their children lives which were both rewarding and noble. To our generation, for the first time in history, is offered the possibility to offer to *our* children, and I mean all children of the family of man, lives of this quality, lives no less rich in adventure and challenge for being secure, healthy, and harmonious, lives during which the age-old promise of "peace on earth and good will to men" might at last begin to be fulfilled.

Is this unrealistic? Of course it may be. Of course it *will* be if we insist on looking no farther than the ends of our hard noses, if we insist on setting no higher aim than national or racial or ideological advantage. In closing, I would argue again that, in light of the miracles, technological or divine, which now permit us to land on the moon, to blow up our planet or to feed the multitudes, the highest realism is to choose soberly among these miraculous new capabilities, to control and root out together those that can enrich and unite us.

A recent British ambassador to Washington remarked that "man is a peculiarly constructed animal who can't read the handwriting on the wall until he has his back to it." Let that not be said of us. Let us read in time both the evil tidings and the good tidings written on the wall and, asking God's help, choose wisely and realistically between them. *Charles W. Yost*

HONOR

628 National honor is national property of the highest value. *James Monroe*

HUMILITY

629 Humility must always be the portion of any man who receives acclaim earned in the blood of his followers and the sacrifices of his friends. *Dwight D. Eisenhower*

630 I had delusions of humility. *Gene Fowler*

HUNGER

631 One half of humanity is hungering at this very moment. There is less food per person on the planet today than there was thirty years ago in the midst of a worldwide depression. *Robert S. McNamara*

IDEALS

632 We are all idealists. We are all visionaries. Let it not be said of this Atlantic generation that we left ideals and visions to the past, nor purpose and determination to our adversaries. We have come too far, we have sacrificed too much, to disdain the future now. *John F. Kennedy*

633 Ideals are like stars; you will not succeed in touching them with your hands. But like the seafaring man on the desert of waters, you choose them as your guides, and following them you will reach your destiny. *Carl Schurz*

INCENTIVES

634 Call it what you will, incentives are what get people to work harder. *Nikita Khrushchev*

INDICTMENT

635 I do not know the method of drawing up an indictment against a whole people. *Edmund Burke*

INDISPENSABLE

636 There is no indispensable man. *Franklin D. Roosevelt*

INDIVIDUALISM

637 I believe in individualism . . . up to the point where the individualist starts to operate at the expense of society. *Ibid.*

INTERNATIONAL JUDGMENT

638 When Kansas and Colorado have a quarrel over the water in the Arkansas River they don't call out the National Guard in each state and go to war over it. They bring a suit in the Supreme Court of the United States and abide by the decision. There isn't a reason in the world why we cannot do that internationally. *Harry S. Truman*

IRON CURTAIN

639 A shadow has fallen upon the scenes so lately lighted by the Allied victory. From Stettin in the Baltic to Trieste in the Adriatic an iron curtain has descended across the Continent. *Winston Churchill*

JUDGMENT

640 Of those to whom much is given, much is required. And when at some future date the high court of history sits in judgment on each one of us—recording whether in our brief span of service we fulfilled our responsibilities to the state—our success or failure, in whatever office we may hold, will be measured by the answers to four questions—were we truly men of courage . . . were we truly men of judgment . . . were we truly men of integrity . . . were we truly men of dedication? *John F. Kennedy*

JUSTICE

641 Why should there not be a patient confidence in the ultimate justice of the people? Is there any equal hope in the world? *Abraham Lincoln*

JOHN F. KENNEDY

642 President Kennedy was so contemporary a man—so involved in our world—so immersed in our times—so responsive to its challenges—so intense a participant in the great events and great decisions of our day,

that he seemed the very symbol of the vitality and exuberance that is the essence of life itself. *Adlai Stevenson*

KNOWLEDGE

643   It is substantially true that virtue or morality is a necessary spring of popular government. The rule indeed extends with more or less force to every species of free government. Who that is a sincere friend to it can look with indifference upon attempts to shake the foundation of the fabric.

Promote then, as an object of primary importance, institutions for the general diffusion of knowledge. In proportion as the structure of a government gives force to public opinion, it is essential that public opinion be enlightened. *George Washington*

LABOR

644   Labor disgraces no man; unfortunately you occasionally find men disgrace labor. *Ulysses S. Grant*

645   Having behind us the producing masses of this nation, and the world, supported by the commercial interests, the laboring interests, and the toilers everywhere, we will answer their demand for a gold standard by saying to them: You shall not press down upon the brow of labor the crown of thorns, you shall not crucify mankind upon a cross of gold. *William Jennings Bryan*

LANGUAGE

646   We live . . . in a sea of semantic disorder in which old labels no longer faithfully describe. Police states are called "people's democracies." Armed conquest of free people is called "liberation." Such slippery slogans make more difficult the problems of communicating true faith, facts, and beliefs. . . . We must use language to enlighten the mind, not as the instrument of the studied innuendo and distorter of truth. And we must live by what we say. *Dwight D. Eisenhower*

LAW

647   Let me not be understood as saying that there are no bad laws, or that grievances may not arise for the redress of which no legal provisions have been made. I mean to say no such thing, but I do mean to say that although bad laws, if they exist, should be repealed as soon as possible, still, while they continue in force, for the sake of example they should be religiously observed. *Abraham Lincoln*

648   All obstructions to the execution of the laws, all combinations and associations under whatever plausible character, with the real design to direct, control, counteract, or awe the regular deliberations and action of the constituted authorities, are destructive of this fundamental principle, and of fatal tendency. *George Washington*

649   I know no method to secure the repeal of bad or obnoxious laws so effective as their strict execution. *Ulysses S. Grant*

LIBERAL

650   What is a liberal? He may be an earnest soul, unimpeachable in his
      fidelity to the roots and anchors of the American system, who wants
      the maximum measure of life, liberty, and happiness for our total
      people. In that sense I want my party to be "liberal."
          On the other hand, he may seek the substitution of socialism for free
      enterprise, and paternalism for individual responsibility. In that sense
      I do not want my party to be "liberal." I am not interested in equality
      of servitude. *Arthur H. Vandenberg*

LIBERTY

651   The war is actually begun! The next gale that sweeps from the north
      will bring to our ears the clash of resounding arms! Our brethren are
      already in the field. Why stand we idle here? . . . Is life so dear, or peace
      so sweet, as to be purchased at the price of chains and slavery? Forbid
      it, Almighty God! I know not what course others may take, but as for
      me, give me liberty, or give me death! *Patrick Henry*

652   The unity of the Government, which constitutes you one people, is also
      now dear to you. It is justly so; for it is a main pillar in the edifice of
      your real independence; the support of your tranquillity at home; your
      peace abroad; of your safety; of your prosperity in every shape; of that
      very liberty which you so highly prize. *George Washington*

653   Let every nation know, whether it wishes us well or ill, that we shall
      pay any price, bear any burden, meet any hardship, support any friend,
      oppose any foe to assure the survival and the success of liberty. *John
      F. Kennedy*

654   Liberty and Union, now and forever, one and inseparable. *Daniel
      Webster*

655   The history of liberty is a history of the limitations of governmental
      power, not the increase of it. *Woodrow Wilson*

656   He that would make his own liberty secure must guard even his enemy
      from oppression. *Thomas Paine*

657   In the name of the Great Jehovah and the Continental Congress.
      Ethan Allen, demanding the surrender of Fort Ticonderoga

LITTLE NATIONS

658   The greatest art of the world was the work of little nations. The most
      enduring literature of the world came from little nations. The heroic
      deeds that thrill humanity through generations were the deeds of little
      nations fighting for their freedom and, yes, the salvation of mankind
      came through a little nation. *John F. Kennedy*

LOYALTY

659   This hour little needs the loyalty that is loyal to one section and yet
      holds the other in enduring suspicion and estrangement. Give us the
      broad and perfect loyalty that loves and trusts Georgia alike with

Massachusetts—that knows no south, no north, no east, no west, but endears with equal and patriotic love every foot of our soil, every state in our Union. *Henry W. Grady*

MAJORITY

660   A majority held in restraint by constitutional checks and limitations, and always changing easily with deliberate changes of popular opinions and sentiments, is the only true sovereign of a free people. Whoever rejects it does, of necessity, fly to anarchy or to despotism. Unanimity is impossible; the rule of a minority, as a permanent arrangement, is wholly inadmissible; so that, rejecting the majority principle, anarchy or despotism in some form is all that is left. *Abraham Lincoln*

661   At the present moment in world history nearly every nation must choose between alternative ways of life. . . . One way of life is based upon the will of the majority. . . . The second way of life is based upon the will of the minority forcibly imposed upon the majority. It relies upon terror and oppression, a controlled press and radio, fixed elections, and the suppression of personal freedom.

I believe that it must be the policy of the United States to support free peoples who are resisting subjugation by armed minorities or by outside pressure. *Harry S. Truman*

MAN

662   A man who is good enough to shed his blood for his country is good enough to be given a square deal afterward. More than that no man is entitled to, and less than that no man shall have. *Theodore Roosevelt*

663   The question is this: Is man an ape or an angel? I, my lord, am on the side of the angels. *Benjamin Disraeli*

MEDIOCRITY

664   The tendencies of democracies are, in all things, to mediocrity, since the tastes, knowledge, and principles of the majority form the tribunal of appeal. This circumstance, while it certainly serves to elevate the average qualities of a nation, renders the introduction of a high standard difficult. Thus do we find in literature, the arts, architecture, and in all acquired knowledge, a tendency in America to gravitate towards the common center in this, as in other things; lending a value and estimation to mediocrity that are not elsewhere given. *James Fenimore Cooper*

MEMORIES

665   I carry with me from this state to that high and lonely office to which I now succeed more than fond memories and firm friendships. The enduring qualities of Massachusetts—the common threads woven by

the Pilgrim and the Puritan, the fisherman and the farmer, the Yankee and the immigrant—will not be and could not be forgotten in this nation's executive mansion. They are an indelible part of my life, my conviction, my view of the past, and my hopes in the future. *John F. Kennedy*

MILK
666 There is no finer investment for any community than putting milk into babies. Healthy citizens are the greatest asset any country can have. *Winston Churchill*

MINORITY
667 The thing we have to fear in this country, to my way of thinking, is the influence of the organized minorities, because somehow or other the great majority does not seem to organize. They seem to feel that they are going to be effective because of their own strength, but they give no expression of it. *Alfred E. Smith*

MUCK-RAKE
668 Men with the muck-rake are often indispensable to the well-being of society, but only if they know when to stop raking the muck. *Theodore Roosevelt*

THE NATION
669 We will serve all the nation, not one section or one sector, or one group, but all Americans. These are the *United* States—a united people with a united purpose. *Lyndon B. Johnson*

670 In this age when there can be no losers in peace and no victors in war —we must recognize the obligation to match national strength with national restraint—we must be prepared at one and the same time for both the confrontation of power and the limitation of power—we must be ready to defend the national interest and to negotiate the common interest. *Ibid.*

NEGRO
671 The Negro says, "Now." Others say, "Never." The voice of responsible Americans . . . says, "Together." There is no other way. Until justice is blind to color, until education is unaware of race, until opportunity is unconcerned with the color of men's skins, emancipation will be a proclamation but not a fact. *Ibid.*

NEIGHBOR
672 In the field of world policy I would dedicate this nation to the policy of the good neighbor. *Franklin D. Roosevelt*

NOBEL PRIZE WINNERS
673 I think this is the most extraordinary collection of talent, of human knowledge, that has ever been gathered together at the White House

—with the possible exception of when Thomas Jefferson dined alone. *John F. Kennedy*

PATERNALISM

674　The lessons of paternalism ought to be unlearned and the better lesson taught that while the people should patriotically and cheerfully support their government, its functions do not include the support of the people. *Grover Cleveland*

PATRIOTISM

675　I venture to suggest that patriotism is not a short and frenzied outburst of emotion but the tranquil and steady dedication of a lifetime. *Adlai Stevenson*

PEACE

676　The mere absence of war is not peace. The mere absence of recession is not growth. *John F. Kennedy*

677　With malice toward none, with charity for all, with firmness in the right as God gives us to see the right, let us finish the work we are in, to bind up the nation's wounds, to care for him who shall have borne the battle, and for his widow and orphans, to do all which may achieve and cherish a just and lasting peace among ourselves and with all nations. *Abraham Lincoln*

678　There must be, not a balance of power, but a community of power; not organized rivalries, but an organized common peace. *Woodrow Wilson*

679　A worthy, righteous peace is the fruit of effort. You don't get peace, you don't retain peace just by being peaceable. You get it, if it is worth having, by a constant willingness to work and sacrifice and risk for it. *Frank Knox*

680　If man does find the solution for world peace, it will be the most revolutionary reversal of his record we have ever known. *George C. Marshall*

681　Too often peace has been thought of as a negative condition—the mere absence of war. We know now that we cannot achieve peace by taking a negative attitude. Peace is positive, and it has to be waged with all our thought, energy, and courage and with the conviction that war is not inevitable. *Dean Acheson*

PEOPLE

682　Why should there not be a patient confidence in the ultimate justice of the people? Is there any better or equal hope in the world? *Abraham Lincoln*

683　It is only governments that are stupid, not the masses of people. *Dwight D. Eisenhower*

684 County judge, chairman of a committee, President of the U.S.; they are all the same kind of jobs. It is the business of dealing with people. *Harry S. Truman*

PLEDGE

685 I pledge you, I pledge myself, to a new deal for the American people. *Franklin D. Roosevelt*

POLITICS

686 That log house did me more good in politics than anything I ever said in a speech. *John Nance Garner*

687 The idea that you can merchandise candidates for high office like breakfast cereal—that you can gather votes like box tops—is, I think, the ultimate indignity to the democratic process. *Adlai Stevenson*

THE POOR

688 To those people in the huts and villages of half the globe struggling to break the bonds of mass misery, we pledge our best efforts to help them help themselves, for whatever period is required—not because the Communists may be doing it, not because we seek their votes, but because it is right. If a free society cannot help the many who are poor, it cannot save the few who are rich. *John F. Kennedy*

POPULATION PROBLEM

689 One-third of mankind today lives in an environment of relative abundance.

But two-thirds of mankind—more than two billion individuals—remain entrapped in a cruel web of circumstances that severely limits their right to the necessities of life. They have not yet been able to achieve the transition to self-sustaining economic growth. They are caught in the grip of hunger and malnutrition; high illiteracy; inadequate education; shrinking opportunity; and corrosive poverty.

The gap between the rich and poor nations is no longer merely a gap. It is a chasm. On one side are nations of the West that enjoy per capita incomes in the $3,000 range. On the other are nations in Asia and Africa that struggle to survive on per capita incomes of less than $100.

What is important to understand is that this is not a static situation. The misery of the underdeveloped world is today a dynamic misery, continuously broadened and deepened by a population growth that is totally unprecedented in history.

This is why the problem of population is an inseparable part of the larger, overall problem of development. *Robert S. McNamara*

690 It required sixteen hundred years to double the world population of 250 million, as it stood in the first century A.D. Today [May 1969], the more than three billion on earth will double in thirty-five years' time,

and the world's population will then be increasing at the rate of an additional billion every eight years.

To project the totals beyond the year 2000 becomes so demanding on the imagination as to make the statistics almost incomprehensible.

A child born today, living on into his seventies, would know a world of fifteen billion. His grandson would share the planet with sixty billion.

In six and a half centuries from now—the same insignificant period of time separating us from the poet Dante—there would be one human being standing on every square foot of land on earth: a fantasy of horror that even the *Inferno* could not match.

Such projections are, of course, unreal. They will not come to pass because events will not permit them to come to pass.

Of that we can be certain.

What is not so certain is precisely what those events will be. They can only be: mass starvation; political chaos; or population planning.

Whatever may happen after the year 2000, what is occurring right now is enough to jolt one into action.

India, for example, is adding a million people a month to its population—and this in spite of the oldest family-planning program in Southeast Asia.

The Philippines currently has a population of thirty-seven million. There is no authorized government family-planning program. At the present rate of growth, these limited islands—in a brief thirty-five years—would have to support over one hundred million human beings.

The average population growth of the world at large is 2 percent. Many underdeveloped countries are burdened with a rate of 3½ percent or more. A population growing at 1 percent doubles itself in seventy years; at 2 percent it doubles in thirty-five years; at 3½ percent it doubles in only twenty years.

Now, if we are to reject mass starvation and political chaos as solutions to this explosive situation, then there are clearly only three conceivable ways in which a nation can deliberately *plan* to diminish its rate of population growth: to increase the death rate; to step up the migration rate; or to reduce the birth rate. *Ibid.*

POWER

691   The greater the power, the more dangerous the abuse. *Edmund Burke*

PRESIDENT

692   I have a theory that in the United States those who seek the presidency never win it. Circumstances rather than a man's ambition determine the result. If he is the right man for the right time, he will be chosen. *Richard M. Nixon*

693 I would not seek your nomination for the presidency, because the burdens of that office stagger the imagination. Its potential for good or evil now, and in the years of our lives, smothers exultation and converts vanity to prayer. *Adlai Stevenson*

694 Sir, I would rather be right than President. *Henry Clay*

695 I happen, temporarily, to occupy the White House. I am a living witness that any one of your children may look to come here as my father's child has. *Abraham Lincoln*

PRESS

696 The extremists of both parts of this country are violent; they mistake loud and violent talk for eloquence and for reason. They think he who talks loudest reasons best. And this we must expect, when the press is free as it is here, and I trust always will be; for, with all its licentiousness and all its evil, the entire and absolute freedom of the press is essential to the preservation of government on the basis of a free constitution. *Daniel Webster*

697 Of all times, in time of war the press should be free. That of all occasions in human affairs calls for a press vigilant and bold, independent and uncensored. Better to lose a battle than to lose the vast advantage of the free press. A free and independent press, as historic incidents show, may be of greater service than any other single feature of a great conflict. *William E. Borah*

698 There is a great disposition in some quarters to say that the newspapers ought to limit the amount of news they print; that certain kinds of news ought not to be published. I do not know how that is. I am not prepared to maintain any abstract position on that line; but I have always felt that whatever the divine Providence permitted to occur, I was not too proud to report. *Charles A. Dana*

PRIDE

699 There is such a thing as a man being too proud to fight. *Thomas W. Wilson*

PRIVATE ENTERPRISE

700 We believe profoundly that constant and unnecessary governmental meddling in our economy leads to a standardized, weakened, and tasteless society that encourages dull mediocrity, whereas private enterprise, dependent upon the vigor of healthful competition, leads to individual responsibility, pride of accomplishment, and, above all, national strength. *Dwight D. Eisenhower*

PROFIT MOTIVE

701 When shallow critics denounce the profit motive inherent in our system of private enterprise, they ignore the fact that it is an economic

support of every human right we possess and without it, all rights would soon disappear. *Ibid.*

PROPERTY

702   In the nature of things, those who have no property and see their neighbors possess much more than they think them to need, cannot be favorable to laws made for the protection of property. When this class becomes numerous, it grows clamorous. It looks on property as its prey and plunder, and is naturally ready, at times, for violence and revolution. *Daniel Webster*

PROSPERITY

703   No country can long endure if its foundations are not laid deep in the material prosperity which comes from thrift, from business energy and enterprise, from hard unsparing effort in the fields of industrial activity; but neither was any nation ever yet truly great if it relied upon material prosperity alone. *Theodore Roosevelt*

PUBLIC OPINION

704   In proportion as the structure of a government gives force to public opinion, it is essential that public opinion should be enlightened. *George Washington*

REGULATION

705   The man who holds that every human right is secondary to his profit must now give way to the advocate of human welfare, who rightly maintains that every man holds his property subject to the general right of the community to regulate its use to whatever degree the public welfare may require it. *Theodore Roosevelt*

RELIEF

706   Continued dependence upon relief induces a spiritual and moral disintegration fundamentally destructive to the national fiber. To dole out relief in this way is to administer a narcotic, a subtle destroyer of the human spirit. *Franklin D. Roosevelt*

RELIGION

707   Of all the dispositions and habits which lead to political prosperity, Religion and Morality are indispensable. In vain would that man claim the tribute of Patriotism, who should labor to subvert these great pillars of human happiness, these firmest props of the duties of Men and Citizens. *George Washington*

708   The great writers to whom the world owes what religious liberty it possesses have mostly asserted freedom of conscience as an indefeasible right, and denied absolutely that a human being is accountable to others for his religious belief. Yet so natural to mankind is intolerance in whatever they really care about, that religious freedom has hardly

anywhere been practically realized, except where religious indifference, which dislikes to have its peace disturbed by theological quarrels, has added its weight to the scale. *John Stuart Mill*

RESPONSIBILITY

709 The first requisite of a good citizen in this republic of ours is that he shall be able and willing to pull his weight. *Theodore Roosevelt*

710 This is a free country. We rely on the individual sense of responsibility of the individual citizen. We are proud of this. It is the basic difference between our system of democracy and the slave system of the Soviet Union. *Charles E. Wilson*

RIGHT

711 Let us have faith that right makes might; and in that faith let us, to the end, dare to do our duty as we understand it. *Abraham Lincoln*

RIGHTEOUS

712 The humblest citizen of all the land, when clad in the armor of a righteous cause, is stronger than all the hosts of Error. *William Jennings Bryan*

RUGGED INDIVIDUALISM

713 While I can make no claim for having introduced the term "rugged individualism," I should be proud to have invented it. It has been used by American leaders for over a half century in eulogy of those God-fearing men and women of honesty whose stamina and character and fearless assertion of rights led them to make their own way in life. *Herbert Hoover*

SECURITY

714 For mere vengeance I would do nothing. This nation is too great to look for mere revenge. But for the security of the future I would do everything. *James A. Garfield*

SIZE

715 I am against all big organizations as such, national ones first and foremost; against all big successes and big results; and in favor of the eternal forces of truth which always work in the individual and immediately unsuccessful way, underdogs always, till history comes, after they are long dead, and puts them on the top. *William James*

SOCIAL PROGRESS

716 Social progress does not have to be bought at the price of individual freedom. *John Foster Dulles*

SONNET

717 A true sonnet goes eight lines and then takes a turn for better or worse and goes six or eight lines more. *Robert Frost*

718 I will sit down now, but the time will come when you will hear me. *Benjamin Disraeli*

719 In my opinion, the vernacular tongue of the country has become greatly vitiated, depraved, and corrupted by the style of our congressional debates. And if it were possible for those debates to vitiate the principles of the people as much as they have depraved their tastes, I should cry out, "God save the Republic!" *Daniel Webster*

720 An after-dinner speech is like a love letter. Ideally, you should begin by not knowing what you are going to say, and end by not knowing what you've said. *Lord Jowitt*

STRENGTH

721 . . . These calculations overlook the decisive element: what counts is not necessarily the size of the dog in the fight—it's the size of the fight in the dog. *Dwight D. Eisenhower*

722 There is a homely adage which runs, "Speak softly and carry a big stick; you will go far." If the American nation will speak softly and yet build and keep at a pitch of the highest training a thoroughly efficient navy, the Monroe doctrine will go far. *Theodore Roosevelt*

STRIKES

723 During strikes it must always be remembered that the public interest is paramount. The safety of great masses of people not parties to the discussion and the functioning of government can never be at stake in any bargaining process. Starvation is not a legitimate weapon for capital to use against labor. It is not more legitimate for labor to use it against the public. *Fiorello H. La Guardia*

STRUGGLE

724 Now the trumpet summons us again—not as a call to bear arms, though arms we need—not as a call to battle, though embattled we are—but as a call to bear the burden of a long twilight struggle year in and year out, "rejoicing in hope, patient in tribulation"—a struggle against the common enemies of man: tyranny, poverty, disease, and war itself. *John F. Kennedy*

TASK

725 What is our task? To make Britain a fit country for heroes to live in. *David Lloyd George*

TEACHER

726 I am not willing that this discussion should close without mention of the value of a true teacher. Give me a log hut, with only a simple bench, Mark Hopkins on one end and I on the other, and you may have all the buildings, apparatus, and libraries without him. *James A. Garfield*

THANKSGIVING

727 As the colors of autumn stream down the wind, scarlet in sumach and maple, spun gold in the birches, a splendor of smoldering fire in the oaks along the hill, and the last leaves flutter away, and the dusk falls briefly about the worker bringing in from the field a late load of its fruit, and Arcturus is lost to sight and Orion swings upward that great sun upon his shoulder, we are stirred once more to ponder the Infinite Goodness that has set apart for us, in all this moving mystery of creation, a time of living and a home. In such a spirit I appoint Thursday, the twenty-fourth of November, a day of *Public Thanksgiving*. In such a spirit I call upon the people to acknowledge heartily in friendly gathering and house of prayer the increase of the season nearing now its close: the harvest of earth, the yield of patient mind and faithful hand, that have kept us fed and clothed and have made for us a shelter even against the storm. It is right that we whose arc of sky has been darkened by no war hawk, who have been forced by no man to stand and speak when to speak was to choose between death and life, should give thanks also for the further mercies we have enjoyed, beyond desert or any estimation, of Justice, Freedom, Loving-kindness, Peace—resolving, as we prize them, to let no occasion go without some prompting or some effort worthy in a way however humble of those proudest among man's ideals, which burn, though it may be like candles fitfully in our gusty world, with a light so clear we name its source divine.

    Given under my hand and seal of the State at the Capitol, in Hartford, this tenth day of November in the year of our Lord one thousand nine hundred and thirty-eight and of the independence of the United States one hundred and sixty-third. Wilbur L. Cross

TREASON

728 Tarquin and Caesar each had his Brutus, Charles the First his Cromwell, and George the Third ["Treason!" cried the Speaker] may profit by their example. If *this* be treason, make the most of it. *Patrick Henry*

TRUST

729 The only way to make a man trustworthy is to trust him; and the surest way to make him untrustworthy is to distrust him and show your distrust. *Henry L. Stimson*

TRUTH

730 Are we disposed to be of the number of those who, having eyes, see not, and having ears, hear not the things which so nearly concern their temporal salvation? For my part, whatever anguish of spirit it might cost, I am willing to know the whole truth; to know the worst and to provide for it. *Patrick Henry*

731 I believe it is an established maxim in morals that he who makes an assertion without knowing whether it is true or false is guilty of false-

hood, and the accidental truth of the assertion does not justify or excuse him. *Abraham Lincoln*

732   We simply have to develop better methods of communication with the people because we know that there is no better system of ultimate reliance on the discriminating choice of the people. But they have to be informed. The first responsibility in information is truth. *Adlai Stevenson*

733   You will find that the truth is often unpopular and the contest between agreeable fancy and disagreeable fact is unequal. For, in the vernacular, we Americans are suckers for good news. *Ibid.*

UNDERDEVELOPED NATIONS

734   We must embark on a bold new program for making the benefits of our scientific advances and industrial progress available for the improvement and growth of underdeveloped areas. . . . And in cooperation with other nations we should foster capital investment in areas needing development. *Harry S. Truman*

UNITY

735   Let us trust God and our better judgment to set us right hereafter. United we stand: divided we fall. Let us not split into factions which must destroy this union upon which our existence depends. Let us preserve our strength . . . and not exhaust it in civil commotions and intensive wars. *Patrick Henry*

WAR

736   I am tired and sick of war. Its glory is all moonshine. It is only those who have neither fired a shot nor heard the shrieks and groans of the wounded who cry aloud for blood, more vengeance, more desolation. War is hell. *William Tecumseh Sherman*

737   Older men declare war. But it is youth that must fight and die. And it is youth that must inherit the tribulation, the sorrow, and the triumphs that are the aftermath of war. *Herbert Hoover*

738   Wars are not "acts of God." They are caused by man, by man-made institutions, by the way in which man has organized his society. What man has made, man can change. *Fred M. Vinson*

739   In war, whichever side may call itself the victor, there are no winners, but all are losers. *Neville Chamberlain*

740   I would say to the House, as I said to those who have joined the Government: "I have nothing to offer but blood, toil, tears, and sweat." *Winston Churchill*

741   We shall not flag or fail. We shall fight in France, we shall fight on the seas and oceans, we shall fight with growing confidence and growing strength in the air, we shall defend our island, whatever the cost may be, we shall fight on the beaches, we shall fight on the landing grounds,

we shall fight in the fields and in the streets, we shall fight in the hills; we shall never surrender. *Ibid.*

742 Never in the field of human conflict was so much owed by so many to so few. *Ibid.*

743 Here is the answer which I will give to President Roosevelt. . . . Give us the tools, and we will finish the job. *Ibid.*

WEAK

744 The concessions of the weak are the concessions of fear. *Edmund Burke*

WISDOM

745 Neither a wise man nor a brave man lies down on the tracks of history to wait for the train of the future to run over him. *Dwight D. Eisenhower*

WOMAN

746 I know I have the body of a weak and feeble woman, but I have the heart and stomach of a King, and of a King of England too. *Elizabeth I*

747 It is by the promulgation of sound morals in the community, and more especially by the training and instruction of the young, that woman performs her part towards the preservation of a free government. *Daniel Webster*

WORLD

748 We live in an age, fellow citizens, when there have been established among the nations a more elevated tribunal than ever before existed on earth; I mean the tribunal of the enlightened public opinion of the world. *Ibid.*

749 My fellow citizens of the world: ask not what your country can do for you—ask what you can do for the freedom of man. *John F. Kennedy*

...5...
Great Quotations from Literature and Other Sources

ACCOMPLISHMENT

750 To accomplish great things, we must not only act but also dream, not only plan but also believe. *Anatole France*

ACTING THE FOOL

751 The most difficult character in comedy is that of the fool, and he must be no simpleton that plays that part. *Miguel de Cervantes Saavedra*

ACTION

752 Trust no future, howe'er pleasant!
Let the dead past bury its dead!
Act—act in the living Present!
Heart within and God o'erhead. *Henry Wadsworth Longfellow*

ADAM

753 What a good thing Adam had—when he said a good thing, he knew nobody had said it before. *Mark Twain*

ADMIRATION

754 Admiration is a very short-lived passion, that immediately decays upon growing familiar with its object. *Joseph Addison*

ADVANTAGE

755 It is the greatest of all advantages to enjoy no advantage at all. *Henry David Thoreau*

ADVERSITY

756 God brings men into deep waters, not to drown them, but to cleanse them. *John Hill Aughey*

757 There is no education like adversity. *Benjamin Disraeli*

758 Sweet are the uses of adversity;
Which, like the toad, ugly and venomous,
Wears yet a precious jewel in its head. *William Shakespeare*

759 Let us be patient! These severe afflictions
Not from the ground arise,
But ofttimes celestial benedictions
Assume this dark disguise. *Henry Wadsworth Longfellow*

AGE

760 If wrinkles must be written upon our brows, let them not be written upon the heart. The spirit should not grow old. *James A. Garfield*

761 The riders in a race do not stop short when they reach the goal. There is a little finishing canter before coming to a standstill. There is time to hear the kind voice of friends and to say to one's self: "The work is done." *Oliver Wendell Holmes, Jr.*

762 The old believe everything: the middle-aged suspect everything: the young know everything. *Oscar Wilde*

763 As a man advances in life he gets what is better than admiration—judgment to estimate things at their own value. *Samuel Johnson*

ALONE

764 Woe unto him that is never alone, and cannot bear to be alone. *P. G. Hamerton*

AMBITION

765 A slave has but one master; an ambitious man has as many as there are people useful to him in making his fortune. *Jean de La Bruyère*

766 The first ambitious man corrupted the earth. *Voltaire*

767 Ambition has but one reward for all:
A little power, a little transient fame,
A grave to rest in, and a fading name! *William Winter*

AMERICA

768 Only those Americans who are willing to die for their country are fit to live. *Douglas MacArthur*

769 I pledge allegiance to the flag of the United States and to the Republic for which it stands, one nation, indivisible, with liberty and justice for all. *James B. Upham and Francis Bellamy*

770 I would not hesitate to say that the United States is the finest society on a grand scale that the world has thus far produced. *Alfred North Whitehead*

771 Your [America's] diffusion of literacy and average comfort and well-being among the masses, in my opinion, is one of the major achievements in human history. *Ibid.*

772 It is a fabulous country, the only fabulous country; it is the only place where miracles not only happen, but where they happen all the time. *Thomas Wolfe*

773 The possible destiny of the United States of America, as a nation of a hundred millions of freemen, stretching from the Atlantic to the Pacific, living under the laws of Alfred, and speaking the language of Shakespeare and Milton, is an august conception. *Samuel Taylor Coleridge*

AMUSEMENT

774 Few of us can bear the theory of our amusements. It is essential to the pride of a man to believe that he is industrious. *Walter Bagehot*

ANCESTRY

775 There is no king who has not had a slave among his ancestors, and no slave who has not had a king among his. *Helen Keller*

ARGUING

776 Anyone who conducts an argument by appealing to authority is not using his intelligence; he is just using his memory. *Leonardo da Vinci*

ART

777 It is the treating of the commonplace with the feeling of the sublime that gives to art its true power. *Jean François Millet*

ARTIST

778 This is the reason that the artist lives and works and has his being: that from life's clay and his own nature, and from his father's common earth of toil and sweat and violence and error and bitter anguish, he may distill the beauty of an everlasting form, enslave and conquer man by his enchantment, cast his spell across the generations, beat death down upon his knees, kill death utterly, and fix eternity with the grappling hooks of his own art. *Thomas Wolfe*

ATHEISM

779 That the universe was formed by a fortuitous concourse of atoms, I will no more believe than that the accidental jumbling of the alphabet would fall into a most ingenious treatise of philosophy. *Jonathan Swift*

780 In a way, the greatest praise of God is his denial by the atheist who thinks creation is so perfect it does not need a creator. *Marcel Proust*

ATTAINMENT

781 The significance of a man is not in what he attains, but rather in what he longs to attain. *Kahlil Gibran*

BATTLE

782 In the long run all battles are lost, and so are all wars. *H. L. Mencken*

BEAUTY

783 She walks in beauty like the night
Of cloudless climes and starry skies;
And all that's best of dark and bright
Meets in her aspect and her eyes:
Thus mellowed to that tender light
Which heaven to gaudy day denies. *Lord Byron*

BEGINNING

784 The first step, my son, which one makes in the world is the one on
which depends the rest of our days. *Voltaire*

BIBLE

785 The Bible is a window in this prison-world, through which we may look
into eternity. *Timothy Dwight*

786 The English Bible—a book which, if everything else in our language
should perish, would alone suffice to show the whole extent of its
beauty and power. *Thomas Babington Macaulay*

BIOGRAPHY

787 To be ignorant of the lives of the most celebrated men of antiquity is
to continue in a state of childhood all our days. *Plutarch*

BIRTH

788 Man alone at the very moment of his birth, cast naked upon the naked
earth, does she abandon to cries and lamentations. *Pliny the Elder*

BLESSING

789 Never undertake anything for which you wouldn't have the courage
to ask the blessings of Heaven. *G. C. Lichtenberg*

790 God bless us every one. *Charles Dickens*

BOOKS

791 All that Mankind has done, thought, gained, or been: it is lying as in
magic preservation in the pages of Books. They are the chosen possession of men. *Thomas Carlyle*

792 God be thanked for books. They are the voices of the distant and the
dead, and make us heirs of the spiritual life of past ages. *William Ellery
Channing*

BORROWING

793 Neither a borrower nor a lender be;
For loan oft loses both itself and friend,
And borrowing dulls the edge of husbandry. *William Shakespeare*

BREVITY

794 Brevity is not only the soul of wit, but the soul of making oneself
agreeable, and of getting on with people, and indeed of everything
that makes life worth having. *Samuel Butler*

BROTHERHOOD

795   While there is a lower class I am in it. While there is a criminal class I am of it. While there is a soul in prison I am not free. *Eugene V. Debs*

BURDEN

796   God burdens no man beyond his powers. *Indian Proverb*

BUSINESS

797   We demand that big business give people a square deal; in return we must insist that when anyone engaged in big business honestly endeavors to do right, he shall himself be given a square deal. *Theodore Roosevelt*

CARE

798   The night shall be filled with music
And the cares that infest the day
Shall fold their tents like the Arabs,
And as silently steal away. *Henry Wadsworth Longfellow*

CAUSE

799   God befriend us, as our cause is just! *William Shakespeare*

CHANGE

800   There is a certain relief in change, even though it be from bad to worse; as I have found in traveling in a stagecoach, that it is often a comfort to shift one's position and be bruised in a new place. *Washington Irving*

801   A social system that cannot be changed cannot be maintained. *Holbrook Jackson*

802   Progress is impossible without change; and those who cannot change their minds cannot change anything. *George Bernard Shaw*

CHARACTER

803   Talent is nurtured in solitude; character is formed in the stormy billows of the world. *Johann Wolfgang von Goethe*

804   E'en as he trod that day to God, so walked he from his birth,
In simpleness and gentleness and honor and clean mirth. *Rudyard Kipling*

805   Fame is what you have taken,
Character's what you give;
When to this truth you have taken,
Then you begin to live. *Bayard Taylor*

806   The true greatness of nations is in those qualities which constitute the greatness of the individual. *Charles Sumner*

CHARITY

807   My poor are my best patients. God pays for them. *Hermann Boerhaave*

808 He who waits to do a great deal of good at once will never do anything. *Samuel Johnson*

CHILDHOOD

809 Better to be driven out from among men than to be disliked of children. *Richard Henry Dana*

810 The childhood shows the man,
As morning shows the day. *John Milton*

811 It is a wise father that knows his own child. *William Shakespeare*

812 How dear to my heart are the scenes of my childhood,
When fond recollection presents them to view. *Samuel Woodworth*

CHILDREN

813 Children are a bridge to heaven. *Persian Proverb*

814 All my children are prodigies. *Yiddish Proverb*

815 Feel the dignity of a child. Do not feel superior to him, for you are not. *Robert Henri*

CHOICE

816 A man following Christ's teaching is like a man carrying a lantern before him at the end of a pole. The light is ever before him, and ever impels him to follow it, by continually lighting up fresh ground and attracting him onward. *Leo Tolstoy*

CHRISTMAS

817 O little town of Bethlehem,
How still we see thee lie!
Above thy deep and dreamless sleep
The silent stars go by. *Phillips Brooks*

818 No Santa Claus! Thank God, he lives, and he lives forever. A thousand years from now, Virginia, nay ten times ten thousand years from now, he will continue to make glad the heart of childhood. *Francis P. Church*

819 I heard the bells on Christmas Day
Their old, familiar carols play,
And wild and sweet
The words repeat
Of peace on earth, goodwill to men! *Henry Wadsworth Longfellow*

820 Let's dance and sing and make good cheer,
For Christmas comes but once a year. *George Macfarren*

CHURCH

821 I never weary of great churches. It is my favorite kind of mountain scenery. Mankind was never so happily inspired as when it made a cathedral. *Robert Louis Stevenson*

CIRCUMSTANCES

822   Man is not the creature of circumstances,
      Circumstances are the creatures of men. *Benjamin Disraeli*

823   The happy combination of fortuitous circumstances. *Sir Walter Scott*

CITIZEN

824   I am a citizen, not of Athens or Greece, but of the world. *Socrates*

CITY

825   It is men who make a city, not walls or ships. *Thucydides*

CIVILIZATION

826   . . . mankind's struggle upwards, in which millions are trampled to
      death, that thousands may mount on their bodies. *Clara L. Balfour*

827   We think our civilization near its meridian, but we are yet only at the
      cock-crowing and the morning star. *Ralph Waldo Emerson*

828   A decent provision for the poor is the true test of civilization. *Samuel
      Johnson*

829   Civilization is, before all, the will to live in common. A man is uncivi-
      lized, barbarian, in the degree in which he does not take others into
      account. *José Ortega y Gasset*

830   Many clever men like you have trusted to civilization. Many clever
      Babylonians, clever Egyptians, many clever men at the end of Rome.
      Can you tell me, in a world that is flagrant with the failures of civiliza-
      tion, what there is particularly immortal about yours? *Gilbert Keith
      Chesterton*

COMMON SENSE

831   Common sense is the measure of the possible. *Henri Frédéric Amiel*

832   This country is where it is today on account of the real common sense
      of the big normal majority. *Will Rogers*

COMMUNISM

833   The theory of Communism may be summed up in one sentence: Abol-
      ish all private property. *Karl Marx and Friedrich Engels*

COMPROMISE

834   All government—indeed, every human benefit and enjoyment, every
      virtue and every prudent act—is founded on compromise and barter.
      Edmund Burke

CONGRESS

835   Every man in it is a great man, an orator, a critic, a statesman; and
      therefore every man upon every question must show his oratory, his
      criticism, and his political abilities. *John Adams*

836 We wholly conquer only what we assimilate. *André Gide*

837 Conquer but don't triumph. *Baroness Ebner-Eschenbach*

CONSCIENCE
838 There is another man within me that's angry with me. *Thomas Browne*

CONSTITUTION
839 Constitutions should consist only of general provisions; the reason is
that they must necessarily be permanent, and that they cannot calculate for the possible change of things. *Alexander Hamilton*

840 We are under a Constitution, but the Constitution is what the judges
say it is. *Charles Evans Hughes*

841 In questions of power let no more be heard of confidence in man, but
bind him down from mischief by the chains of the Constitution.
Thomas Jefferson

CONVICTION
842 Conviction is the conscience of the mind. *Nicolas Chamfort*

CREATION
843 The world embarrasses me, and I cannot dream
That this watch exists and has no watchmaker. *Voltaire*

CRITICS
844 Critics are the men who have failed in literature and art. *Benjamin
Disraeli*

CRUSADER
845 Not every crusader is a saint. *Russian Proverb*

CURIOSITY
846 Curiosity is one of the permanent and certain characteristics of a vigorous intellect. *Samuel Johnson*

CYNICS
847 Cynics are only happy in making the world as barren for others as they
have made it for themselves. *George Meredith*

DEATH
848 But whether on the scaffold high
Or in the battle's van,
The fittest place where man can die
Is where he dies for man! *Michael Joseph Barry*

849 No more; and by a sleep to say we end
The heartache and the thousand natural shocks
That flesh is heir to, 'tis a consummation
Devoutly to be wished. *William Shakespeare*

850 Death lies on her like an untimely frost
Upon the sweetest flower of all the field. *Ibid.*

851 God's finger touched him, and he slept. *Alfred Lord Tennyson*

852 We don't know life: how can we know death? *Confucius*

853 As a well-spent day brings happy sleep, so a life well used brings happy death. *Leonardo da Vinci*

854 First our pleasures die—and then
Our hopes, and then our fears—and when
These are dead, the debt is due,
Dust claims dust—and we die too. *Percy Bysshe Shelley*

DECISION

855 Once to every man and nation comes the moment to decide,
In the strife of Truth with Falsehood, for the good or evil side. *James Russell Lowell*

DESPAIR

856 We need not despair of any man as long as he lives. *St. Augustine*

857 Despair is the conclusion of fools. *Benjamin Disraeli*

DESTINY

858 People born to be hanged are safe in water. *Mark Twain's Mother*

859 Lots of folks confuse bad management with destiny. *Frank McKinney*

860 Men heap together the mistakes of their lives and create a monster they call destiny. *John Oliver Hobbes*

DISCOURAGEMENT

861 Discouragement serves no possible purpose; it is simply the despair of wounded self-love. *François de Fénelon*

DISCRETION

862 Great ability without discretion comes almost invariably to a tragic end. *Léon Gambetta*

863 The better part of valor is discretion. *William Shakespeare*

DISGRACE

864 Whatever disgrace we may have deserved, it is almost always in our power to reestablish our character. *Titus Maccius Plautus*

DOCTOR

865 There's another advantage of being poor—a doctor will cure you faster. *Frank McKinney*

866 One of the most advanced types of human being on earth today is the good American doctor. *Alfred North Whitehead*

DOING

867 It is doubtless a formidable advantage never to have done anything.
But it can be carried too far. *Antoine Rivarol*

DONE

868 Nothing is done. Everything in the world remains to be done or done
over. *Lincoln Steffens*

DOUBT

869 To be, or not to be, that is the question:
Whether 'tis nobler in the mind to suffer
The slings and arrows of outrageous fortune;
Or to take arms against a sea of troubles,
And by opposing end them? *William Shakespeare*

EARLY RISING

870 He who is known as an early riser can stay in bed till noon. *Yiddish
Proverb*

EARNESTNESS

871 Earnestness is the salt of eloquence. *Victor Hugo*

EASY

872 What is easy is seldom excellent. *Samuel Johnson*

ECONOMY

873 Buy not what you want, but what you have need of; what you do not
want is dear at a farthing. *Marcus Porcius Cato*

EGOTISM

874 If a man lacks a streak of kindly egotism, beware of him. *Charles
Horton Cooley*

ENEMY

875 He who has a thousand friends has not a friend to spare,
And he who has one enemy will meet him everywhere. *Ralph Waldo
Emerson*

876 To get rid of an enemy, one must love him. *Leo Tolstoy*

877 A man cannot be too careful in the choice of his enemies. *Oscar Wilde*

ENGLAND

878 In England, if something goes wrong—say, if one finds a skunk in the
garden—he writes to the family solicitor, who proceeds to take
the proper measures, whereas in America, you telephone the fire
department. Each satisfies a characteristic need; in the English,
love of order and legalistic procedure; and here in America, what
you like is something vivid, and red, and swift. *Alfred North Whitehead*

ENGLISH LANGUAGE

879 I would make boys all learn English: and then I would let the clever ones learn Latin as an honor and Greek as a treat. But the only thing I would whip them for is not knowing English. I would whip them hard for that. *Winston Churchill*

ENJOYMENT

880 The fullest possible enjoyment is to be found by reducing our ego to zero. *Gilbert Keith Chesterton*

ENTHUSIASM

881 The sense of this word among the Greeks affords the noblest definition of it: enthusiasm signifies God in us. *Mme. de Staël*

882 There are incompetent enthusiasts, and they are a mighty dangerous lot. *G. C. Lichtenberg*

EQUALITY

883 Your levelers wish to level down as far as themselves, but they cannot bear leveling up to themselves. *Samuel Johnson*

884 One man alone was brought forth at the time of Creation in order that thereafter none should have the right to say to another, "My father was greater than your father." *Talmud*

885 Men are born unequal. The great benefit of society is to diminish this inequality, as much as possible by procuring for everybody security, the necessary property, education, and succor. *Joseph Joubert*

886 In sport, in courage, and the sight of Heaven, all men meet on equal terms. *Winston Churchill*

ERRORS

887 We have to pay dearly to get rid of our errors and even then we are lucky. *Johann Wolfgang von Goethe*

EVENTS

888 When we are young, we think that the important and blessed events and people in our life will appear with drum rolls and trumpet calls. But when we look back on life in old age, we find that they came in silently and almost unnoticed through the back door. *Arthur Schopenhauer*

EVIL

889 The evil that men do lives after them;
The good is oft interred with their bones. *William Shakespeare*

EXPERIENCE

890 We always exempt ourselves from the common laws. When I was a boy and the dentist pulled out a second tooth, I thought to myself that I would grow a third if I needed it. Experience discouraged this prophecy. *Oliver Wendell Holmes, Jr.*

891 Has any man ever attained to inner harmony by pondering the experience of others? Not since the world began! He must pass through the fire. *Norman Douglas*

FAILURE

892 We need to teach the highly educated person that it is not a disgrace to fail and that he must analyze every failure to find its cause. He must learn how to fail intelligently, for failing is one of the greatest arts in the world. *Charles F. Kettering*

893 But to him who tries and fails and dies,
I give great honor and glory and tears. *Joaquin Miller*

894 Here's to the men who lose!
What though their work be e'er so nobly planned
And watched with zealous care;
No glorious halo crowns their efforts grand—
Contempt is Failure's share! *G. L. Scarborough*

FAITH

895 To win true peace, a man needs to feel himself directed, pardoned, and sustained by a supreme power, to feel himself in the right road, at the point where God would have him be—in order with God and the universe. This faith gives strength and calm. I have not got it. *Henri Frédéric Amiel*

FAME

896 The fame of great men ought always to be estimated by the means used to acquire it. *François de La Rochefoucauld*

FAULTS

897 Men so like to be talked about that a discussion of their faults delights them. *André Maurois*

898 We keep on deceiving ourselves in regard to our faults, until we at last come to look upon them as virtues. *Heinrich Heine*

FIFTY

899 He that has seen both sides of fifty has lived to little purpose if he has not other views of the world than he had when he was much younger. *William Cowper*

FISHING

900 The charm of fishing is that it is the pursuit of what is elusive but attainable, a perpetual series of occasions for hope. *John Buchan*

FLOWERS

901 Flowers have an expression of countenance as much as men or animals. Some seem to smile; some have a sad expression; some are pensive and

diffident; others again are plain, honest, and upright, like the broad-faced sunflower and the hollyhock. *Henry Ward Beecher*

902 I know not which I love the most,
Nor which the comeliest shows,
The timid, bashful violet
Or the royal-hearted rose;

The pansy in her purple dress,
The pink with cheek of red,
Or the faint, fair heliotrope, who hangs,
Like a bashful maid, her head. *Phoebe Cary*

903 The buttercups, bright-eyed and bold,
Held up their chalices of gold
To catch the sunshine and the dew. *Julia C. R. Dorr*

904 To me the meanest flower that blows can give
Thoughts that do often lie too deep for tears. *William Wordsworth*

FOIBLES

905 A man's foibles are what make him lovable. *Johann Wolfgang von Goethe*

FOLLY

906 He has spent all his life in letting down empty buckets into empty wells, and he is frittering away his age in trying to draw them up again. *Sydney Smith*

FOOL

907 There are well-dressed foolish ideas just as there are well-dressed fools. *Nicolas Chamfort*

908 If forty million people say a foolish thing it does not become a wise one, but the wise man is foolish to give them the lie. *W. Somerset Maugham*

FORGETFULNESS

909 There is no remembrance which time does not obliterate, nor pain which death does not terminate. *Miguel de Cervantes Saavedra*

910 Almost anything in the world is readily forgotten after ten years. After the passage of fifty years a happening so falls into the mists of antiquity that little is known about it except by those who took part in it; and that little is mostly wrong. *Kenneth Roberts*

911 The tumult and the shouting dies,
The captains and the kings depart;
Still stands thine ancient sacrifice,
A humble and a contrite heart.
Lord God of Hosts, be with us yet,
Lest we forget—lest we forget. *Rudyard Kipling*

912 Who is the Forgotten Man? He is the clean, quiet, virtuous, domestic citizen, who pays his debts and his taxes and is never heard of out of his little circle. *William Graham Sumner*

FREEDOM

913 The cause of freedom is the cause of God. *Samuel Bowles*

914 When Freedom from her mountain height
Unfurled her standard to the air,
She tore the azure robe of night,
And set the stars of glory there. *Joseph Rodman Drake*

915 Ay, call it holy ground,
The soil where first they trod;
They have left unstained, what there they found—
Freedom to worship God. *Felicia D. Hemans*

916 Freedom is that faculty which enlarges the usefulness of all other faculties. *Immanuel Kant*

917 Many politicians are in the habit of laying it down as a self-evident proposition that no people ought to be free till they are fit to use their freedom. The maxim is worthy of the fool in the old story who resolved not to go into the water till he had learned to swim. *Thomas Babington Macaulay*

918 The only freedom which deserves the name is that of pursuing our own good in our own way, so long as we do not attempt to deprive others of theirs or impede their efforts to obtain it. *John Stuart Mill*

919 I would rather sit on a pumpkin, and have it all to myself, than to be crowded on a velvet cushion. *Henry David Thoreau*

920 Freedom is more precious than any gifts for which you may be tempted to give it up. *Baltasar Gracian*

921 It is my certain conviction that no man loses his freedom except through his own weakness. *Mahatma Gandhi*

922 The basic test of freedom is perhaps less in what we are free to do than in what we are free not to do. *Eric Hoffer*

FRIENDSHIP

923 Of all the things which wisdom provides to make life entirely happy, much the greatest is the possession of friendship. *Epicurus*

924 A friend must not be injured, even in jest. *Publilius Syrus*

FUTURE

925 I never think of the future. It comes soon enough. *Albert Einstein*

926 There was a wise man in the East whose constant prayer was that he might see today with the eyes of tomorrow. *Alfred Mercier*

927 There was the Door to which I found no key;
There was the Veil through which I might not see. *Omar Khayyám*

GENEROSITY

928 Generosity always has admirers but rarely imitators, since it is too expensive a virtue. *Johann Nestroy*

GOD

929 Man proposes, but God disposes. *Thomas a Kempis*

930 They that deny a God destroy man's nobility; for certainly man is of kin to the beasts by his body; and, if he be not of kin to God by his spirit, he is a base and ignoble creature. *Francis Bacon*

931 God's in His Heaven—
All's right with the world! *Robert Browning*

932 A mighty fortress is our God,
A bulwark never failing,
Our helper he amid the flood
Of mortal ills prevailing. *Martin Luther*

GOLDEN RULE

933 My duty towards my neighbor is to love him as myself, and to do to all men as I would they should do unto me. *Book of Common Prayer*

934 We have committed the Golden Rule to memory; let us now commit it to life. *Edward Markham*

GOVERNMENT

935 Experience teaches us to be most on our guard to protect liberty when the government's purposes are beneficent. *Louis D. Brandeis*

936 Government is a trust, and the officers of the government are trustees; and both the trust and the trustees are created for the benefit of the people. *Henry Clay*

937 No man undertakes a trade he has not learned, even the meanest; yet everyone thinks himself sufficiently qualified for the hardest of all trades—that of government. *Socrates*

938 When Tzu Lu asked about the art of government, the Master replied: "Be in advance of the people; show them how to work." On his asking for something more, the Master added: "Untiringly." *Confucius*

939 It is a maxim of wise government to deal with men not as they ought to be but as they are. *Johann Wolfgang von Goethe*

GRAVE

940 Teach me to live that I may dread
The grave as little as my bed. *Bishop Thomas Ken*

941 Oh, how small a portion of earth will hold us when we are dead, who ambitiously seek after the whole world while we are living! *Philip of Macedon*

GREAT MEN

942 A great man is he who has not lost the heart of a child. *Mencius*

943 Eminent posts make great men greater, and little men less. *Jean de La Bruyère*

944 No really great man ever thought himself so. *William Hazlitt*

945 Eleven out of twelve great men of history were only agents of a great cause. *Friedrich Nietzsche*

GRIEF

946 What's gone and what's past help
Should be past grief. *William Shakespeare*

HAPPINESS

947 Happy creatures do not know a great deal about life. *Anatole France*

HEART

948 Still stands thine ancient sacrifice—
An humble and a contrite heart. *Rudyard Kipling*

949 Great ideas come from the heart. *Luc de Vauvenargues*

950 It is wisdom to believe the heart. *George Santayana*

HEREDITY

951 Heredity is nothing but stored environment. *Luther Burbank*

HISTORY

952 What history tells us is the long, heavy, confused dream of mankind. *Arthur Schopenhauer*

953 We must consider how very little history there is; I mean real authentic history. That certain kings reigned, and certain battles were fought, we can depend upon as true; but all the coloring, all the philosophy of history, is conjecture. *Samuel Johnson*

HONOR

954 For Brutus is an honorable man;
So are they all, all honorable men. *William Shakespeare*

HOPE

955 The natural flights of the human mind are not from pleasure to pleasure, but from hope to hope. *Samuel Johnson*

956 Hope says to us constantly, "Go on, go on," and leads us thus to the grave. *Mme. de Maintenon*

HUMAN NATURE

957 It is in human nature to think wisely and to act in an absurd fashion. *Anatole France*

HUMILITY

958   Do not consider yourself to have made any spiritual progress, unless you account yourself the least of all men. *Thomas a Kempis*

959   Many people want to be devout, but no one wants to be humble. *François de La Rochefoucauld*

960   Humility is the solid foundation of all the virtues. *Confucius*

961   After crosses and losses, men grow humbler and wiser. *Benjamin Franklin*

IDEAS

962   No army can withstand the strength of an idea whose time has come. *Victor Hugo*

IGNORANCE

963   When ignorance is bliss,
'Tis folly to be wise. *Thomas Gray*

964   Wisdom and truth come to a man who truly says, "I am ignorant, I do not know." *J. Krishnamurti*

IMMORTALITY

965   The nearer I approach the end, the plainer I hear around me the immortal symphonies of the worlds which invite me. It is marvelous, yet simple. *Victor Hugo*

IMPORTANCE

966   Every individual has a place to fill in the world, and is important, in some respect, whether he chooses to be so or not. *Nathaniel Hawthorne*

967   The longer one lives, the less importance one attaches to things, and also the less importance to importance. *Jean Rostand*

INFORMATION

968   As a general rule the most successful man in life is the man who has the best information. *Benjamin Disraeli*

JOURNALISM

969   The best use of a journal is to print the largest practical amount of important truth—truth which tends to make mankind wiser, and thus happier. *Horace Greeley*

970   We live under a government of men and morning newspapers. *Wendell Phillips*

JUSTICE

971   Justice is always violent to the party offending, for every man is innocent in his own eyes. *Daniel Defoe*

972   Justice is the right of the weaker. *Joseph Joubert*

KINDNESS

973 The kindness of the American people is, so far as I know, something unique in the history of the world, and it is the justification of your existence. *Alfred North Whitehead*

KNOW THYSELF

974 How can you come to know yourself? Never by thinking; always by doing. Try to do your duty, and you'll know right away what you amount to. And what is your duty? Whatever the day calls for. *Johann Wolfgang von Goethe*

KNOWLEDGE

975 Men are four:
He who knows not and knows not he knows not; he is a fool—shun him;
Hewhoknowsnotandknowssheknowsnot;heissimple—teachhim;
He who knows and knows not he knows; he is asleep—wake him;
He who knows and knows he knows; he is wise—follow him! *Arabic Apothegm*

LABOR

976 Labor, if it were not necessary for the existence, would be indispensable for the happiness of man. *Samuel Johnson*

977 If you want knowledge, you must toil for it; if food, you must toil for it; and if pleasure, you must toil for it; toil is the law. *John Ruskin*

LACK OF UNDERSTANDING

978 Lack of understanding is a great power. Sometimes it enables men to conquer the world. *Anatole France*

LAW

979 Written laws are like spiders' webs, and will like them only entangle and hold the poor and weak, while the rich and powerful will easily break through them. *Anacharsis*

980 When men are pure, laws are useless; when men are corrupt, laws are broken. *Benjamin Disraeli*

981 Law is a statement of circumstances in which the public force will be brought to bear upon men through the courts. *Oliver Wendell Holmes, Jr.*

982 There is but one law for all; namely, that law which governs all law—the law of our Creator, the law of humanity, justice, equity; the law of nature and of nations. *Edmund Burke*

LEARNING

983 And still they gazed, and still the wonder grew,
That one small head should carry all it knew. *Oliver Goldsmith*

984 All wish to be learned, but no one is willing to pay the price. *Juvenal*

985   Who is a wise man? He that learns from all men. *Talmud*

986   The man who is too old to learn was probably always too old to learn.
       Henry S. Haskins

987   A little learning is a dangerous thing;
       Drink deep, or taste not the Pierian spring:
       There shallow draughts intoxicate the brain,
       And drinking largely sobers us again. *Alexander Pope*

LIBERTY

988   The people never give up their liberties but under some delusion.
       Edmund Burke

989   Give me the liberty to know, to think, to believe, and to utter freely
       according to conscience, above all other liberties. *John Milton*

990   Liberty can neither be got nor kept but by so much care that mankind
       are generally unwilling to give the price for it. *Lord Halifax*

991   Liberty means responsibility. That is why most men dread it. *George
       Bernard Shaw*

992   Personal liberty is the paramount essential to human dignity and hu-
       man happiness. *Bulwer-Lytton*

LIFE

993   Every man's life is a fairy tale written by God's fingers. *Hans Christian
       Andersen*

994   It is a misery to be born, a pain to live, a trouble to die. *St. Bernard
       of Clairvaux*

995   One life—a little gleam of Time between two Eternities. *Thomas
       Carlyle*

996   My candle burns at both ends;
       It will not last the night;
       But, ah, my foes, and, oh, my friends—
       It gives a lovely light. *Edna St. Vincent Millay*

LIGHT

997   Lead, kindly Light, amid the encircling gloom,
       Lead Thou me on!
       The night is dark, and I am far from home—
       Lead Thou me on!
       Keep Thou my feet; I do not ask to see
       The distant scene—one step enough for me. *John Henry Newman*

LIMITS

998   As we advance in life, we learn the limits of our abilities. *James An-
       thony Froude*

999   Men are apt to mistake the strength of their feeling for the strength
of their argument. The heated mind resents the chill touch and relentless scrutiny of logic. *William Gladstone*

MAN

1000   Every man is the descendant of every king and every slave that ever
lived. *Kahlil Gibran*

1001   He who doesn't think too much of himself is much more than he
thinks. *Johann Wolfgang von Goethe*

1002   Perhaps the only true dignity of man is his capacity to despise himself.
George Santayana

1003   God give us men. A time like this demands
Strong minds, great hearts, true faith, and ready hands!
Men whom the lust of office does not kill,
Men whom the spoils of office cannot buy,
Men who possess opinions and a will,
Men who love honor, men who cannot lie. *Josiah Gilbert Holland*

1004   He was a man, take him for all in all,
I shall not look upon his like again. *William Shakespeare*

MATRIMONY

1005   To have and to hold from this day forward, for better, for worse, for
richer, for poorer, in sickness and in health, to love and to cherish, till
death us do part. *Book of Common Prayer*

MEDITATION

1006   No great work has ever been produced except after a long interval
of still and musing meditation. *Walter Bagehot*

MEMORIES

1007   After enough time has passed, all memories are beautiful. *August
Strindberg*

MERCY

1008   Among the attributes of God, although they are all equal, mercy
shines with even more brilliancy than justice. *Miguel de Cervantes
Saavedra*

1009   The quality of mercy is not strained,
It droppeth as the gentle rain from heaven
Upon the place beneath. It is twice blessed:
It blesseth him that gives and him that takes.
'Tis mightiest in the mightiest; it becomes
The throned monarch better than his crown;
His scepter shows the force of temporal power,
The attribute to awe and majesty,

Wherein doth sit the dread and fear of kings;
But mercy is above this sceptered sway;
It is enthroned in the hearts of kings,
It is an attribute to God himself;
And earthly power doth then show likest God's
When mercy seasons justice. *William Shakespeare*

MIDDLE AGE

1010   Perhaps middle age is, or should be, a period of shedding shells; the shell of ambition, the shell of material accumulations and possessions, the shell of the ego. *Anne Morrow Lindbergh*

MINORITY

1011   Everything great and intelligent is in the minority. *Johann Wolfgang von Goethe*

MISERY

1012   Misery is almost always the result of thinking. *Joseph Joubert*

MONEY

1013   Make all you can, save all you can, give all you can. *John Wesley*

MORTALITY

1014   Oh, why should the spirit of mortal be proud?
Like a fast-flitting meteor, a fast-flying cloud,
A flash of the lightning, a break of the wave,
He passes from life to his rest in the grave. *William Knox*

MOTHER

1015   A mother who is really a mother is never free. *Honoré de Balzac*

MOTIVES

1016   Man sees your actions, but God your motives. *Thomas a Kempis*

NATION

1017   Nation: a group of men who speak one language and read the same newspapers. *Friedrich Nietzsche*

NO

1018   If you can't say no, you can't expect to live within your income. *William Feather*

NOVEL

1019   History is a novel that did happen; the novel is history as it might have happened. *Brothers Goncourt*

NOVICE

1020   Man comes as a novice to each age in his life. *Nicolas Chamfort*

OBLIGATIONS

1021 To serve God is not to pass our lives on our knees in prayer; it is to discharge on earth those obligations which our duty requires. *Jean Jacques Rousseau*

OBVIOUS

1022 No question is so difficult to answer as that to which the answer is obvious. *George Bernard Shaw*

OFFICE

1023 He that holds public office is no more or less than a public slave. *Baltasar Gracian*

1024 The very essence of a free government consists in considering offices as public trusts, bestowed for the good of the country, and not for the benefit of an individual or a party. *John C. Calhoun*

OLD AGE

1025 The evening of life brings with it its lamp. *Joseph Joubert*

1026 The greatest compensation of old age is its freedom of spirit. . . . Another compensation is that it liberates you from envy, hatred, and malice. *W. Somerset Maugham*

OPPORTUNITY

1027 There is a tide in the affairs of men,
Which, taken at the flood, leads on to fortune. *William Shakespeare*

PARTY

1028 He serves his party best who serves the country best. *Rutherford B. Hayes*

PAST

1029 Those who cannot remember the past are condemned to repeat it. *George Santayana*

PAST AND FUTURE

1030 A European who goes to New York and Chicago sees the future; when he goes to Asia, he sees the past. *Bertrand Russell*

PEACE

1031 The war drum throbbed no longer, and the battle flags were furled In the parliament of man, the federation of the world. *Alfred Lord Tennyson*

PESSIMISM

1032 Show me a person with plenty of worries and troubles and I will show you a person who, whatever he is, is not a pessimist. *Gilbert Keith Chesterton*

1033   Politics is the greatest of all sciences. *Luc de Vaugenargues*

1034   The basis of politics is compromise. *Gustav Freytag*

1035   Nothing is politically right which is morally wrong. *Daniel O'Connell*

1036   I thank fate for having made me born poor. Poverty taught me the true value of the gifts useful to life. *Anatole France*

1037   If you've ever really been poor you remain poor at heart all your life. I've often walked when I could very well afford to take a taxi because I simply couldn't bring myself to waste the shilling it would cost. *Arnold Bennett*

1038   Republics come to an end by luxurious habits; monarchies by poverty. *Montesquieu*

1039   Poverty destroys pride. It is difficult for an empty bag to stand upright. *Alexandre Dumas fils*

1040   Great tranquillity of heart is his who cares for neither praise nor blame. *Thomas a Kempis*

1041   He prays well who is so absorbed with God that he does not know he is praying. *St. Francis de Sales*

1042   Prayer does not change God, but changes him who prays. *Sören Kierkegaard*

1043   Prayer is the very soul and essence of religion and therefore prayer must be the very core of the life of man, for no man can live without religion. *Mahatma Gandhi*

1044   Grant, we beseech thee, merciful Lord, to thy faithful people pardon and peace, that they may be cleansed from all their sins, and serve thee with a quiet mind; through Jesus Christ our Lord. Amen. *Book of Common Prayer*

1045   Few men progress, except as they are pushed along by events. *Edgar Watson Howe*

1046   Progress is the mother of problems. *Gilbert Keith Chesterton*

1047   About things on which the public thinks long, it commonly attains to think right. *Samuel Johnson*

1048   Ignorant men raise questions that wise men answered a thousand years ago. *Johann Wolfgang von Goethe*

1049 The "silly question" is the first intimation of some totally new development. *Alfred North Whitehead*

READING

1050 I have sometimes dreamt that when the Day of Judgment dawns and the great conquerors and lawyers and statesmen come to receive their awards—their crowns, their laurels, their names carved indelibly upon imperishable marble—the Almighty will turn to Peter and will say, not without a certain envy when He sees us coming with our books under our arms, "Look, these need no reward. We have nothing to give them here. They have loved reading." *Virginia Woolf*

REASON

1051 Nothing has an uglier look to us than reason, when it is not on our side. *Lord Halifax*

REFORM

1052 Every reform, however necessary, will by weak minds be carried to an excess which will itself need reforming. *Samuel Taylor Coleridge*

REPENT

1053 To many people virtue consists mainly in repenting sins, not avoiding them. *G. C. Lichtenberg*

RESURRECTION

1054 Shall man alone, for whom all else revives,
No resurrection know? Shall man alone,
Imperial man! be sown in barren ground,
Less privileged than grain, on which he feeds? *Edward Long*

RIDICULE

1055 Resort is had to ridicule only when reason is against us. *Thomas Jefferson*

RUIN

1056 While in the progress of their long decay,
Thrones sink to dust, and nations pass away. *Earl of Carlyle*

RULES OF LIFE

1057 My son, resolve to do the will of others rather than your own.
Always choose to possess less rather than more.
Always take the lowest place, and regard yourself as less than others.
Desire and pray always that God's will may be perfectly fulfilled in you.
A man who observes these rules shall come to enjoy peace and tranquillity of soul. *Thomas a Kempis*

SACRIFICE

1058 Blessed is he who has learned to bear what he cannot change and to sacrifice with dignity what he cannot save. *Friedrich von Schiller*

1059   It is only well with me when I have a chisel in my hand. *Michelangelo*

1060   There is a skeleton in every house. *Anonymous*

1061   If you would wish another to keep your secret, first keep it yourself.
Lucius Annaeus Seneca

1062   The root of all morality is self-control. *Johann Gottlieb Fichte*

1063   He who knows himself best esteems himself least. *H. G. Bohn*

1064   If you wish in this world to advance,
Your merits you're bound to exhance;
You must stir it and stump it,
And blow your own trumpet,
Or trust me, you haven't a chance. *William Schwenck Gilbert*

1065   It astounds us to come upon other egoists, as though we alone had the
right to be selfish and be filled with eagerness to live. *Jules Renard*

1066   His [Macaulay's] enemies might have said before that he talked rather
too much; but now he has occasional flashes of silence, that make his
conversation perfectly delightful. *Sydney Smith*

1067   All the great things are simple, and many can be expressed in a single
word: freedom; justice; honor; duty; mercy; hope. *Winston Churchill*

1068   There is
One great society alone on earth:
The noble Living and noble Dead. *William Wordsworth*

1069   Socrates was famed for wisdom not because he was omniscient but
because he realized at the age of seventy that he still knew nothing.
Robert Staughton Lynd

1070   Some people think that whatever is done solemnly must make sense.
G. C. Lichtenberg

1071   The happiest of all lives is a busy solitude. *Voltaire*

1072   Solitude makes us tougher toward ourselves and tenderer toward others: in both ways it improves our character. *Friedrich Nietzsche*

1073   We enter the world alone, we leave it alone. *James Anthony Froude*

1074   Solitude affects some people like wine; they must not take too much of it, for it flies to the head. *Mary Coleridge*

1075   The thoughtful Soul to Solitude retires. *Omar Khayyám*

SPEAKING

1076   There are not many situations more incessantly uneasy than that in which the man is placed who is watching an opportunity to speak, without courage to take it. *Samuel Johnson*

SPEECH

1077   A vessel is known by the sound, whether it be cracked or not; so men are proved by their speech, whether they be wise or foolish. *Demosthenes*

SPIRIT

1078   When my spirit soars, my body falls on its knees. *G. C. Lichtenberg*

SPRING

1079   Spring hangs her infant blossoms on the trees,
        Rocked in the cradle of the western breeze. *William Cowper*

STATE

1080   A thousand years scarce serve to form a state;
        An hour may lay it in the dust. *Lord Byron*

STATESMANSHIP

1081   The politician says: "I will give you what you want." The statesman says: "What you think you want is this. What it is possible for you to get is that. What you really want, therefore, is the following." *Walter Lippmann*

STUPID

1082   There are people whose only merit consists in saying and doing stupid things at the right time, and who ruin all if they change their manners. *François de La Rochefoucauld*

STYLE

1083   In composing, as a general rule, run your pen through every other word you have written; you have no idea what vigor it will give your style. *Sydney Smith*

SUMMER

1084   Oh, the summer night
        Has a smile of light
        And she sits on a sapphire throne. *B. W. Procter*

1085 There are three marks of a superior man: being virtuous, he is free
from anxiety; being wise, he is free from perplexity; being brave, he
is free from fear. *Confucius*

1086 Superiority is always detested. *Baltasar Gracian*

1087 When we are not sure, we are alive. *Graham Greene*

1088 We seldom repent talking too little, but very often talking too much;
this is a common and well-known maxim which everybody knows and
nobody practices. *Jean de La Bruyère*

1089 "The time has come," the Walrus said,
"To talk of many things:
  Of shoes—and ships—and sealing wax—
  Of cabbages—and kings—
  And why the sea is boiling hot—
  And whether pigs have wings." *Lewis Carroll*

1090 To please, one must make up his mind to be taught many things
which he already knows, by people who do not know them. *Nicolas
Chamfort*

1091 Taxes are the price we pay for civilized society. *Oliver Wendell
Holmes, Jr.*

1092 The teacher is like the candle which lights others in consuming itself.
Giovanni Ruffini

1093 Beggar that I am, I am even poor in thanks. *William Shakespeare*

1094 So once in every year we throng
Upon a day apart,
To praise the Lord with feast and song
In thankfulness of heart. *Arthur Guiterman*

1095 Heap high the board with plenteous cheer, and gather to the feast,
And toast the sturdy Pilgrim band whose courage never ceased.
Give praise to that All-Gracious One by whom their steps were
  led,
And thanks unto the harvest's Lord who sends our "daily bread."
Alice Williams Brotherton

THINKING

1096 "Really, now you ask me," said Alice, very much confused, "I don't think—"
"Then you shouldn't talk," said the Hatter. *Lewis Carroll*

THOUGHT

1097 Thought pure and simple is as near to God as we can get; it is through this that we are linked with God. *Samuel Butler*

1098 Yon Cassius has a lean and hungry look;
He thinks too much: such men are dangerous. *William Shakespeare*

TIME

1099 Nothing really belongs to us but time, which even he has who has nothing else. *Baltasar Gracian*

1100 You are not born for fame if you don't know the value of time. *Luc de Vauvenargues*

1101 We all find time to do what we really want to do. *William Feather*

TOLERANCE

1102 One has only to grow older to become more tolerant. I see no wrong that I might not have committed myself. *Johann Wolfgang von Goethe*

TRANQUILLITY

1103 Periods of tranquillity are seldom prolific of creative achievement. Mankind has to be stirred up. *Alfred North Whitehead*

TRAVEL

1104 Only fools want to travel all the time; sensible men want to arrive. *Klemens von Metternich*

TROUBLE

1105 To take arms against a sea of troubles . . . *William Shakespeare*

TRUTH

1106 Truth crushed to earth shall rise again:
The eternal years of God are hers;
But Error, wounded, writhes in pain,
And dies among his worshipers. *William Cullen Bryant*

1107 Truth ever lovely—since the world began,
The foe of tyrants, and the friend of man. *Thomas Campbell*

TYRANNY

1108 Bad laws are the worst sort of tyranny. *Edmund Burke*

1109 Unlimited power corrupts the possessor; and this I know, that where law ends, there tyranny begins. *William Pitt*

UNION

1110 By union the smallest states thrive, by discord the greatest are destroyed. *Gaius Sallustius Crispus Sallust*

UNKNOWN

1111 Not a day passes over the earth, but men and women of no note do great deeds, speak great words, and suffer noble sorrows. *Charles Reade*

VICTORY

1112 Avoid victories over superiors. *Baltasar Gracian*

1113 There is nothing so dreadful as a great victory—except a great defeat. *Attributed to Duke of Wellington*

VIRTUE

1114 You are a man, not God; you are human, not an angel. How can you expect to remain always in a constant state of virtue, when this was not possible even for an angel of Heaven, nor for the first man in the Garden? *Thomas a Kempis*

WALKING

1115 Take long walks in stormy weather or through deep snow in the fields and woods, if you would keep your spirits up. Deal with brute nature. Be cold and hungry and weary. *Henry David Thoreau*

WAR

1116 Where troops have been quartered, brambles, and thorns spring up. In the track of great armies there must follow lean years. *Lao-tzu*

1117 The belief in the possibility of a short decisive war appears to be one of the most ancient and dangerous of human illusions. *Robert Lynd*

1118 War is the science of destruction. *John S. C. Abbott*

1119 By the rude bridge that arched the flood,
Their flag to April's breeze unfurled;
Here once the embattled farmers stood,
And fired the shot heard round the world. *Ralph Waldo Emerson*

WEALTH

1120 Surplus wealth is a sacred trust which its possessor is bound to administer in his lifetime for the good of the community. *Andrew Carnegie*

WISDOM

1121 The heart is wiser than the intellect. *Josiah Gilbert Holland*

1122 Nine-tenths of wisdom consists in being wise in time. *Theodore Roosevelt*

WOMAN

1123 Nature is in earnest when she makes a woman. *Oliver Wendell Holmes*

WORDS

1124 Words are the only things that last forever. *William Hazlitt*

1125 But yesterday the word of Caesar might
Have stood against the world; now lies he there,
And none so poor to do him reverence. *William Shakespeare*

WORK

1126 In every rank, or great or small,
'Tis industry supports us all. *John Gay*

1127 And only the Master shall praise us, and only the Master shall blame;
And no one shall work for money, and no one shall work for fame;
But each for the joy of the working, and each, in his separate star,
Shall draw the Thing as he sees It, for the God of Things as They Are!
Rudyard Kipling

1128 One must work, nothing but work. And one must have patience. *Auguste Rodin*

1129 Happiness, I have discovered, is nearly always a rebound from hard work. *David Grayson*

WORLD

1130 Man draws the nearer to God as he withdraws further from the consolations of the world. *Thomas a Kempis*

1131 The world is but a perpetual see-saw. *Michel de Montaigne*

YOUTH

1132 One of the hardest things to realize, specially for a young man, is that our forefathers were living men who really knew something. *Rudyard Kipling*

1133 I remember my youth and the feeling that will never come back any more—the feeling that I could last forever, outlast the sea, the earth, and all men. *Joseph Conrad*

1134 As I approve of a youth that has something of the old man in him, so I am no less pleased with an old man that has something of the youth. He that follows this rule may be old in body, but can never be so in mind. *Marcus Tullius Cicero*

1135 Youth! youth! how buoyant are thy hopes! They turn,
Like marigolds, toward the sunny side. *Jean Ingelow*

...6...

Excerpts from Significant Speeches

1136 I am not a Virginian, but an American. *Patrick Henry*

1137 Every artist dips his brush in his own soul, and paints his own nature into the pictures. *Henry Ward Beecher*

1138 In all the circumstances of his life, the writer can recapture the feeling of a living community that will justify him. But only if he accepts as completely as possible the two trusts that constitute the nobility of his calling: the service of truth and the service of freedom. *Albert Camus*

1139 Make sure you generate a reasonable number of mistakes. I know that comes naturally to some people, but too many executives are so afraid of error that they rigidify their organization with checks and counter-checks, discourage innovation, and, in the end, so structure themselves that they will miss the kind of offbeat opportunity that can send a company skyrocketing. So take a look at your record, and if you can come to the end of a year and see that you haven't made any mistakes, then I say, brother, you just haven't tried everything you should have tried.

It is a cliché to say that we learn by our mistakes, but I'll state the case more strongly than that: I'll say you can't learn without mistakes. Consider how the baby learns to walk. He's getting along fine on all fours. He can crawl under, around, and through at a good clip. Why tamper with success? Then one day he gets up on his two hind legs, he takes a couple of steps, and the first thing you know, there he is flat on the floor, bawling, with a lump on his noggin. But that one look at the wonderful world of upright locomotion is enough for him, and he tries it again and again, until he masters it. *Fletcher L. Byrom, President, Koppers Company, Inc.*

THE CHOICE

1140 It is my conviction that you will find in the vast storehouse of learning no chamber that will provide more treasures for your purpose than in the American heritage. Khrushchev's message to the people of the outer world was, "We will bury you!" The American message to the people of the outer world was and is, "We will exalt you."

Each of us has the choice to opt for the shoestrings or the stars. *Dr. John A. Howard, President, Rockford College*

CONFUSION IN OUR SOCIETY

1141 The confusion in our society runs deep and many of our intellectual institutions are frozen in thoughtless obedience to unworkable or unexamined assumptions.

It is, in my judgment, only by a painstaking reexamination and redefinition of the purposes and the priorities of our educational institutions and by a recognition that the student must be trained for responsible citizenship that the university can justify society's support. And the society will be pretty stupid if it does not demand this change. *Ibid.*

CONTINUE PUSHING EACH FRONTIER

1142 Many years before there was a space program my father had a favorite quotation: "He who would bring back the wealth of the Indies must take the wealth of the Indies with him." This we have done. We have taken to the moon the wealth of this nation, the vision of its political leaders, the intelligence of its scientists, the dedication of its engineers, the careful craftsmanship of its workers and the enthusiastic support of its people. We have brought back rocks and I think it's a fair trade. For just as the Rosetta Stone revealed the language of ancient Egypt, so may these rocks unlock the mystery of the origin of the moon, of our earth, and even of our solar system. . . .

We can ignore neither the wealth of the Indies nor the realities of the immediate needs of our cities, our citizens, or our civics. We cannot launch our planetary probes from a springboard of poverty, discrimination, or unrest. But neither can we wait until each and every terrestrial problem has been solved. Such logic two hundred years ago would have prevented expansion westward past the Appalachian Mountains, for assuredly the Eastern Seaboard was beset by problems of great urgency then, as it is today. *Michael Collins*

DAY OF TRIAL

1143 In moods of doubt and frustration in the face of injustice and wretchedness, I think of the counsel of the most sagacious man I have ever known, Justice Brandeis. "The way to deal with the irresistible," he would say, "is to resist it." To his impatient daughter he said, "My dear, if you would only recognize that life is hard, things would be so much easier for you." And throughout a life singularly fruitful and fraught with more than one man's share of sharp encounters, a career that began as "the people's lawyer" in Boston, he maintained his commitment to his formula for achievement: brains, rectitude, singleness of purpose, and time.

Justice Holmes, who served the Union in the Civil War and lived to see the inauguration of Franklin Roosevelt, expressed the same thought with a touch of the poet. . . .

"We are all very near despair. The sheathing that floats us over its waves is compounded of hope, faith in the unexplainable worth and sure issue of effort, and the deep, subconscious content which comes from the exercise of our powers. In the words of a touching Negro song—

"Sometimes I's up, sometimes I's down,
Sometimes I's almost to the groun'."

Paul A. Freund, Harvard Law Professor

ECONOMIC PROGRESS

1144   This nation is in the early years of an era whose rate of economic progress should be close to a full percentage point higher than its historical average. In the first two-thirds of this century, real incomes and output doubled about every twenty years. In the period ahead we shall probably double output and real purchasing power in about sixteen years. *Paul W. McCracken, Chairman, Council of Economic Advisers*

EDUCATION

1145   Certainly no school or community of any kind can solve all the problems of this or any other society. But the school is our chief formal agency for education, and if it be organized and operated as a center for extensive community education, it can do far more, and better too, than has even been dreamed of in conventional thinking. And we had better start to make it do so. Our schools are in crisis, not only financial, but also programatic. For in the eloquent words of Muriel Crosby, prime mover of Wilmington, Delaware's, comprehensive school-community improvement program:

We look at children
And see ourselves.
Hope for the future,
Or despair.
High expectations,
Or resignation.

Builders of the dream,
Or despoilers.
Creators of a new city,
Or vandals,
Seeking to destroy the old.
We look at children
And see ourselves.

What do you see? And what will you do about what you do see?
Edward G. Olsen, Professor of Education, California State College

EVIL

1146 Those who corrupt the public mind are just as evil as those who steal from the public purse. *Adlai E. Stevenson*

EXTREMISM AND MODERATION

1147 I would thus remind you that extremism in the defense of liberty is no vice. And let me remind you also that moderation in the pursuit of justice is no virtue! *Barry M. Goldwater*

THE FARM OF TOMORROW

1148 And now let's take a quick look at what this farm of tomorrow may be.

Most of the seers agree on a picture something like this:

Computer-controlled machines will plant the crops, fertilize by prescription, determine the right time to market, harvest on order, and grade and package commodities for delivery to automated warehouses.

Livestock will be kept in environmentally controlled shelters. Cattle, hogs, and sheep will grow to market size on one-third less feed and in one-third less time.

In the fields, crop rows will be separated by impervious strips that catch rainfall and drain it to nourish the plants. Crops will need only a fraction of the water now required. Irrigation will be completely automated. Weeds will be laboratory curiosities.

Combinations of biological and specific chemical methods will have wiped out the dozen or so insects that cause most of our losses today and will control most of the other crop-damaging bugs.

All this will take lots of capital. This presents a great challenge to the financial community. You as the managers of credit and finance have the responsibility and the opportunity to help devise credit institutions that will enable the farmer to have access to very large amounts of capital on a continuing basis without depriving him of his decision-making role.

The crossroads question you can help answer is: Who will own and operate the farms of the future—will agriculture still be a family-owned, family-operated enterprise?

I believe you will come up with the right answer. *J. Phil Campbell, Undersecretary of Agriculture*

FOREIGN INVESTMENT

1149   Foreign investment is an organic affair. To hold one's market position one must keep feeding existing operations as well as developing new ones. This is the meaning of the organic concept of foreign investment as distinct from the marginalist incremental viewpoint. This movement overseas is the great international movement of this century and it is changing the world. It is not just an American movement. British, German, Dutch, French, and Japanese firms are moving in the same direction. So Washington should stop worrying about trade fairs, exhortations to export, and such—not that these are totally unimportant—but it should get with the modern movement. Exports are running at over 30 billion dollars annually, but U.S. production overseas is running at about 120 to 150 billion dollars and the profits are remitted home.

Moreover, the free deployment of investment overseas by any nation works toward the maximization of world resources. Controls are bound to distort this allocation of capital. Let our objective be to maximize the use of world resources for world peace and prosperity. This would be a really effective contribution to the brotherhood of man. Perhaps this is what I mean by applying the ecumenical spirit to such mundane matters as world trade and investment. No man and no nation is an island entire to itself. Here, I believe, is the great chance for the world. But we must see the present in terms of the future, not of the past. We must grasp the *zeitgeist* and we do not do that by meditating on the past nor by considering alone our own immediate interests. A world view is, I believe, the road to peace. And peace in our time is more than a dream. *John J. Powers, Jr., Chairman of the Board and President, Charles Pfizer & Co., Inc.*

THE FORGOTTEN MAN

1150   Wealth comes only from production, and all that the wrangling grabbers, loafers, and jobbers get to deal with comes from somebody's toil and sacrifice. Who, then, is he who provides it all? The Forgotten Man . . . delving away in patient industry, supporting his family, paying his taxes, casting his vote, supporting the church and the school. . . . *William Graham Sumner*

FREEDOM

1151   We have confused the free with the free and easy. *Adlai E. Stevenson*

THE FUTURE OF OUR COUNTRY

1152   Remember, my son, that any man who is a bear on the future of his country will go broke. *J. P. Morgan*

GOD

1153   I just want to lobby for God. *Reverend Billy Graham*

GREAT LIVES

1154   Great lives never go out. They go on. *Benjamin Harrison*

GUIDELINES

1155   What about guidelines? You will by now be aware that some of us in
Washington have been able to restrain our admiration about the role
of direct intervention in wage and price decisions. For one thing
there is a basic question of principle. How far is it legitimate for
government to impose rules that come to have the force of law without ever having passed the legislative process? Moreover, the real
effectiveness of this approach is far from clear. High-level man hours
spent in cajolery might, at least so history suggests, better be spent
on dealing with the fundamentals that produce an inflationary environment. The union leader persuaded to show restraint this time may
be so on the defensive intramurally that the next time he must go all
out. While an average is an average of a dispersion which, in a market
system, itself has an allocative function to perform, it has seemed
difficult tactically to concede that a settlement ought to be above
average—and impossible politically to suggest that one ought to be
below par. And in any case this approach never has come to grips with
some major dimensions of the problem here—e.g., sharply rising costs
in markets ranging from construction to medical services.

Finally, the approach seemed to be most clear-cut when it was least
needed—namely, during the noninflationary period of the early
1960s. When the price-cost level began to rise, and counteraction was
needed, no one could be certain what it all meant operationally—as
indicated by the fact that recommended figures were then dropped
from Economic Reports. *Paul W. McCracken, Chairman, Council of
Economic Advisers*

HUNGER

1156   A hungry man is not a free man. *Adlai E. Stevenson*

IF THEY'D PLAYED IT COOL IN 1776

1157   Our great country was discovered, put together, fought for, and saved
by men who would be quite disgusted in a group of modern "angle
players" and "goofers." It is quite easy to prove that Nathan Hale,
Patrick Henry, Paul Revere, George Washington, Benjamin Franklin,
Robert E. Lee, and almost anyone else you care to include among our
national heroes would be classed as different, odd, peculiar, and far
behind the times by modern groups of angle-playing, stupidly con-
ceited young people, who are exactly the opposite of what I urge each
of you to be.

Nathan Hale never saw his twenty-second birthday. He could have blamed George Washington and lived to a ripe old age.

Paul Revere could have said: "Why pick on me? It is the middle of the night. I cannot ride through every Middlesex village. Besides, I am not the only man in Boston with a horse."

Patrick Henry could have said: "Yes, I am for liberty but we must be realistic. We are small compared to the British, and someone is going to get hurt."

George Washington could have said: "Gentlemen, you honor me. I am just getting some personal matters settled and have much to do at Mount Vernon. Why don't you try General Gates? Also, you might say I have served my time."

Benjamin Franklin could have said: "I'm over seventy-five years old. What you need as a minister to France in these strenuous times is a younger man. Let a new generation take over. I want to rest." Instead he negotiated most brilliantly the Treaty of Alliance.

After Appomattox, Robert E. Lee could have said: "I've gone through the worst strain a man could endure. I've lost the cause, and my personal affairs have suffered. I could cash in on my reputation and put myself and my family into continued wealth." Instead he turned down the most lucrative of offers.

Our country today needs patriotism, nationalism, morality, courage, dedication, and religion, as never before. These verities are eternal. They are necessities if we are to survive as a free people, and they should be taught from kindergarten through college. *James E. Palmer, Jr., Professional Staff Member, U.S. Senate Committee on Banking and Currency*

THOMAS JEFFERSON

1158 Thomas Jefferson was quite versatile. So, when the late President Kennedy had a group of internationally known scientists in the White House, he said to them that they represented the greatest concentration of talent in the history of the world except when Thomas Jefferson was in the same room. He mentioned that Jefferson was "a young man of thirty-two who could tie an artery, break a horse, calculate an eclipse, build an edifice, try a cause, play the violin, dance the minuet, and write the Declaration of Independence."

This is the kind of flexibility and vocational capability we'd like to see in young people—particularly people at thirty-two who are being asked to lead the nation into bigger and better things, as well as into a more perilous future. *L. C. Michelon, Vice-President, Republic Industrial Education Institute*

LAW

1159 Law is the crystallization of the habit and thought of society. *Woodrow Wilson*

LIBERTY

1160   The broad goal of our foreign policy is to enable the people of the
United States to enjoy in peace the blessings of liberty. *John Foster
Dulles*

1161   Our country has liberty without license, and authority without despotism. *Cardinal James Gibbons*

MAN

1162   I believe that man will not merely endure: he will prevail. He is
immortal, not because he alone among creatures has an inexhaustible
voice, but because he has a soul, a spirit capable of compassion and
sacrifice and endurance. *William Faulkner (Nobel Prize acceptance
speech)*

MAN AND NATURE

1163   We tend to forget the extent to which nature destroys—and pollutes
—segments of itself, sporadically and violently—with man often a
major victim in these upheavals. Witness the great earthquakes, volcanic eruptions, tidal waves, floods, and epidemics that have been
recorded. Among the greatest of these were: The earthquake in
Shensi Province of China in 1556, killing an estimated 800,000 people, and the one in Japan in 1923 which took close to 150,000 lives
and destroyed more than half a million houses; the volcanic eruption
of 1470 B.C. that destroyed much of the Minoan civilization; the 1833
explosion of Krakatoa, an island in Indonesia, which in addition to
wiping out 163 villages and killing 36,000 people sent rock and dust
falling for ten days as far as 3,000 miles away; the great flood of the
Hwang Ho River in 1887 that swept 900,000 people to their death;
the famine in India in 1770 that claimed the lives of a third of the
country's population—tens of millions of people—and the 1877–1878
famine in northern China that killed 9 million. And centuries before
man seriously tampered with nature through modern medicine, between 1347 and 1351, the Black Death (bubonic plague) wiped out
75 million people in Europe. History records numerous other types
of plagues and natural disasters that have periodically destroyed various forms of life and changed the face of the earth—and most of this,
I remind you, long before man and his new technology interfered
with the balance of nature.

I state all this not to offend nature lovers, or decry the beauty and
mystery of mother nature, but only to point out that she is not always
goodness and light, and like many women can be fickle and tempes-
tuous. What we must realize, though, is that it is not a matter of
"You can't live with her and you can't live without her." We are a
part of nature. We have no choice but to coexist with her, and in
view of our own creative evolution, which does produce some rapid
and extreme change, this is going to take a lot more understanding

and effort than we have put forth in the past.

Part of this understanding can be gained from a brief look at man and his technology, and their effect on the natural environment. To read some material popular today you would get the feeling that man-made pollution is a brand-new phenomenon. What is new is the extent to which we are contaminating our environment and our current reaction to it. The rest is almost as old as recorded history. Man has caused and been affected by pollution throughout the ages. In the Holy Bible, passages in Revelation [9:2, 18] tell us:

". . . and from the shaft rose smoke, like the smoke of a great furnace, and the sun and the air were darkened with the smoke from the shaft. . . . By these three plagues a third of mankind was killed by the fire and smoke and sulphur issuing from their mouths." *Dr. Glenn T. Seeborg*

THE PEOPLE
1164 Government . . . cannot be wiser than the people. *Adlai Stevenson*

PRIDE AND HUMILITY
1165 It is with a great sense of pride as an American and with humility as a human being that I say to you today what no men have been privileged to say before: "We walked on the moon." But the footprints at Tranquility Base belong to more than the crew of Apollo 11. They were put there by hundreds of thousands of people across this country, people in government, industry, and universities, the teams and crews that preceded us, all who strived throughout the years with Mercury, Gemini, and Apollo.

Those footprints belong to the American people and you, their representatives, who accept it and support it, the inevitable challenge of the moon. And since we came in peace for all mankind, those footprints belong also to all people of the world. As the moon shines impartially on all those looking up from our spinning earth, so do we hope the benefits of space exploration will be spread equally with a harmonizing influence to all mankind.

Scientific exploration implies investigating the unknown. The result can never be wholly anticipated. Charles Lindbergh said, "Scientific accomplishment is a path, not an end; a path leading to and disappearing in mystery."

The first step on the moon was a step toward our sister planets and ultimately toward the stars. "A small step for a man" was a statement of a fact; "a giant leap for mankind" is a hope for the future. *Edwin E. Aldrin*

REFORM
1166 A reformer is a guy who rides through a sewer in a glass-bottom boat. *James Walker*

RESPONDING TO CHALLENGE

1167   We landed on the Sea of Tranquility, in the cool of the early lunar morning, when the long shadows would aid our perception.

The sun was only ten degrees above the horizon, while the earth turned through nearly a full day during our stay, the sun at Tranquility Base rose barely eleven degrees—a small fraction of the month-long lunar day. There was a peculiar sensation of the duality of time—the swift rush of events that characterizes all our lives, and the ponderous parade which makes the aging of the universe.

Both kinds of time were evident: the first by the routine events of the flight—whose planning and execution were detailed to fractions of a second—the latter by rocks round us, unchanged throughout the history of man, whose three-billion-year-old secrets made them the treasures we sought. . . .

Mystery creates wonder and wonder is the basis for man's desire to understand. Who knows what mysteries will be solved in our lifetime, and what new riddles will become the challenge of the new generations? Science has not mastered prophecy. We predict too much for next year yet far too little for the next ten. Responding to challenge is one of democracy's great strengths. Our successes in space lead us to hope that this strength can be used in the next decade in the solution of many of our planet's problems. *Neil A. Armstrong*

A RIGHTEOUS CAUSE

1168   The humblest citizen of all the land, when clad in the armor of a righteous cause, is stronger than all the hosts of error. *William Jennings Bryan*

SELF-HELP

1169   Men are made stronger on realization that the helping hand they need is at the end of their own right arm. *Sidney J. Phillips*

SUCCESS

1170   There is nothing in the world really beneficial that does not lie within the reach of an informed understanding and a well-directed pursuit. *Edmund Burke*

TO SERVE HIS COUNTRY AND HIS PEOPLE

1171   We are looking at our shoestrings when we should have our eyes fixed on the stars. Pollution is a subject of some concern nowadays. This morning I would like to suggest that the pollution that may well be our greatest curse, even a greater threat to the survival of mankind than the slowly spreading contamination of air, water, and food, *is the pollution of ideals*. A man without aspirations is not a whole man. A society without a shared and cherished vision of what might be is a desolate society, and one lacking in vitality and cohesiveness.

In the Godkin Lectures at Harvard University last March, John

Gardner asserted, "A high level of morale is essential if a society is to succeed in the arduous tasks of renewal." A high level of morale is exactly what we do not have in the United States. It will be my endeavor to examine some possible causes and consequences of this phenomenon and suggest that we begin the difficult decontamination process which will enable our ideals to be revitalized and our humanity to be restored. *John A. Howard, President, Rockford College*

TRADE

1172   There is an old tradition which requires that speakers submit a title for their speech long before they know what they are going to talk about. Consistent with this Dr. Braile asked me, last July, for a title and I told him it was "Trade: A Vision for the Seventies."

I thought that had a nice ring.

After all, if you ask a man to leave his family for the evening, and pay fourteen dollars for dinner, the least you can promise is a vision.

I did have another title: "Trade Policy at the Crossroads." I dropped that because I was afraid one of you would remember that I gave the same speech two years ago.

Still it is an honest title. Whatever my credentials as a visionary, I ought to be an expert on trade crossroads. As President of the International Chamber of Commerce I spent two years at one. I don't think things have moved much since I left office last June.

The crossroads, if you will forgive a tired metaphor, is between protectionism and free trade. It is, more broadly, between two visions of the world.

One is an old vision, a vision of the nation state, sovereign, self-sufficient, self-seeking and grandly unconcerned about much of anything beyond its borders.

The other is the vision of an economically interdependent world where man, goods, and capital move freely from one country to another.

Neither camp, free trader nor protectionist, ever carries its arguments to their logical extreme. Protectionism, pushed to its extreme, is impossible. There are now 140 nations more or less in the world and new ones are coined constantly. They all have to buy from the world, so they all have to sell to it. As a further embarrassment, times of high protectionism have usually coincided with economic stagnation and often with political disaster. We ought to remember that the Smoot-Hawley Tariff—with rates so high it stopped trade cold—was passed in 1930.

The free trade camp, and I consider myself a member in good standing, is also uneasy about its ultimate vision. However fine it might be, it is hard to imagine a world where man, capital, and goods really move with unfettered freedom. To function, this would need a world of closely integrated social, economic, and governmental institutions.

With a Common Market that cannot agree on a common monetary policy, with a Latin American Free Trade Area that cannot agree on much of anything, the free trade idea borders, I would have to admit, on the visionary.

Still, if I must choose, I'll take the visionary.

As the old joke goes, show me a man with both feet on the ground and I'll show you a man who can't put his pants on.

Furthermore, the decision is not between the extremes, it is one of direction. Of trend. And that is the significance of the crossroads and the danger of this protracted pause. *Arthur K. Watson*

TRUTH

1173 It is true, no age can restore life, whereof perhaps there is no great loss; and revolutions of ages do not oft recover the loss of a rejected truth, for the want of which whole nations fare the worse. *John Milton*

1174 For who knows not that truth is strong, next to the Almighty; she needs no policies, nor stratagems, nor licensings to make her victorious; those are the shifts and the defenses that error uses against her power: give her but room, and do not bind her when she sleeps. *Ibid.*

TWO KINDS OF PEOPLE

1175 Ever since wealth appeared, there have been two significant kinds of people in society. One, the wealthy and powerful; the other, the poor and dependent.

Those who wished to enjoy wealth and power, in the feudal days, accepted fully the responsibility to feed and look after the citizens of the realm. This is the way the system worked.

In retrospect, we view it with distaste and even horror because of the ruthless domination of the lords and the squalor of the serfs.

But at least the serfs had a contract that was recognized on both sides: It was up to the lords to take care of them.

In a lengthy historical convulsion, this state of affairs was abolished. The serf became free. He no longer owed to the lord a big slice of what he was able to scratch together. But, by the same token, he was on his own. And that's the way it has been since the dawn of the Industrial Revolution.

Almost all the time, this supplanting of one system by another has been described as progress. But at rare intervals of dire misfortune the erstwhile serfs have been so ill-cared-for, so hungry, and so desperate, that they have challenged the new and better way.

All this is by way of explaining that the publicly approved institution of business and industry—the functional way in which people for the last few centuries have earned their living—similarly rests on a convention. This convention is that the conditions that make it possible for businessmen to operate, for investors to reap rewards, and for the wealthy to enjoy their wealth, must also in some way take care of the less fortunate rest of the populace.

This convention, we must be willing to admit, was *not* invented by Franklin D. Roosevelt. It has been there all the time since the last serf was freed and so-called private enterprise took over.

If we have discerned it rather dimly until recently, the outline is becoming much clearer now. The rapid organization of welfare recipients and their ability to enforce, first, their appeals and then their demands is evidence of this fact.

We are simply validating a newer form of social contract. My guess is that we will have to become accustomed to the application in the field of welfare of labor's simple criterion: *more.* That's because, again, as in the case of the labor movement, organization of large numbers of voters in our representative democracy brings pressure on the elected decision-maker to give them what they say they want. *George Hammond, Chairman, Carl Byoir & Associates*

UNSELFISH PURPOSE

1176 A day of unselfish purpose is always a day of confident hope. *Woodrow Wilson*

WAR

1177 I know war as few other men now living know it, and nothing to me is more revolting. I have long advocated its complete abolition, as its very destructiveness on both friend and foe has rendered it useless as a method of settling international disputes. *Douglas MacArthur (Address to Congress, April 19, 1951)*

...7...

Inspiring Quotations from the Bible

ABILITY

1178 If ye have faith as a grain of mustard seed . . . nothing shall be impossible unto you. *Matthew 17:20*

1179 With men this is impossible; but with God all things are possible. *Matthew 19:26*

1180 God is faithful, who will not suffer you to be tempted above that ye are able; but will with the temptation also make a way to escape, that ye may be able to bear it. *I Corinthians 10:13*

ABSENCE

1181 The Lord watch between me and thee, when we are absent one from another. *Genesis 31:49*

ACCUSATION

1182 Blessed are ye, when men shall revile you, and persecute you, and shall say all manner of evil against you falsely, for my sake. *Matthew 5:11*

ACHIEVEMENT

1183 God saw everything that he had made, and, behold, it was very good. *Genesis 1:31*

1184 I have fought a good fight, I have finished my course, I have kept the faith. *II Timothy 4:7*

AFFLICTION

1185 In my distress I called upon the Lord, and cried to my God; and he did hear my voice out of his temple. *II Samuel 22:7*

1186 If thou faint in the day of adversity, thy strength is small. *Proverbs 24:10*

1187 Blessed are they that mourn: for they shall be comforted. . . . Blessed are they which are persecuted for righteousness' sake: for theirs is the kingdom of heaven. Blessed are ye, when men shall revile you, and persecute you, and shall say all manner of evil against you falsely, for my sake. Rejoice, and be exceeding glad: for great is your reward in heaven: for so persecuted they the prophets which were before you. *Matthew 5:4, 10–12*

1188   Come unto me, all ye that labour and are heavy laden, and I will give you rest. *Matthew 11:28*

1189   O my Father, if it be possible, let this cup pass from me: nevertheless, not as I will, but as thou wilt. *Matthew 26:39*

1190   These things I have spoken unto you, that in me ye might have peace. In the world ye shall have tribulation; but be of good cheer; I have overcome the world. *John 16:33*

1191   We know that all things work together for good to them that love God, to them who are called according to his purpose. *Romans 8:28*

1192   Who shall separate us from the love of Christ? shall tribulation, or distress, or persecution? *Romans 8:35*

1193   The Lord is my helper, and I will not fear what man shall do unto me. *Hebrews 13:6*

AGE

1194   Thou shalt rise up before the hoary head, and honour the face of the old man. *Leviticus 19:32*

1195   With the ancient is wisdom; and in length of days understanding. *Job 12:2*

1196   We spend our years as a tale is told. *Psalms 90:9*

1197   So teach us to number our days, that we may apply our hearts unto wisdom. *Psalms 90:12*

1198   The fear of the Lord prolongeth days. *Proverbs 10:27*

1199   We all do fade as a leaf. *Isaiah 64:6*

AMBITION

1200   Let us make us a name. *Genesis 11:4*

1201   Labour not to be rich. . . . Wilt thou set thine eyes upon that which is not? for riches certainly make themselves wings; they fly away as an eagle toward heaven. *Proverbs 23:4–5*

1202   The last shall be first, and the first last. *Matthew 20:16*

1203   He that is greatest among you shall be your servant. And whosoever shall exalt himself shall be abased; and he that shall humble himself shall be exalted. *Matthew 23:11–12*

1204   If any man desire to be first, the same shall be last of all, and servant of all. *Mark 9:35*

1205 Whosoever will be great among you, shall be your minister: and whosoever of you will be the chiefest, shall be servant of all. *Mark 10:43–44*

ANGER

1206 A soft answer turneth away wrath: but grievous words stir up anger. *Proverbs 15:1*

1207 He that is slow to anger is better than the mighty; and he that ruleth his spirit than he that taketh a city. *Proverbs 16:32*

1208 Be not hasty in thy spirit to be angry: for anger resteth in the bosom of fools. *Ecclesiastes 7:9*

1209 Be ye angry, and sin not: let not the sun go down upon your wrath. *Ephesians 4:26*

1210 Let all bitterness, and wrath, and anger, and clamour, and evil speaking, be put away from you, with all malice. *Ephesians 4:31*

ANXIETY

1211 Yea, though I walk through the valley of the shadow of death, I will fear no evil: for thou art with me; thy rod and thy staff they comfort me. *Psalms 23:4*

1212 Take therefore no thought for the morrow: for the morrow shall take thought for the things of itself. Sufficient unto the day is the evil thereof. *Matthew 6:34*

1213 Let not your heart be troubled: ye believe in God, believe also in me. *John 14:1*

1214 God hath not given us the spirit of fear; but of power, and of love, and of a sound mind. *II Timothy 1:7*

ASPIRATION

1215 This is the generation of them that seek him. *Psalms 24:6*

1216 I will lift up mine eyes unto the hills, from whence cometh my help. *Psalms 121:1*

1217 Forgetting those things which are behind, and reaching forth unto those things which are before, I press toward the mark. *Philippians 3:13–14*

BACKSLIDING

1218 If the salt have lost his savour, wherewith shall it be salted? It is thenceforth good for nothing, but to be cast out, and to be trodden under foot of men. *Matthew 5:13*

1219 No man, having put his hand to the plough, and looking back, is fit for the kingdom of God. *Luke 9:62*

BEAUTY

1220 Beauty is a fading flower. *Isaiah 28:1*

1221   Consider the lilies of the field, how they grow; they toil not, neither do they spin: And yet I say unto you, That even Solomon in all his glory was not arrayed like one of these. *Matthew 6:28–29*

BEHAVIOR

1222   Whatsoever ye would that men should do to you, do ye even so to them. *Matthew 7:12*

BENEDICTION

1223   The Lord bless thee, and keep thee: The Lord make his face shine upon thee, and be gracious unto thee: The Lord lift up his countenance upon thee, and give thee peace. *Numbers 6:24–26*

1224   Now the God of patience and consolation grant you to be like minded one toward another according to Christ Jesus: That ye may with one mind and one mouth glorify God, even the Father of our Lord Jesus Christ. *Romans 15:5–6*

1225   Now the God of hope fill you with all joy and peace in believing, that ye may abound in hope, through the power of the Holy Ghost. *Romans 15:13*

1226   The grace of our Lord Jesus Christ be with you. *Romans 16:20*

1227   Grace be unto you, and peace, from God our Father, and from the Lord Jesus Christ. *I Corinthians 1:3*

1228   The grace of the Lord Jesus Christ, and the love of God, and the communion of the Holy Ghost, be with you all. *II Corinthians 13:14*

1229   Brethren, the grace of our Lord Jesus Christ be with your spirit. *Galatians 6:18*

1230   He lifted up his hands, and blessed them. *Luke 24:50*

1231   Now the God of peace, that brought again from the dead our Lord Jesus, that great shepherd of the sheep, through the blood of the everlasting covenant, make you perfect in every good work to do his will, working in you that which is well pleasing in his sight, through Jesus Christ; to whom be glory for ever and ever. Amen. *Hebrews 13:20–21*

BIGOTRY

1232   Ye blind guides, which strain at a gnat, and swallow a camel. *Matthew 23:24*

1233   The sabbath was made for man, and not man for the sabbath. *Mark 2:27*

BLESSED

1234   Blessed is the man that maketh the Lord his trust. *Psalms 40:4*

1235   Blessed is he that considereth the poor: the Lord will deliver him in time of trouble. *Psalms 84:5*

1236   Blessed is the man that endureth temptation: for when he is tried, he shall receive the crown of life. *James 1:12*

BLESSING

1237   The Lord thy God blesseth thee, as he promised thee. *Deuteronomy 15:6*

1238   The Lord hath blessed his people. *II Chronicles 31:10*

1239   Stand up and bless the Lord your God for ever and ever. *Nehemiah 9:5*

1240   Thou preparest a table before me in the presence of mine enemies: thou anointest my head with oil; my cup runneth over. *Psalms 23:5*

1241   He that hath clean hands, and a pure heart . . . shall receive the blessing from the Lord, and righteousness from the God of his salvation. *Psalms 24:4–5*

1242   God be merciful unto us, and bless us; and cause his face to shine upon us. *Psalms 67:1*

1243   Blessed be the Lord, who daily loadeth us with benefits. *Psalms 68:19*

1244   Seek ye first the kingdom of God, and his righteousness; and all these things shall be added unto you. *Matthew 6:33*

1245   Eye hath not seen, nor ear heard, neither have entered into the heart of man, the things which God hath prepared for them that love him. *I Corinthians 2:9*

1246   Blessed be the Father of our Lord Jesus Christ, who hath blessed us with all spiritual blessings. *Ephesians 1:3*

BOASTING

1247   Boast not thyself of tomorrow; for thou knowest not what a day may bring forth. *Proverbs 27:1*

1248   Let another man praise thee, and not thine own mouth; a stranger, and not thine own lips. *Proverbs 27:2*

BODY

1249   I am fearfully and wonderfully made. *Psalms 139:14*

BORROWING

1250   The wicked borroweth, and payeth not again. *Psalms 37:21*

1251   Give to him that asketh thee, and from him that would borrow of thee turn not thou away. *Matthew 5:42*

BROTHERHOOD

1252   Let there be no strife, I pray thee, between me and thee . . . for we be brethren. *Genesis 13:8*

1253   Have we not all one father? hath not one God created us? *Malachi 2:10*

1254   Inasmuch as ye have done it unto one of the least of these my brethren, ye have done it unto me. *Matthew 25:40*

1255   They that go down to the sea in ships, that do business in great waters . . . *Psalms 107:23*

1256   Follow me, and I will make you fishers of men. *Matthew 4:19*

1257   The harvest truly is great, but the labourers are few: pray ye therefore the Lord of the harvest, that he would send forth labourers into his harvest. *Luke 10:2*

1258   Humble yourselves therefore under the mighty hand of God . . . casting all your care upon him; for he careth for you. *I Peter 5:6–7*

1259   Why beholdest thou the mote that is in thy brother's eye, but considerest not the beam that is in thine own eye? *Matthew 7:3*

1260   Judge not, and ye shall not be judged: condemn not, and ye shall not be condemned: forgive, and ye shall be forgiven. *Luke 6:37*

1261   As ye would that men should do to you, do ye also to them likewise. *Luke 6:31*

1262   Knowledge puffeth up, but charity edifieth. *I Corinthians 8:1*

1263   Though I speak with the tongues of men and of angels, and have not charity, I am become as sounding brass, or a tinkling cymbal. And though I have the gift of prophecy, and understand all mysteries, and all knowledge; and though I have all faith, so that I could remove mountains, and have not charity, I am nothing. And though I bestow all my goods to feed the poor, and though I give my body to be burned, and have not charity, it profiteth me nothing. *I Corinthians 13:1–3*

1264   Charity suffereth long, and is kind; charity envieth not; charity vaunteth not itself, is not puffed up; Doth not behave itself unseemly, seeketh not her own, is not easily provoked, thinketh no evil; Rejoiceth not in iniquity, but rejoiceth in the truth; Beareth all things, believeth all things, hopeth all things, endureth all things. *I Corinthians 13:4–7*

1265   And now abideth faith, hope, charity, these three; but the greatest of these is charity. *I Corinthians 13:13*

1266   Happy is the man whom God correcteth: therefore despise not thou the chastening of the Almighty. *Job 5:17*

1267 Surely it is meet to be said unto God, I have borne chastisement, I will not offend any more: That which I see not teach thou me: if I have done iniquity, I will do no more. *Job 34:31–32*

1268 It is good for me that I have been afflicted; that I might learn thy statutes. *Psalms 119:71*

CHEERFULNESS

1269 A merry heart maketh a cheerful countenance. *Proverbs 15:13*

1270 A merry heart doeth good like a medicine. *Proverbs 17:22*

CHILDREN

1271 As arrows are in the hand of a mighty man; so are children of the youth. *Psalms 127:4*

1272 A wise son maketh a glad father: but a foolish son is the heaviness of his mother. *Proverbs 10:1*

1273 A wise son heareth his father's instruction. *Proverbs 13:1*

1274 Children's children are the crown of old men; and the glory of children are their fathers. *Proverbs 17:6*

1275 A foolish son is a grief to his father, and bitterness to her that bare him. *Proverbs 17:25*

1276 Train up a child in the way he should go: and when he is old, he will not depart from it. *Proverbs 22:6*

1277 Suffer little children, and forbid them not, to come unto me: for of such is the kingdom of heaven. *Matthew 19:14*

1278 When I was a child, I spake as a child, I understood as a child, I thought as a child: but when I became a man, I put away childish things. *I Corinthians 13:11*

CHRIST

1279 This is my beloved Son, in whom I am well pleased. *Matthew 17:5*

1280 I am the way, the truth, and the life. *John 14:6*

CHURCH

1281 Mine house shall be called a house of prayer for all people. *Isaiah 56:7*

1282 Upon this rock I will build my church; and the gates of hell shall not prevail against it. *Matthew 16:18*

COMFORT

1283 Naked came I out of my mother's womb, and naked shall I return thither: the Lord gave, and the Lord hath taken away; blessed be the name of the Lord. *Job 1:21*

1284 They that know thy name will put their trust in thee: for thou, Lord, hast not forsaken them that seek thee. *Psalms 9:10*

1285   Cast thy burden upon the Lord, and he shall sustain thee: he shall never suffer the righteous to be moved. *Psalms 55:22*

COMPANIONS

1286   I had rather be a doorkeeper in the house of my God, than to dwell in the tents of wickedness. *Psalms 84:10*

1287   He that walketh with wise men shall be wise: but a companion of fools shall be destroyed. *Proverbs 13:20*

CONFESSION

1288   He that covereth his sins shall not prosper: but whoso confesseth and forsaketh them shall have mercy. *Proverbs 28:13*

CONSCIENCE

1289   The wicked flee when no man pursueth: the righteous are bold as a lion. *Proverbs 28:1*

CONTENTION

1290   Agree with thine adversary quickly, whiles thou art in the way with him. *Matthew 5:25*

1291   Whosoever shall smite thee on thy right cheek, turn to him the other also. *Matthew 5:39*

1292   Every kingdom divided against itself is brought to desolation; and every city or house divided against itself shall not stand. *Matthew 12:25*

CONTENTMENT

1293   Better is a dry morsel, and quietness therewith, than an house full of sacrifices with strife. *Proverbs 17:1*

CONVERSION

1294   Except ye be converted, and become as little children, ye shall not enter into the kingdom of heaven. *Matthew 18:3*

1295   I will arise and go to my father, and will say unto him, Father, I have sinned against heaven, and before thee. *Luke 22:32*

1296   Behold, I stand at the door and knock: if any man hear my voice, and open the door, I will come in to him, and will sup with him, and he with me. *Revelation 3:20*

COUNSEL

1297   Give instruction to a wise man, and he will be yet wiser: teach a just man, and he will increase in learning. *Proverbs 9:9*

COURAGE

1298   If God be for us, who can be against us? *Romans 8:31*

1299   Watch ye, stand fast in the faith, quit you like men, be strong. *I Corinthians 16:13*

CREATION

1300 God created man in his own image, in the image of God created he him. *Genesis 1:27*

1301 My help cometh from the Lord, which made heaven and earth. *Psalms 121:2*

DEATH

1302 Dust thou art, and unto dust shalt thou return. *Genesis 3:19*

1303 Lord, make me to know mine end, and the measure of my days, what it is; that I may know how frail I am. *Psalms 39:4*

1304 O death, where is thy sting? O grave, where is thy victory? *I Corinthians 15:55*

DESPAIR

1305 My God, my God, why hast thou forsaken me? *Psalms 22:1*

DISCONTENT

1306 Let us not be desirous of vain glory, provoking one another, envying one another. *Galatians 5:26*

DUTY

1307 Fear God, and keep his commandments: for this is the whole duty of man. *Ecclesiastes 12:13*

1308 What doth the Lord require of thee, but to do justly, and to love mercy, and to walk humbly with thy God? *Micah 6:8*

ENEMY

1309 Rejoice not when thine enemy falleth, and let not thine heart be glad when he stumbleth. *Proverbs 24:17*

1310 If thine enemy be hungry, give him bread to eat: and if he be thirsty, give him water to drink. *Proverbs 25:21*

ETERNITY

1311 Before the mountains were brought forth, or ever thou hadst formed the earth and the world, even from everlasting to everlasting, thou art God. *Psalms 90:2*

EXAMPLE

1312 Let your light so shine before men, that they may see your good works, and glorify your Father which is in heaven. *Matthew 5:16*

FAITH

1313 Commit thy way unto the Lord; trust also in him; and he shall bring it to pass. *Psalms 37:5*

1314 The Lord is good, a strong hold in the day of trouble; and he knoweth them that trust in him. *Nahum 1:7*

1315   All things, whatsoever ye shall ask in prayer, believing, ye shall receive. *Matthew 21:22*

1316   Shew me thy faith without thy works, and I will shew thee my faith by my works. *James 2:18*

FALSEHOOD

1317   Thou shalt not bear false witness against thy neighbour. *Exodus 20:16*

FLATTERY

1318   Many will intreat the favour of the prince: and every man is a friend to him that giveth gifts. *Proverbs 19:6*

1319   Meddle not with him that flattereth with his lips. *Proverbs 20:19*

1320   Woe unto you, when all men shall speak well of you! for so did their fathers to the false prophets. *Luke 6:26*

FOLLY

1321   Every one that heareth these sayings of mine, and doeth them not, shall be likened unto a foolish man, which built his house upon the sand. *Matthew 7:26*

1322   God hath chosen the foolish things of the world to confound the wise. *I Corinthians 1:27*

FORGIVENESS

1323   Say not, I will do so to him as he hath done to me: I will render to the man according to his work. *Proverbs 24:29*

1324   Forgive us our debts, as we forgive our debtors. *Matthew 6:12*

1325   If ye forgive men their trespasses, your heavenly Father will also forgive you. *Matthew 6:14*

FRIENDSHIP

1326   Greater love hath no man than this, that a man lay down his life for his friends. *John 15:13*

GIVING

1327   He that hath pity upon the poor lendeth unto the Lord; and that which he hath given will he pay him again. *Proverbs 19:17*

1328   Take heed that ye do not your alms before men, to be seen of them . . . But when thou doest alms, let not thy left hand know what thy right hand doeth. *Matthew 6:1, 3*

1329   Whosoever shall give you a cup of water to drink in my name . . . shall not lose his reward. *Mark 9:41*

1330   He that hath two coats, let him impart to him that hath none; and he that hath meat, let him do likewise. *Luke 3:11*

1331   It is more blessed to give than to receive. *Acts 20:35*

1332   God loveth a cheerful giver. *II Corinthians 9:7*

1333   If any provide not for his own, and specially for those of his own house, he hath denied the faith, and is worse than an infidel. *I Timothy 5:8*

1334   God forbid that I should glory, save in the cross of our Lord Jesus Christ. *Galatians 6:14*

1335   The eternal God is thy refuge, and underneath are the everlasting arms. *Deuteronomy 33:27*

1336   The Lord seeth not as man seeth; for man looketh on the outward appearance, but the Lord looketh on the heart. *I Samuel 16:7*

1337   In whose hand is the soul of every living thing, and the breath of all mankind. *Job 12:10*

1338   The heavens declare the glory of God: and the firmament sheweth his handywork. *Psalms 19:1*

1339   The Lord is my shepherd; I shall not want. *Psalms 23:1*

1340   Thou art my father, my God, and the rock of my salvation. *Psalms 89:26*

1341   The Lord is good; his mercy is everlasting; and his truth endureth to all generations. *Psalms 100:5*

1342   One God and Father of all, who is above all, and through all, and in you all. *Ephesians 4:6*

1343   Who only hath immortality, dwelling in the light which no man can approach unto; whom no man hath seen, nor can see: to whom be honour and power everlasting. *I Timothy 6:16*

1344   Thou shalt not covet thy neighbour's house, thou shalt not covet thy neighbour's wife, nor his manservant, nor his maidservant, nor his ox, nor his ass, nor any thing that is thy neighbour's. *Exodus 20:17*

1345   The love of money is the root of all evil. *I Timothy 6:10*

1346   What is a man profited, if he shall gain the whole world, and lose his own soul? *Matthew 16:26*

1347   The spirit indeed is willing, but the flesh is weak. *Matthew 26:41*

1348   First be reconciled to thy brother, and then come and offer thy gift. *Matthew 5:24*

1349   A new commandment I give unto you, That ye love one another; as I have loved you, that ye also love one another. *John 13:34*

HARVEST

1350 Every good tree bringeth forth good fruit; but a corrupt tree bringeth forth evil fruit. *Matthew 7:17*

1351 The harvest truly is plenteous, but the labourers are few. *Matthew 9:37*

1352 One soweth, and another reapeth. *John 4:37*

1353 He which soweth sparingly shall reap also sparingly; and he which soweth bountifully shall reap also bountifully. *II Corinthians 9:6*

1354 Whatsoever a man soweth, that shall he also reap. *Galatians 6:7*

HATRED

1355 Thou shalt not hate thy brother in thine heart. *Leviticus 19:17*

1356 Love your enemies, bless them that curse you, do good to them that hate you, and pray for them which despitefully use you, and persecute you. *Matthew 5:44*

1357 If a man say, I love God, and hateth his brother, he is a liar: for he that loveth not his brother whom he hath seen, how can he love God whom he hath not seen? *I John 4:20*

HEART

1358 Create in me a clean heart, O God; and renew a right spirit within me. *Psalms 51:10*

1359 Blessed are the pure in heart: for they shall see God. *Matthew 5:8*

1360 Those things which proceed out of the mouth come forth from the heart; and they defile the man. *Matthew 15:18*

HEAVEN

1361 Lay up for yourselves treasures in heaven, where neither moth nor rust doth corrupt, and where thieves do not break through nor steal. *Matthew 6:20*

HELP

1362 God is our refuge and strength, a very present help in trouble. *Psalms 46:1*

HUMILITY

1363 Take my yoke upon you, and learn of me; for I am meek and lowly in heart: and ye shall find rest unto your souls. *Matthew 11:29*

1364 Whosoever therefore shall humble himself as this little child, the same is greatest in the kingdom of heaven. *Matthew 18:4*

1365 Whosoever will be great among you, let him be your minister; And whosoever will be chief among you, let him be your servant. *Matthew 20:26–27*

1366 Whosoever shall exalt himself shall be abased; and he that shall humble himself shall be exalted. *Matthew 23:12*

1367   He hath put down the mighty from their seats, and exalted them of low degree. *Luke 1:52*

HYPOCRISY

1368   When thou doest thine alms, do not sound a trumpet before thee, as the hypocrites do in the synagogues and in the streets, that they may have glory of men. *Matthew 6:2*

1369   When thou prayest, thou shalt not be as the hypocrites are: for they love to pray standing in the synagogues and in the corners of the streets, that they may be seen of men. *Matthew 6:5*

1370   No man can serve two masters: for either he will hate the one, and love the other; or else he will hold to the one, and despise the other. Ye cannot serve God and mammon. *Matthew 6:24*

1371   Thou hypocrite, first cast out the beam out of thine own eye; and then shalt thou see clearly to cast out the mote out of thy brother's eye. *Matthew 7:5*

1372   Woe unto you, scribes and Pharisees, hypocrites! for ye are like unto whited sepulchres, which indeed appear beautiful outward, but are within full of dead men's bones, and of all uncleanness. *Matthew 23:27*

1373   The Pharisee stood and prayed thus with himself, God, I thank thee, that I am not as other men are. *Luke 18:11*

IDLENESS

1374   Go to the ant, thou sluggard; consider her ways, and be wise. *Proverbs 6:6*

1375   He becometh poor that dealeth with a slack hand: but the hand of the diligent maketh rich. *Proverbs 10:4*

1376   The sluggard will not plow by reason of the cold; therefore shall he beg in harvest, and have nothing. *Proverbs 20:4*

1377   Love not sleep, lest thou come to poverty. *Proverbs 20:13*

1378   Drowsiness shall clothe a man with rags. *Proverbs 23:21*

1379   If any would not work, neither should he eat. *II Thessalonians 3:10*

IGNORANCE

1380   Poverty and shame shall be to him that refuseth instruction. *Proverbs 13:18*

1381   The simple inherit folly: but the prudent are crowned with knowledge. *Proverbs 14:18*

1382   That the soul be without knowledge, it is not good. *Proverbs 19:2*

IMMORTALITY

1383   The Lord shall preserve thy going out and thy coming in from this time forth, and even for evermore. *Psalms 121:8*

1384   He shall receive . . . in the world to come eternal life. *Mark 10:30*

1385   For God so loved the world, that he gave his only begotten Son, that whosoever believeth in him should not perish, but have everlasting life. *John 3:16*

1386   I am the living bread which came down from heaven; if any man eat of this bread, he shall live for ever. *John 6:51*

1387   The last enemy that shall be destroyed is death. *I Corinthians 15:26*

IMPARTIALITY

1388   He maketh his sun to rise on the evil and on the good, and sendeth rain on the just and on the unjust. *Matthew 5:45*

1389   God is no respecter of persons. *Acts 10:34*

IMPERFECTION

1390   There is none that doeth good, no, not one. *Psalms 14:3*

1391   He that is without sin among you, let him first cast a stone. *John 8:7*

IMPERMANENCE

1392   One generation passeth away, and another generation cometh. *Ecclesiastes 1:4*

1393   All flesh is grass, and all the goodliness thereof is as the flower of the field: The grass withereth, the flower fadeth. *Isaiah 40:6–7*

1394   What is your life: It is even a vapour, that appeareth for a little time and then vanisheth away. *James 4:14*

INDECISION

1395   How long halt ye between two opinions: if the Lord be God, follow him: but if Baal, then follow him. *I Kings 18:21*

INDUSTRY

1396   In all labour there is profit. *Proverbs 14:23*

1397   Seest thou a man diligent in his business? He shall stand before kings; he shall not stand before mean men. *Proverbs 22:29*

1398   He that tilleth his land shall have plenty of bread. *Proverbs 28:19*

1399   Whatsoever thy hand findeth to do, do it with thy might. *Ecclesiastes 9:10*

INFIDELITY

1400   Shall the day say to him that fashioneth it, What makest thou? or thy work, He hath no hands? *Isaiah 45:9*

1401   He that is not with me is against me; and he that gathereth not with me scattereth. *Luke 11:23*

1402   O man, who art thou that repliest against God? Shall the thing formed say to him that formed it, Why hast thou made me thus? *Romans 9:20*

INFIRMITY

1403 The Lord upholdeth all that fall, and raiseth up all those that be bowed down. *Psalms 145:14*

1404 He healeth the broken in heart, and bindeth up their wounds. *Psalms 147:3*

1405 Take heed lest by any means this liberty of yours become a stumbling-block to them that are weak. *I Corinthians 8:9*

INSTABILITY

1406 Be no more children, tossed to and fro, and carried about with every wind of doctrine, by the sleight of men, and cunning craftiness, whereby they lie in wait to deceive. *Ephesians 4:14*

1407 A double minded man is unstable in all his ways. *James 1:8*

INSTRUCTION

1408 The fear of the Lord is the beginning of knowledge: but fools despise wisdom and instruction. *Proverbs 1:7*

1409 Wisdom is the principal thing; therefore get wisdom: and with all thy getting get understanding. *Proverbs 4:7*

INTEGRITY

1410 The integrity of the upright shall guide them. *Proverbs 11:3*

1411 The just man walketh in his integrity: his children are blessed after him. *Proverbs 20:7*

IRREVERENCE

1412 Thou shalt not take the name of the Lord thy God in vain. *Exodus 20:7*

1413 Whosoever curseth his God shall bear his sin. *Leviticus 24:15*

JOY

1414 Weeping may endure for a night, but joy cometh in the morning. *Psalms 30:5*

1415 Serve the Lord with gladness: come before his presence with singing. *Psalms 100:2*

1416 Happy is that people, whose God is the Lord. *Psalms 144:15*

1417 Whoso trusteth in the Lord, happy is he. *Proverbs 16:20*

JUDGMENT

1418 Teach me good judgment. *Psalms 119:66*

1419 Many seek the ruler's favour; but every man's judgment cometh from the Lord. *Proverbs 29:26*

1420 With what judgment ye judge, ye shall be judged: and with what measure ye mete, it shall be measured to you again. *Matthew 7:2*

1421   Judge not according to the appearance, but judge righteous judgment. *John 7:24*

1422   Speak not evil one of another. *James 4:11*

JUSTICE

1423   He that ruleth over men must be just. *II Samuel 23:3*

1424   If a man be just, and do that which is lawful and right . . . he shall surely live, saith the Lord God. *Ezekiel 18:5, 9*

JUSTIFICATION

1425   For all have sinned and come short of the glory of God; Being justified freely by his grace, through the redemption that is in Christ Jesus. *Romans 3:23–24*

KINDNESS

1426   A word spoken in due season, how good it is! *Proverbs 15:23*

1427   As we have therefore opportunity, let us do good unto all men. *Galatians 6:10*

KNOWLEDGE

1428   Wise men lay up knowledge. *Proverbs 10:14*

LAW

1429   He that keepeth the law, happy is he. *Proverbs 29:18*

1430   The law was given by Moses, but grace and truth came by Jesus Christ. *John 1:17*

1431   The law is not made for a righteous man, but for the lawless and disobedient. *I Timothy 1:9*

1432   This is the love of God, that we keep his commandments. *I John 5:3*

LIBERTY

1433   Ye shall know the truth, and the truth shall make you free. *John 8:32*

1434   Use not liberty for an occasion to the flesh. *Galatians 5:13*

LIFE

1435   All that a man hath will he give for his life. *Job 2:4*

1436   None of us liveth to himself, and no man dieth to himself. *Romans 14:7*

LIGHT

1437   The Lord shall be thine everlasting light. *Isaiah 60:20*

1438   I am the light of the world: he that followeth me shall not walk in darkness, but shall have the light of life. *John 8:12*

LOVE

1439   Thou shalt love thy neighbour as thyself. *Leviticus 19:18*

1440 Thou shalt love the Lord thy God with all thine heart, and with all thy soul, and with all thy might. *Deuteronomy 6:5*

1441 If ye love them which love you, what thank have ye? for sinners also love those that love them. *Luke 6:32*

LUST

1442 Whosoever looketh on a woman to lust after her hath committed adultery with her already in his heart. *Matthew 5:28*

1443 All that is in the world, the lust of the flesh, and the lust of the eyes, and the pride of life, is not of the Father, but is of the world. *I John 2:16*

1444 The world passeth away, and the lust thereof: but he that doeth the will of God abideth for ever. *I John 2:17*

MAN

1445 Man that is born of woman is of few days, and full of trouble. He cometh forth like a flower, and is cut down: he fleeth also as a shadow, and continueth not. *Job 14:1–2*

1446 O Lord, thou art our Father; we are the clay, and thou our potter; and we all are the works of thy hand. *Isaiah 64:8*

MARRIAGE

1447 The Lord God said, It is not good that the man should be alone; I will make him an help meet for him. *Genesis 2:18*

1448 Therefore shall a man leave his father and his mother, and shall cleave unto his wife: and they shall be one flesh. *Genesis 2:23*

1449 Unto the woman he said . . . thy desire shall be to thy husband, and he shall rule over thee. *Genesis 3:16*

1450 Husbands, love your wives, even as Christ also loved the church, and gave himself for it. *Ephesians 5:25*

MEDITATION

1451 Whatsoever things are true, whatsoever things are honest, whatsoever things are just, whatsoever things are pure, whatsoever things are lovely, whatsoever things are of good report; if there be any virtue, and if there be any praise, think on these things. *Philippians 4:8*

MEEKNESS

1452 The meek shall inherit the earth. *Psalms 37:11*

1453 Blessed are the meek: for they shall inherit the earth. *Matthew 5:5*

1454 Bless them which persecute you: bless, and curse not. *Romans 12:14*

MERCY

1455 Surely goodness and mercy shall follow me all the days of my life. *Psalms 23:6*

1456 Be ye therefore merciful, as your Father also is merciful. *Luke 6:36*

1457 Blessed are the merciful: for they shall obtain mercy. *Matthew 5:7*

MINISTRY

1458 The harvest is great, but the labourers are few: pray ye therefore the Lord of the harvest, that he should send forth labourers into his harvest. *Luke 10:1*

1459 How beautiful are the feet of them that preach the gospel of peace, and bring glad tidings of good things! *Romans 10:15*

NATURE

1460 In the beginning God created the heaven and the earth. *Genesis 1:1*

1461 The earth is the Lord's and the fulness thereof. *Psalms 24:1*

1462 The flowers appear on the earth; the time of the singing of birds is come. *Song of Solomon 2:12*

OBEDIENCE

1463 The mercy of the Lord is from everlasting to everlasting upon them that fear him . . . and to those that remember his commandments to do them. *Psalms 103:17–18*

1464 Blessed is the man that feareth the Lord, that delighteth greatly in his commandments. *Psalms 112:1*

1465 Why call ye me, Lord, Lord, and do not the things which I say? *Luke 6:46*

1466 If ye love me, keep my commandments. *John 14:15*

OPPORTUNITY

1467 God speaketh once, yea twice, yet man perceiveth it not. *Job 33:14*

1468 The harvest is past, the summer is ended, and we are not saved. *Jeremiah 8:20*

1469 I must work the works of him that sent me, while it is day: the night cometh, when no man can work. *John 9:4*

1470 Behold, now is the accepted time; behold, now is the day of salvation. *II Corinthians 6:2*

PARENTS

1471 Honour thy father and thy mother. *Exodus 10:12*

1472 My son, hear the instruction of thy father, and forsake not the law of thy mother. *Proverbs 1:8*

1473 Whom the Lord loveth he correcteth; even as a father the son in whom he delighteth. *Proverbs 3:12*

1474 Who curseth his father or his mother, his lamp shall be put out in obscure darkness. *Proverbs 20:20*

1475   If a son shall ask bread of any of you that is a father, will ye give him a stone? *Luke 11:11*

1476   Children, obey your parents in the Lord: for this is right. *Ephesians 6:1*

PATIENCE

1477   Those that wait upon the Lord, they shall inherit the earth. *Psalms 37:9*

1478   To them who by patient continuance in well doing seek for glory and honour and immortality, eternal life. *Romans 2:7*

1479   Let us not be weary in well doing: for in due season we shall reap, if we faint not. *Galatians 6:9*

1480   Let us run with patience the race that is set before us. *Hebrews 12:1*

PEACE

1481   They shall beat their swords into plowshares, and their spears into pruninghooks. *Isaiah 2:4*

1482   Blessed are the peacemakers: for they shall be called the children of God. *Matthew 5:9*

1483   Glory to God in the highest, and on earth peace, good will toward men. *Luke 2:14*

1484   Peace I leave with you, my peace I give unto you: not as the world giveth, give I unto you. Let not your heart be troubled, neither let it be afraid. *John 14:27*

1485   The peace of God, which passeth all understanding, shall keep your hearts and minds through Christ Jesus. *Philippians 4:7*

PERFECTION

1486   Now the God of peace . . . Make you perfect in every good work to do his will, working in you that which is well pleasing in his sight. *Hebrews 13:20–21*

1487   If we love one another, God dwelleth in us, and his love is perfected in us. *I John 4:12*

PERSECUTION

1488   Blessed are they which are persecuted for righteousness' sake: for theirs is the kingdom of heaven. Blessed are ye, when men shall revile you, and persecute you, and shall say all manner of evil against you falsely, for my sake. Rejoice, and be exceeding glad: for great is your reward in heaven: for so persecuted they the prophets which were before you. *Matthew 5:10–12*

1489   Whosoever will save his life shall lose it; but whosoever shall lose his life for my sake and the gospel's, the same shall save it. *Mark 8:35*

1490 If the world hate you, ye know that it hated me before it hated you. *John 15:18*

PESSIMISM

1491 All is vanity. *Ecclesiastes 1:2*

1492 In much wisdom is much grief; and he that increaseth knowledge increaseth sorrow. *Ecclesiastes 1:18*

1493 Sorrow is better than laughter. *Ecclesiastes 7:3*

1494 There is not a just man upon earth, that doeth good, and sinneth not. *Ecclesiastes 7:20*

PIETY

1495 Blessed are they which do hunger and thirst after righteousness; for they shall be filled. *Matthew 5:6*

1496 Not every one that saith unto me, Lord, Lord, shall enter into the kingdom of heaven; but he that doeth the will of my Father which is in heaven. *Matthew 7:21*

1497 To love him with all the heart, and with all the understanding, and with all the soul, and with all the strength, and to love his neighbour as himself, is more than all whole burnt offerings and sacrifices. *Mark 12:33*

PLEASURE

1498 He that loveth pleasure shall be a poor man: he that loveth wine and oil shall not be rich. *Proverbs 21:17*

1499 A time to weep, and a time to laugh; a time to mourn, and a time to dance. *Ecclesiastes 3:4*

PLENTY

1500 Honour the Lord with thy substance . . . So shall thy barns be filled with plenty. *Proverbs 3:9–10*

1501 Give and it shall be given unto you: good measure, pressed down, and shaken together, and running over. *Luke 6:38*

POSSESSION

1502 All things come of thee, and of thine own have we given thee. *I Chronicles 29:14*

1503 Where your treasure is, there will your heart be also. *Matthew 6:21*

POVERTY

1504 The needy shall not always be forgotten: the expectation of the poor shall not perish forever. *Psalms 9:18*

1505 The poor is hated even of his own neighbour: but the rich hath many friends. *Proverbs 14:20*

1506 He that hath mercy on the poor, happy is he. *Proverbs 14:21*

1507 I will bless the Lord at all times: his praise shall continually be in my mouth. *Psalms 34:1*

1508 I will praise the name of God with a song, and will magnify him with thanksgiving. *Psalms 69:30*

1509 Praise ye the Lord. O give thanks unto the Lord; for he is good: for his mercy endureth for ever. *Psalms 106:1*

PRAYER
1510 As for me, I will call upon God; and the Lord shall save me. *Psalms 55:16*

1511 In the day of my trouble I will call upon thee: for thou wilt answer me. *Psalms 86:7*

1512 He will regard the prayer of the destitute, and not despise their prayer. *Psalms 102:17*

1513 The Lord is nigh unto all them that call upon him, to all that call upon him in truth. *Psalms 145:18*

1514 Let us lift up our heart with our hands unto God in the heavens. *Lamentations 3:41*

1515 When thou prayest, enter into thy closet, and when thou hast shut thy door, pray to thy Father which is in secret; and thy Father which seeth in secret shall reward thee openly. *Matthew 6:6*

1516 Our Father which art in heaven, Hallowed be thy name. Thy kingdom come. Thy will be done in earth, as it is in heaven. Give us this day our daily bread. And forgive us our debts, as we forgive our debtors. And lead us not into temptation, but deliver us from evil: For thine is the kingdom, and the power, and the glory, for ever. *Matthew 6:9–13*

1517 Ask, and it shall be given you; seek, and ye shall find; knock, and it shall be opened unto you. *Matthew 7:7*

1518 All things, whatsoever ye shall ask in prayer, believing, ye shall receive. *Matthew 21:22*

1519 Whatsoever ye shall ask the Father in my name, he will give it you. *John 16:23*

1520 Pray one for another. *James 5:16*

PRIDE
1521 Every one that is proud in heart is an abomination to the Lord. *Proverbs 16:5*

1522 Before destruction the heart of man is haughty, and before honour is humility. *Proverbs 18:12*

1523 Let not the wise man glory in his wisdom, neither let the mighty man glory in his might, let not the rich man glory in his riches: But let him that glorieth glory in this, that he understandeth and knoweth me, that I am the Lord which exercise loving-kindness, judgment, and righteousness, in the earth: for in these things I delight, saith the Lord. *Jeremiah 9:23–24*

1524   God resisteth the proud, but giveth grace unto the humble. *James 4:6*

PROVIDENCE

1525   Behold the fowls of the air: for they sow not, neither do they reap, nor gather into barns; yet your heavenly Father feedeth them. Are ye not much better than they? *Matthew 6:26*

PRUDENCE

1526   Give not that which is holy unto the dogs, neither cast ye your pearls before swine, lest they trample them under their feet, and turn again and rend you. *Matthew 7:6*

1527   Which of you, intending to build a tower, sitteth not down first, and counteth the cost, whether he have sufficient to finish it? *Luke 14:28*

REDEMPTION

1528   The Son of man came not to be ministered unto, but to minister, and to give his life a ransom for many. *Matthew 20:28*

1529   I am the good shepherd: the good shepherd giveth his life for the sheep. *John 10:11*

1530   There is one God, and one mediator between God and men, the man Christ Jesus; Who gave himself a ransom for all. *I Timothy 2:5–6*

REMISSION

1531   Though your sins be as scarlet, they shall be as white as snow; though they be red like crimson, they shall be as wool. *Isaiah 1:18*

1532   Even as Christ forgave you, so also do ye. *Colossians 3:13*

REMORSE

1533   The Lord is nigh unto them that are of a broken heart; and saveth such as be of a contrite spirit. *Psalms 34:18*

1534   The sacrifices of God are a broken spirit: a broken and a contrite heart, O God, thou wilt not despise. *Psalms 51:17*

REPENTANCE

1535   The Lord your God is gracious and merciful, and will not turn away his face from you, if ye return unto him. *II Chronicles 30:9*

1536   Lord, be merciful unto me; heal my soul; for I have sinned against thee. *Psalms 41:4*

1537   Let the wicked forsake his way, and the unrighteous man his thoughts; and let him return unto the Lord, and he will have mercy upon him; and to our God, for he will abundantly pardon. *Isaiah 55:7*

1538   Except ye repent, ye shall all likewise perish. *Luke 13:3*

1539   Joy shall be in heaven over one sinner that repenteth, more than over ninety and nine just persons, which need no repentance. *Luke 15:7*

1540   I will arise and go to my father, and will say unto him, Father, I have sinned against heaven, and before thee, and am no more worthy to be called thy Son. *Luke 15:18–19*

1541   God be merciful to me a sinner. *Luke 18:13*

RESIGNATION

1542   Teach me to do thy will; for thou art my God. *Psalms 143:10*

RESOLUTION

1543   As for me and my house, we will serve the Lord. *Joshua 24:15*

RESPONSIBILITY

1544   Am I my brother's keeper? *Genesis 4:9*

1545   Every one of us shall give account of himself to God. *Romans 14:12*

RETRIBUTION

1546   Be sure your sin will find you out. *Numbers 32:23*

1547   How oft is the candle of the wicked put out! and how oft cometh their destruction upon them! *Job 21:17*

REVERENCE

1548   The place whereon thou standest is holy ground. *Exodus 3:5*

1549   Ye shall keep my sabbaths, and reverence my sanctuary. *Leviticus 19:30*

1550   What doth the Lord thy God require of thee, but to fear the Lord thy God, to walk in all his ways, and to love him, and to serve the Lord thy God with all thy heart and with all thy soul. *Deuteronomy 10:12*

1551   Let all the earth fear the Lord: let all the inhabitants of the world stand in awe of him. *Psalms 33:8*

1552   The fear of the Lord is the beginning of wisdom. *Psalms 111:10*

REWARD

1553   If thou wilt walk in my ways, to keep my statutes and my commandments . . . then I will lengthen thy days. *I Kings 3:14*

1554   The righteous shall inherit the earth. *Psalms 37:29*

1555   Blessings are upon the head of the just. *Proverbs 10:6*

1556   He shall reward every man according to his works. *Matthew 16:27*

1557   Well done, thou good and faithful servant: thou hast been faithful over a few things, I will make thee ruler over many things: enter thou into the joy of the Lord. *Matthew 25:21*

1558   Come, ye blessed of my Father, inherit the kingdom prepared for you from the foundation of the world: For I was an hungred, and ye gave me meat: I was thirsty, and ye gave me drink: I was a stranger, and ye took me in. *Matthew 25:34–35*

SACRIFICE

1559   He that loseth his life for my sake shall find it. *Matthew 10:39*

1560   If thou wilt be perfect, go and sell that thou hast, and give to the poor, and thou shalt have treasure in heaven: and come and follow me. *Matthew 19:21*

1561   He that loveth his life shall lose it. *John 12:25*

SADNESS

1562   Heaviness in the heart of man maketh it stoop: but a good word maketh it glad. *Proverbs 12:25*

SALVATION

1563   And it shall come to pass, that whosoever shall call on the name of the Lord shall be delivered. *Joel 2:32*

1564   God sent not his Son into the world to condemn the world; but that the world through him might be saved. *John 3:17*

1565   I am the bread of life: he that cometh to me shall never hunger; and he that believeth on me shall never thirst. *John 6:35*

1566   I am the resurrection and the life: he that believeth in me, though he were dead, yet shall he live. And whosoever liveth and believeth in me shall never die. *John 11:25*

SCRIPTURE

1567   Man doth not live by bread only, but by every word that proceedeth out of the mouth of the Lord doth man live. *Deuteronomy 8:3*

1568   Seek ye out of the book of the Lord, and read. *Isaiah 34:16*

1569   Whosoever heareth these sayings of mine, and doeth them, I will liken him unto a wise man, which built his house upon a rock. *Matthew 7:24*

1570   Blessed are they that hear the word of God and keep it. *Luke 11:28*

SELFISHNESS

1571   Whoso hath this world's good, and seeth his brother have need, and shutteth up his bowels of compassion from him, how dwelleth the love of God in him? *I John 3:17*

SELF-RIGHTEOUSNESS

1572   There is a way which seemeth right unto a man, but the end thereof are the ways of death. *Proverbs 14:12*

1573   Most men will proclaim every one his own goodness: but a faithful man who can find? *Proverbs 20:6*

1574   Every way of a man is right in his own eyes: but the Lord pondereth the hearts. *Proverbs 21:2*

1575   Woe unto them that are wise in their own eyes, and prudent in their own sight! *Isaiah 5:21*

1576   God, I thank thee, that I am not as other men are. *Luke 18:9*

SIN

1577   As he thinketh in his heart, so is he. *Proverbs 23:7*

1578   All we like sheep have gone astray; we have turned every one to his own way. *Isaiah 53:6*

1579   The wages of sin is death. *Romans 6:23*

SLANDER

1580   Deliver my soul, O Lord, from lying lips, and from a deceitful tongue. *Psalms 120:2*

SPIRIT

1581   We know that if our earthly house of this tabernacle were dissolved, we have a building of God, an house not made with hands, eternal in the heavens. *II Corinthians 5:1*

STRENGTH

1582   Be strong, and quit yourselves like men. *I Samuel 4:9*

1583   The race is not to the swift, nor the battle to the strong. *Ecclesiastes 9:11*

1584   They that wait on the Lord shall renew their strength; they shall mount up with wings as eagles; they shall run, and not be weary; and they shall walk, and not faint. *Isaiah 11:32*

1585   The floods came, and the winds blew, and beat upon that house; and it fell not: for it was founded upon a rock. *Matthew 7:25*

SUFFERING

1586   Are ye able to drink of the cup that I shall drink of, and to be baptized with the baptism that I am baptized with? *Matthew 20:22*

1587   Being reviled, we bless; being persecuted, we suffer it. *I Corinthians 4:12*

TALENT

1588   Neglect not the gift that is in thee. *I Timothy 4:14*

TEMPTATION

1589   Can a man take fire in his bosom, and his clothes not be burned? *Proverbs 6:27*

1590   Be not overcome of evil, but overcome evil with good. *Romans 12:21*

1591   Resist the devil, and he will flee from you. *James 4:7*

THANKSGIVING

1592   It is a good thing to give thanks unto the Lord, and to sing praises unto thy name, O most High. *Psalms 92:1*

1593   O give thanks unto the Lord, for he is good, for his mercy endureth for ever. *Psalms 107:1*

1594   In every thing give thanks. *I Thessalonians 5:18*

1595   Be patient toward all men. *I Thessalonians 5:14*

1596   Speak evil of no man. *Titus 3:2*

TROUBLE

1597   Have mercy upon me, O Lord, for I am in trouble. *Psalms 31:9*

UNBELIEF

1598   The fool hath said in his heart, There is no God. *Psalms 14:1*

1599   Increase our faith. *Luke 17:5*

1600   He was in the world, and the world was made by him, and the world knew him not. *John 1:10*

UNSELFISHNESS

1601   We then that are strong ought to bear the infirmities of the weak, and not to please ourselves. *Romans 15:1*

1602   I will very gladly spend and be spent for you. *II Corinthians 12:15*

VIGILANCE

1603   The watchman said, The morning cometh, and also the night. *Isaiah 21:12*

1604   Watch therefore: for ye know not what hour your Lord doth come. *Matthew 24:42*

1605   Take ye heed, watch and pray: for ye know not when the time is. *Mark 13:33*

WANT

1606   Your Father knoweth what things ye have need of, before ye ask him. *Matthew 6:8*

WAR

1607   Wisdom is better than weapons of war. *Ecclesiastes 9:18*

1608   The mighty . . . are gone down to hell with their weapons of war. *Ezekiel 32:27*

WEALTH

1609   Thou shalt remember the Lord thy God: for it is he that giveth thee power to get wealth. *Deuteronomy 8:18*

1610   He that trusteth in his riches shall fall. *Proverbs 11:28*

1611   Better is little with the fear of the Lord than great treasure and trouble therewith. *Proverbs 15:16*

1612   It is easier for a camel to go through the eye of a needle, than for a rich man to enter into the Kingdom of God. *Matthew 19:24*

1613   Ye cannot serve God and mammon. *Luke 16:13*

WISDOM

1614 Behold the fear of the Lord, that is wisdom: and to depart from evil is understanding. *Job 28:28*

1615 Get wisdom, get understanding; forget it not. *Proverbs 4:5*

WORKS

1616 What doth it profit, my brethren, though a man say he hath faith, and have not works? *James 2:14*

1617 Faith, if it hath not works, is dead. *James 2:17*

WORLDLINESS

1618 Take no thought for your life, what ye shall eat, or what ye shall drink; nor yet for your body, what ye shall put on. Is not life more than meat, and the body more than raiment? *Matthew 6:25*

1619 The wisdom of this world is foolishness with God. *I Corinthians 3:19*

WORSHIP

1620 O come, let us worship and bow down: let us kneel before the Lord our maker. *Psalms 95:6*

1621 I was glad when they said unto me, Let us go into the house of the Lord. *Psalms 122:1*

1622 The Lord is in his holy temple: let all the earth keep silence before him. *Habakkuk 2:20*

1623 All nations shall come and worship before thee. *Revelation 15:4*

ZEAL

1624 With my whole heart have I sought thee. *Psalms 119:10*

1625 I must work the works of him that sent me, while it is day: the night cometh, when no man can work. *John 9:14*

...8...

The Wit and Wisdom of Statesmen

1626 I was not discouraged by the seeming magnitude of the undertaking, as I have always thought that one man of tolerable abilities may work great changes, and accomplish great affairs among mankind. If he first forms a good plan, and cutting off all amusements or other employments that would divert his attention, makes the execution of that same plan his sole study and business. *Benjamin Franklin*

1627 Advice is seldom welcome; and those who want it the most always like it the least. *Lord Chesterfield*

1628 I have one yardstick by which I test every major problem—and that yardstick is: Is it good for America? *Dwight D. Eisenhower*

1629 No explanation is necessary because none would be satisfactory. *Ibid.*

1630 He seems determined to make a trumpet sound like a tin whistle. . . . He brings to the fierce struggle of politics the tepid enthusiasm of a lazy summer afternoon at a cricket match. *Aneurin Bevan*

1631 Mr. Attlee is a very modest man. But then he has much to be modest about. *Winston Churchill*

1632 We do not live in the Bavarian forests. We do not live on the west bank of the Rhine. We live behind the Communist guns in this encircled city. This is a geographical fact. But we belong to the West and we will continue belonging to the West. *Willy Brandt*

BEST
1633 I have not permitted myself, gentlemen, to conclude that I am the best man in the country; but I am reminded in this connection of the story of an old Dutch farmer, who remarked to a companion once that it was not best to swap horses when crossing a stream. *Abraham Lincoln*

BIOGRAPHY
1634 There is no romance nor is there anything heroic in my early life. The story of my life can be condensed into one line, and that line you can find in Gray's "Elegy": "The short and simple annals of the poor." *Ibid., answering a request for information for a campaign biography*

BLESSING
1635 An honest heart being the first blessing, a knowing head is the second. *Thomas Jefferson*

BREAD
1636 And having looked to government for bread, on the very first scarcity they will turn and bite the hand that fed them. *Edmund Burke*

BRINK
1637 You have to take chances for peace, just as you must take chances in war. . . . The ability to get to the verge without getting into the war is the necessary art. If you try to run away from it, if you are scared to go to the brink, you are lost. *John Foster Dulles*

BRUTUS
1638 You too, Brutus? *Julius Caesar*

CAMPAIGNING
1639 When Taft was campaigning, someone threw a cabbage at him. It rolled to a stop at Taft's feet. "I see," was his comment, "that one of my adversaries has lost his head." *William Howard Taft*

NEVILLE CHAMBERLAIN
1640 He has the lucidity which is the by-product of a fundamentally sterile mind. . . . He does not have to struggle, like Churchill has, for example, with the crowded pulsations of a fecund imagination. On the contrary he is almost devoid of imagination. Listening to a speech by Chamberlain is like paying a visit to Woolworth's; everything in its place and nothing above sixpence. *Aneurin Bevan*

CHARACTERISTICS
1641 I think there is only one quality worse than hardness of heart and that is softness of head. *Theodore Roosevelt*

CHIVALRY

1642 But the age of chivalry is gone. That of sophisters, economists, and calculators has succeeded; and the glory of Europe is extinguished forever. *Edmund Burke*

WINSTON CHURCHILL

1643 His ear is so sensitively attuned to the bugle note of history that he is often deaf to the more raucous clamor of contemporary life, a defect which his Conservative upbringing and background tend to reinforce. The seven-league-boot tempo of his imagination hastens him on to the "sunny uplands" of the future; he is apt to forget that the slow steps of humanity must travel every inch of the weary road that leads there. . . .

He mistakes verbal felicities for mental inspirations. . . .

A man suffering from petrified adolescence . . .

He refers to a defeat as a disaster as though it came from God, but to a victory as though it came from himself. . . .

The mediocrity of his thinking is concealed by the majesty of his language. *Aneurin Bevan*

COMMUNISM

1644 A strange, a perverted creed that has a queer attraction both for the most primitive and for the most sophisticated societies. . . . Once the bear's hug has got you, it is apt to be for keeps. *Harold Macmillan*

1645 Each year humanity takes a step toward Communism. Maybe not you, but at all events your grandson will surely be a Communist. *Nikita Khrushchev*

1646 Whether you like it or not, history is on our side. We will bury you! *Ibid.*

1647 If we could have the revolution over again, we would carry it out more sensibly and with smaller losses. But history does not repeat itself. The situation is favorable for us. If God existed, we would thank Him for it. *Ibid.*

CONFERENCE

1648 Conferences at the top level are always courteous. Name-calling is left to the foreign ministers. *Averell Harriman*

CONFIDENCE

1649 I do not object to Gladstone always having the ace of trumps up his sleeve but merely to his belief that God Almighty put it there. *Henry Labouchère*

1650 If you once forfeit the confidence of your fellow citizens, you can never regain their respect and esteem. It is true that you may fool all the people some of the time; you can even fool some of the people all the time; but you can't fool all of the people all the time. *Abraham Lincoln*

CONFIRMATION

1651 I am grateful for the overwhelming vote of confirmation in the Senate. We must now wait until the dirt settles. My difficulties, of course, go some years back when Senator Wayne Morse was kicked in the head by a horse. *Clare Boothe Luce*

CONGRESS

1652 Oh! the wisdom, the foresight and the hindsight and the rightsight and the leftsight, the northsight and the southsight, and the eastsight and the westsight that appeared in that august assembly. *John Adams, in a letter to a friend*

1653 In a body where there are more than one hundred talking lawyers, you can make no calculation upon the termination of any debate and frequently, the more trifling the subject, the more animated and protracted the discussion. *Franklin Pierce*

CONGRESSMAN

1654 Will Rogers once said it is not the original investment in a congressman that counts; it is the upkeep. *John F. Kennedy*

CONSERVATION

1655 To the use of the natural resources, renewable or nonrenewable, each generation has the first right. Nevertheless no generation can be allowed needlessly to damage or reduce the future general wealth and welfare by the way it uses or misuses any natural resource. *Gifford Pinchot*

CONSERVATISM

1656 Conservatism is the policy of make no change and consult your grandmother when in doubt. *Woodrow Wilson*

1657 A conservative man is a man who just sits and thinks, mostly sits. *Ibid.*

CONSTITUTION

1658 Our Constitution is in actual operation; everything appears to promise that it will last; but in this world nothing is certain but death and taxes. *Benjamin Franklin*

1659 There is a higher law than the Constitution. *William Henry Seward*

COST OF LIVING

1660 It's hard nowadays for a man with five children and eleven servants to make a living. *Franklin D. Roosevelt*

COURTESY

1661 I don't care what people call me. I've been called everything. But I instructed the White House staff always to call Mr. Hoover "Mr. President" and I did myself. *Harry S. Truman*

STAFFORD CRIPPS

1662 Neither of his colleagues can compare with him in that acuteness or energy of mind with which he devotes himself to so many topics injurious to the strength and welfare of the state. *Winston Churchill*

CRITICISM

1663 I refer you to the second term of President Washington. . . . When I compare the weak, inconsequential things they say about me, compared to what they say about the man who I think is the greatest human the English-speaking race has produced, then I can be quite philosophical about it. *Dwight D. Eisenhower*

DEATH

1664 I still have enjoyment in the company of my friends; and, being easy in my circumstances, have many reasons to like living. But the course of nature must soon put a period to my present mode of existence. This I shall submit to with less regret, as having seen, during a long life, a good deal of the world, I feel a growing curiosity to be acquainted with some other; and can cheerfully, with filial confidence, resign my spirit to the conduct of that great and good Parent of mankind who created it, and who has so graciously protected and prospered me from my birth to the present hour.

I am ready to meet my Maker. Whether my Maker is prepared for the great ordeal of meeting me is another matter. *Winston Churchill*

DEFENSE

1665 There is only one defense; a defense compounded of eternal vigilance, sound policies, and high courage. *John Foster Dulles*

DEMOCRAT

1666 Ask no man whether he is a Democrat or a Republican. Ask him to *vote* Democratic. *Lyndon B. Johnson*

DESCRIPTION

1667 Butler—donnish, dignified, and dull; Maudling—manly, matey, and money wise; and Hailsham—ebullient, erudite, and erratic. *Gerald Nabarro*

1668 A man walking backward with his face to the future. *Aneurin Bevan, about Walter Elliot, Minister of Agriculture*

DETERMINATION

1669 The die was now cast; I had passed the Rubicon. Swim or sink, live or die, survive or perish with my country was my unalterable determination. *John Adams*

DUTY

1670 Little more than sixteen years had elapsed since I had landed on these shores, a homeless waif. . . . And here I was now, a member of the highest lawmaking body of the greatest of republics. Should I ever be able . . . to accomplish this, my conception of duty could not be pitched too high. I recorded a vow in my own heart that I would at least honestly endeavor to fulfill that duty; that I would conscientiously adhere to the principle *salus populi suprema lex esto;* that I would never be a sycophant of power nor a flatterer of the multitude; that, if need be, I would stand up alone for my conviction of truth and right. *Carl Schurz*

ECONOMY

1671 I place economy among the first and most important of republican virtues. *Thomas Jefferson*

EDUCATION

1672 Modern cynics and skeptics . . . see no harm in paying those to whom they entrust the minds of their children a smaller wage than is paid to those to whom they entrust the care of their plumbing. *John F. Kennedy*

1673 If the condition of man is to be progressively ameliorated, as we fondly hope and believe, education is to be the chief instrument in effecting it. *Thomas Jefferson*

ELECTION

1674 I voted for Buchanan because I didn't know him and voted against Frémont because I did know him. *Ulysses S. Grant*

1675 If you think too much about being reelected, it is very difficult to be worth reelecting. *Woodrow Wilson*

1676 During a political campaign, everyone is concerned with what a candidate will do on this or that question if he is elected, except the candidate; he's too busy wondering what he'll do if he isn't elected. *Everett McKinley Dirksen*

EMPLOYMENT

1677 I will undoubtedly have to seek what is happily known as gainful employment, which I am glad to say does not describe holding public office. *Dean Acheson*

ENEMY

1678 Doing an injury puts you below your enemy; revenging one makes you even with him; forgiving one sets you above him. *Benjamin Franklin*

ENGLISH

1679 This is the sort of English up with which I will not put. *Winston Churchill*

ENTHUSIASM

1680 It is unfortunate, considering that enthusiasm moves the world, that so few enthusiasts can be trusted to speak the truth. *Arthur Balfour*

EVENTS

1681 The pace of events is moving so fast that unless we can find some way to keep our sights on tomorrow, we cannot expect to be in touch with today. *Dean Rusk*

FAILURE

1682 My father was not a failure. After all, he was the father of a President of the United States. *Harry S. Truman*

FARMER

1683 I understand nearby there is a farmer who planted some corn. He said to his neighbor, "I hope I break even this year. I really need the money." *John F. Kennedy*

FAVORITE PRAYER

1684 Oh! Almighty and Everlasting God, Creator of Heaven, Earth and the Universe:

Help me to be, to think, to act what is right, because it is right; make me truthful, honest, and honorable in all things; make me intellectually honest for the sake of right and honor and without thought of reward to me. Give me the ability to be charitable, forgiving, and patient with my fellow men—help me to understand their motives and their shortcomings—even as thou understandest mine! Amen, Amen, Amen. *Harry S. Truman*

FOOL

1685 It has been said that there is no fool like an old fool—except a young fool. But the young fool has first to grow up to be an old fool to realize what a damn fool he was when he was a young fool. *Harold Macmillan*

FOOTBALL

1686 An atheist is a guy who watches a Notre Dame–SMU football game and doesn't care who wins. *Dwight D. Eisenhower*

FORGOTTEN MAN

1687 Minority groups now speak much more loudly than do majority groups, which I classify as the forgotten American, the man who pays his taxes, prays, behaves himself, stays out of trouble, and works for his government. *Barry M. Goldwater*

1688 The Forgotten Man is delving away in patient industry, supporting his family, paying his taxes, casting his vote, supporting the church and school, reading his newspaper, and cheering for the politician of his admiration, but he is the only one for whom there is no provision in the great scramble and the big divide. Such is the Forgotten Man. He works, he votes, generally he prays—but he always pays—yes, above all, he pays. *William Graham Sumner*

FORM LETTERS

1689 No form letters are sent out from this office. No husband was ever Section 3, Paragraph IIa to his wife. *Anna Rosenberg*

FRANCE

1690 How can you be expected to govern a country that has 246 kinds of cheese? *Charles de Gaulle*

FREEDOM

1691 Necessity is the plea for every infringement of human freedom. It is the argument of tyrants; it is the creed of slaves. *William Pitt*

FUTURE

1692 You cannot fight against the future. Time is on our side. *William Gladstone*

LLOYD GEORGE

1693 He spent his whole life in plastering together the true and the false and therefrom manufacturing the plausible. *Stanley Baldwin*

GOD

1694 I tremble for my country when I reflect that God is just. *Thomas Jefferson*

1695 If to please the people, we offer what we ourselves disapprove, how can we afterward defend our work? Let us raise a standard to which the wise and honest can repair. The event is in the hands of God. *George Washington*

1696 We say the name of God, but that is only habit. We are atheists. *Nikita Khrushchev*

1697 I have lived, sir, a long time; and the longer I live, the more convincing proofs I see of this truth, that God governs in the affairs of men. And if a sparrow cannot fall to the ground without his notice, is it probable that an empire can rise without his aid? *Benjamin Franklin*

GOLF

1698 An ineffectual attempt to put an elusive ball into an obscure hole with implements ill adapted to the purpose. *Woodrow Wilson*

GOVERNMENT

1699 Without exhaustive debate, even heated debate of ideas and programs, free government would weaken and wither. But if we allow ourselves to be persuaded that every individual or party that takes issue with our own convictions is necessarily wicked or treasonous, then indeed, we are approaching the end of freedom's road. *Dwight D. Eisenhower*

1700   If men were angels, no government would be necessary. If angels were to govern men, neither external nor internal controls on government would be necessary. In framing a government which is to be administered by men over men, the great difficulty lies in this: You must first enable the government to control the governed: and in the next place oblige it to control itself. *Alexander Hamilton*

1701   Why has government been instituted at all? Because the passions of men will not conform to the dictates of reason and justice, without constraint. *Ibid.*

1702   It is not the function of the State to make men happy. They must make themselves happy in their own way, and at their own risk. The functions of the State lie entirely in the conditions or chances under which the pursuit of happiness is carried on. *William Graham Sumner*

GREATNESS

1703   Your dad will never be reckoned among the great. But you can be sure he did his level best and gave all he had to his country. There is an epitaph in Boothill Cemetery in Tombstone, Arizona, which reads, "Here lies Jack Williams; he done his damndest." What more can a person do? *Harry Truman, in letter to Margaret Truman*

1704   It is Easter day—pouring and raw. I suppose you are out sleighing in a samovar! Pin a rose on Lenin when you attend the May first celebration. He is a great man because dead! *Franklin D. Roosevelt, in letter to the U.S. ambassador to Russia*

HAIRCUT

1705   A man of my limited resources cannot presume to have a hair style. Get on and cut it. *Winston Churchill*

HEAD

1706   I will make you shorter by a head. *Elizabeth I*

HISTORY

1707   That great dustheap called history. *Augustine Birrell*

HONESTY

1708   And I will lay the cards out just as straight for them as I do for you. That way everyone will know the score—like the conversation at the card game when one of the boys looked across the table and said, "Now, Reuben, play the cards fair. I know what I dealt you." *Lyndon B. Johnson*

1709   I have not observed men's honesty to increase with their riches. *Thomas Jefferson*

HORSE RACE

1710 You people know a great deal about horse races in Lexington, and you know it doesn't matter which horse is ahead or behind at any given moment, it's the horse that comes out ahead at the finish that counts. *Harry S. Truman*

HOUSE OF LORDS

1711 It's nice to keep in touch—besides, it's the only place in London where you can park a car. *Clement Attlee*

1712 We are fortunate to have inherited an institution [the House of Lords] which we certainly should never have had the intelligence to create. We might have been landed with something like the American Senate. *Lord Esher*

HUMAN RACE

1713 The other night, my little teen-age daughter came home and said— and I don't think she was being very original—"Daddy, as an outsider, how do you feel about the human race?" *Lyndon B. Johnson*

HUNDRED-DOLLAR-A-PLATE DINNERS

1714 I am deeply touched—not as deeply touched as you have been by coming to this dinner, but nevertheless, it is a sentimental occasion. *John F. Kennedy*

HYDROGEN BOMB

1715 It may be that we shall by a process of sublime irony have reached a stage in this story where safety will be the sturdy child of error, and survival the twin brother of annihilation. *Winston Churchill*

IGNORANCE

1716 He was distinguished for ignorance; for he had only one idea and that was wrong. *Benjamin Disraeli*

1717 If a nation expects to be ignorant and free, in a state of civilization, it expects what never was and never will be. *Thomas Jefferson*

INAUGURAL BALL

1718 Never before have so many paid so much to dance so little. *Lyndon B. Johnson*

INCOME TAX

1719 The one thing that hurts more than paying an income tax is not having to pay an income tax. *Lord Dewar*

INJUSTICE

1720 It is of great importance in a republic not only to guard the society against the oppression of its rulers, but to guard one part of the society against the injustice of the other part. *James Madison*

INNOVATION

1721   Continuity does not rule out fresh approaches to fresh situations. *Dean Rusk*

INSPIRATION

1722   I have never accepted what many people have kindly said, namely that I inspired the nation. It was the nation and the race dwelling all around the globe that had the lion heart. I had the luck to be called upon to give the roar. *Winston Churchill*

INTELLIGENTSIA

1723   The intelligent are to the intelligentsia what a gentleman is to a gent. *Stanley Baldwin*

IRON CURTAIN

1724   I view with profound misgivings the retreat of the American Army to our line of occupation in the central sector, thus bringing Soviet power into the heart of Western Europe and the descent of an iron curtain between us and everything to the eastward. *Winston Churchill*

KNOWLEDGE

1725   Whenever the people are well informed, they can be trusted with their own government. *Thomas Jefferson*

1726   He who knows nothing is nearer the truth than he whose mind is filled with falsehoods and errors. *Ibid.*

1727   To be conscious that you are ignorant is a great step to knowledge. *Benjamin Disraeli*

LAUGHTER

1728   In my mind, there is nothing so illiberal and so ill bred as audible laughter. *Lord Chesterfield.*

LEARNING

1729   You ain't learnin' nothin' when you're talkin'. *Lyndon B. Johnson*

LETTER TO THE U.S. AMBASSADOR TO GREAT BRITAIN

1730   When you feel that British accent creeping up on you and your trousers riding up to the knee, take the first steamer home for a couple of weeks' holiday. *Franklin D. Roosevelt.*

LIBERTY

1731   Liberty, too, must be limited in order to be possessed. *Edmund Burke*

1732   Among a people generally corrupt, liberty cannot long exist. *Ibid.*

1733   They that give up essential liberty to obtain a little temporary safety deserve neither liberty nor safety. *Benjamin Franklin*

1734   Natural liberty is a gift of the beneficent Creator, to the whole human race, and . . . civil liberty is founded in that, and cannot be wrested from any people without the most manifest violation of justice. *Alexander Hamilton*

1735 Our liberty cannot be guarded but by the freedom of the press, nor that be limited without danger of losing it. *Thomas Jefferson*

1736 We are not to expect to be translated from despotism to liberty in a featherbed. *Ibid.*

LIFE

1737 I'd rather give my life than be afraid to give it. *Lyndon B. Johnson*

1738 An hour late and a dollar short—that's the way I've been all my life. *Ibid.*

LOUD

1739 Back in the days when I performed my part as a keelboatman, I made the acquaintance of a trifling little steamboat which used to bustle and puff and wheeze about the Sangamon River. It had a five-foot boiler and seven-foot whistle, and every time it whistled, it stopped. *Abraham Lincoln*

LOUIS XVI

1740 He hunts one half of the day, is drunk the other, and signs whatever he is bid. *Thomas Jefferson*

LUCK

1741 The only thing you have to worry about is bad luck. I never have bad luck. *Harry S. Truman*

RAMSAY MacDONALD

1742 I remember when I was a child being taken to the celebrated Barnum's circus. The exhibit which I most desired to see was the one described as the "Boneless Wonder." My parents judged that the spectacle would be too revolting and demoralizing for my youthful eyes. I have waited fifty years to see the Boneless Wonder sitting on the Treasury Bench. *Winston Churchill*

MASSES

1743 All the world over, I will back the masses against the classes. *William Gladstone*

THE MAYFLOWER COMPACT

1744 In the name of God, Amen. We, whose names are underwritten, the loyal subjects of our dread sovereign lord, King James, by the grace of God, of Great Britain, France, and Ireland king, defender of the faith, etc., having undertaken for the glory of God, the advancement of the Christian faith, and honor of our king and country, a voyage to plant the first colony in the northern parts of Virginia, do, by these presents, solemnly and mutually in the presence of God, and of one another, covenant and combine ourselves together into a civil body politic, for our better ordering and preservation and furtherance of the ends aforesaid; and by virtue hereof to enact, constitute, and frame such just and equal laws, ordinances, acts, constitutions, and offices, from time to time, as shall be thought most meet and convenient for the general good of the Colony unto which we promise all due submission and obedience. In witness whereof we have hereunder subscribed our names at Cape Cod the 11 of November, in the year of the reign of our sovereign lord, King James, of England, France, and Ireland, the eighteenth, and of Scotland the fifty-fourth. Anno Dom. 1620. *William Bradford*

MEDAL

1745   I pinned a medal on General MacArthur the other day, and told him I wished I had a medal like that, and he said that it was my duty to give the medals, not receive them. That is always the way. About all I receive is the bricks. It's a good thing I have got a pretty hard head or it would have been broken a long time ago. *Harry S. Truman*

MINISTER OF FINANCE

1746   A minister of finance is a legally authorized pickpocket. *Paul Ramadier*

MISFORTUNE

1747   Well, if Mr. Gladstone fell into the Thames it would be a misfortune; but if someone pulled him out it would be a calamity. *Benjamin Disraeli*

MODERATION

1748   So numerous indeed and so powerful are the causes which serve to give a false bias to the judgment, that we, upon many occasions, see wise and good men on the wrong as well as on the right side of questions of the first magnitude to society. This circumstance, if duly attended to, would furnish a lesson of moderation to those who are ever so much persuaded of their being in the right, in any controversy. *Alexander Hamilton*

MONEY

1749   Millions for defense, but not one cent for tribute. *Charles C. Pinckney*

1750   Too often our Washington reflex is to discover a problem and then throw money at it, hoping it will somehow go away. *Kenneth B. Keating*

1751   As quickly as you start spending federal money in large amounts, it looks like free money. *Dwight D. Eisenhower*

NONSENSE

1752 The wisest thing to do with a fool is to encourage him to hire a hall and discourse to his fellow citizens. Nothing chills nonsense like exposure to the air. *Woodrow Wilson*

OPPONENT'S SPEECH

1753 There were some things in it meant seriously which were humorous and there were others meant humorously which were serious. *Arthur Balfour*

PARTISAN

1754 This is not a partisan dinner. It is open to any member of any political party who wants to contribute one hundred dollars to the Democratic Party in November. *Lyndon B. Johnson*

PATRIOTISM

1755 I don't think the United States needs superpatriots. We need patriotism, honestly practiced by all of us, and we don't need these people that are more patriotic than you or anybody else. *Dwight D. Eisenhower*

PEACE

1756 It should be our endeavor to cultivate the peace and friendship of every nation, even of that which has injured us most, when we shall have carried our point against her. *Thomas Jefferson*

1757 Peace is the goal of my life. I'd rather have lasting peace in the world than be President. I wish for peace, I work for peace, and I pray for peace continually. *Harry S. Truman*

PERSONALITY

1758 I am a vague, conjectural personality, more made up of opinions and academic prepossessions than of human traits and red corpuscles. *Woodrow Wilson*

POLITICAL PARTIES

1759 The nest of office being too small for all of them to cuddle into at once, the contest is eternal which shall crowd the other out. For this purpose, they are divided into two parties, the Ins and the Outs. *Thomas Jefferson*

POLITICIAN

1760 An important maxim to remember is "don't be an amateur." The job of being a professional politician, in spite of the odium which some persons have falsely attached to it, is a high and difficult one. *Henry Cabot Lodge, Jr.*

POLITICS

1761 I seldom think of politics more than eighteen hours a day. *Lyndon B. Johnson*

1762   When a leader is in the Democratic Party he's a boss, when he's in the Republican Party he's nothing but a leader. But there's no difference. *Harry S. Truman*

1763   No popularity lives long in a democracy. *John Quincy Adams*

1764   A Yankee always thinks that he is right, a Scotch-Irishman *knows* that he is right. *Woodrow Wilson*

1765   Power gradually extirpates from the mind every humane and gentle virtue. *Edmund Burke*

1766   Unlimited power is apt to corrupt the minds of those who possess it. *William Pitt*

1767   I know that when things don't go well they like to blame the Presidents, and that is one of the things which Presidents are paid for. *John F. Kennedy*

1768   I have my own ideas, as everyone else does, of what is a proper sphere of activity for the President of the United States. One of them . . . is that he doesn't go out barnstorming for himself under any condition. *Dwight D. Eisenhower*

1769   Oh, that lovely title, ex-President . . . *Ibid.*

1770   The thing I enjoyed most were visits from children. They did not want public office. *Herbert Hoover*

1771   There are some valuable privileges attached to being President— among them the duty and right to terminate all interviews, conferences, social parties, and receptions. Therefore, he can go to bed whenever he likes. *Ibid.*

1772   Are you seeing everything you want while in Washington? If not, let me know. I am pretty well known around here. Perhaps I can fix it up for you. *Ibid.*

1773   The buck stops here. *Harry S. Truman*

1774   I felt as if I had lived five lifetimes in my first five days as President. *Ibid.*

1775   Some of the Presidents were great and some of them weren't. I can say that, because I wasn't one of the great Presidents, but I had a good time trying to be one, I can tell you that. *Ibid.*

1776   Harry [Truman], they'll try to put you behind a wall down here. There will be people that will surround you and cut you off from any ideas but theirs. They'll try to make you think that the President is the smartest man in the world. And, Harry, you know he ain't and I know he ain't. *Sam Rayburn*

1777   My White House job pays more than public school systems but the tenure is less certain. *Lyndon B. Johnson*

1778   The work was killing me; they called me out of bed at all hours of the night to receive resignations of prime ministers. *Vincent Auriol, former president of France*

PRESIDENTS (RETIRED)

1779   We spend our time taking pills and dedicating libraries. *Herbert Hoover, as he helped Harry S. Truman dedicate the Presidential Library at Independence, Missouri*

PRESS

1780   Whenever the press quits abusing me, I know I'm in the wrong pew. *Harry S. Truman*

PROMISE

1781   I will do my best. That is all I can do. I ask for your help—and God's. *Lyndon B. Johnson*

PROPHET

1782   Prognostics do not always prove prophecies—at least, the wisest prophets make sure of the event first. *Horace Walpole*

PUBLICITY

1783   What kills a skunk is the publicity it gives itself. *Abraham Lincoln*

PUBLIC SPEAKING

1784   I heard a fellow tell a story about how he felt when he had to make speeches. He said when he has to make a speech, he felt like the fellow who was at the funeral of his wife, and the undertaker had asked him if he would ride down to the cemetery in the same car with his mother-in-law. He said, "Well, I can do it, but it's just going to spoil the whole day for me." *Harry S. Truman*

RADICAL

1785   A radical is a man with both feet firmly planted in the air. *Franklin D. Roosevelt*

READING

1786   I smoked tobacco and read Milton at the same time, and from the same motive—to find out what was the recondite charm in them which gave my father so much pleasure. After making myself four or five times sick with smoking, I mastered that accomplishment. . . . But I did not master Milton. *John Quincy Adams*

REALIST

1787   In Israel, in order to be a realist you must believe in miracles. *David Ben-Gurion*

RELIGION

1788   Man is by his constitution a religious animal. *Edmund Burke*

1789   There being no Episcopal minister present in the place, I went to hear morning service performed in the Dutch Reformed Church—which, being in that language not a word of which I understood, I was in no danger of becoming a proselyte to its religion by the eloquence of the preacher. *George Washington*

REPUBLICAN

1790   I think it is very important that we have a two-party country. I am a fellow who likes small parties and the Republican Party is about the size I like. *Lyndon B. Johnson*

REPUTATION

1791   Associate yourself with men of good quality if you esteem your own reputation; for 'tis better to be alone than in bad company. *George Washington*

RESPONSIBILITY

1792   The Secretary of Labor is in charge of finding you a job, the Secretary of the Treasury is in charge of taking half the money you make away from you, and the Attorney General is in charge of suing you for the other half. *Lyndon B. Johnson*

1793   This desk of mine is one at which a man may die, but from which he cannot resign. *Dwight D. Eisenhower*

1794   Whatever the ultimate future may hold, it is certainly true that the prospects for the immediate years before us are not bright. In their social actions men are indeed curious, blundering, and at times malevolent children. With one side of their nature they build up a flourishing material civilization embellished by beauty and by culture. With another side they seek to tear down and to befoul all that is fine. Perhaps there never was a time when the creative aspects of life were more widely menaced by these darker forces than now. Upon our generation is laid the heavy task of mastering these baser elements and of building a more secure and more gracious life, not only for the few, but for the multitude as well. *Paul Douglas*

ROLE OF WOMEN

1795   It will be the same, I trust, as it has been since the days of Adam and Eve. *Winston Churchill*

SALUTATION

1796   If you and he are in complete agreement, you address him merely as "The Senator from such and such a state."

      If you are not too sure he agrees with you, you should refer to him as "The able Senator from———."

      But if you know there is violent disagreement on an issue, then there is only one way to address him: "The able and distinguished Senator, my friend from———." *Edmund Muskie*

SENSE

1797   One of the wisest things my daddy ever told me was that "so-and-so is a damned smart man, but the fool's got no sense." *Lyndon B. Johnson*

SOVIET RUSSIA

1798   You start out giving your hat, then you give your coat, then your shirt, then your skin, and finally your soul. *Charles de Gaulle*

SPEECH

1799   [Herbert H.] Asquith's lucidity of style is a positive disadvantage when he has nothing to say. *Arthur Balfour*

1800   Please don't be deterred in the fanatical application of your sterile logic. *Aneurin Bevan*

1801   Well, the speech seems to have made a hit according to all the papers. Shows you never can tell. I thought it was rotten. *Harry S. Truman*

1802   I have to deliver an address of a bipartisan nature that will be entirely satisfactory to the Democrats of Minnesota. *Ibid.*

1803   Those last couple of paragraphs are fine and ringing but I can't get away from the feeling that they make me sound like St. Peter. *Dwight D. Eisenhower*

1804   If you have an important point to make, don't try to be subtle or clever. Use a pile driver. Hit the point once. Then come back and hit it again. Then hit it a third time—a tremendous whack. *Winston Churchill*

SPENDING

1805   It's a terribly hard job to spend a billion dollars and get your money's worth. *George Humphrey*

1806   I don't think you can spend yourself rich. *Ibid.*

STAMP

1807   We cannot put the face of a person on a stamp unless said person is deceased. My suggestion, therefore, is that you drop dead. *James Edward Day*

1808   In North Wales we measure a man from the chin up. You evidently measure from the chin down. *David Lloyd George*

1809   It is only a step from the sublime to the ridiculous. *Napoleon Bonaparte*

1810   I wish to preach, not the doctrine of ignoble ease, but the doctrine of the strenuous life. *Theodore Roosevelt*

1811   No English minister has ever been so popular; and the mediocrity of his talents has been one of the principal causes of his success. *John Quincy Adams*

1812   Caesar's wife must be above suspicion. *Julius Caesar*

1813   Taxation without representation is tyranny. *James Otis*

1814   In 1790, the nation which had fought a revolution against taxation without representation discovered that some of its citizens weren't much happier about taxation with representation. *Lyndon B. Johnson*

1815   There is one difference between a tax collector and a taxidermist— the taxidermist leaves the hide. *Mortimer Caplan*

1816   If you were buying a second-hand car, would you buy it from Harold Wilson? *Anthony Barber*

1817   Nothing should impede the truth save a substantial sum of money. *Hilaire Belloc*

1818   Truth is the proper and sufficient antagonist to error and has nothing to fear from the conflict, unless by human interposition, disarmed of her natural weapons, free argument and debate. *Thomas Jefferson*

1819   Truth is generally the best vindication against slander. *Ibid.*

1820   I have sworn upon the altar of God eternal hostility against every form of tyranny over the mind of man. *Thomas Jefferson*

1821   Poincaré knows everything and understands nothing—Briand understands everything and knows nothing. *David Lloyd George*

UNITED NATIONS

1822 I have now come to believe that the United Nations will best serve the cause of peace if its Assembly is representative of what the world actually is and not merely representative of the parts which we like. *John Foster Dulles*

1823 This organization is created to prevent you from going to hell. It isn't created to take you to heaven. *Henry Cabot Lodge, Jr.*

1824 The first principle of a free society is an untrammeled flow of words in an open forum. *Adlai Stevenson*

VICE-PRESIDENT

1825 People come by here to see me. . . . They expect to see some big, imposing man. And it's me, I'm just a little old Democrat. *John Nance Garner*

VICTOR

1826 It is now some 3 months, 9 days, 19 hours, and 47 minutes since we conceded the election to General Eisenhower. In that interval, General Eisenhower has had the honors of victory and also the misery, while I have had the miseries of defeat and also a vacation. But, as the newspapers say, to the victor belongs the toil. *Adlai Stevenson*

VOTES

1827 There is no city in the United States in which I get a warmer welcome and less votes than Columbus, Ohio. *John F. Kennedy*

WASHINGTON, D.C.

1828 People only leave by way of the box—ballot or coffin. *Claiborne Pell*

WEALTH

1829 The way to wealth, if you desire it, is as plain as the way to market. It depends chiefly on two words, *industry* and *frugality;* that is, waste neither *time* nor *money,* but make best use of both. Without industry and frugality, nothing will do, and with them everything. *Benjamin Franklin*

1830 Stand not too near the rich man lest he destroy thee—and not too far away lest he forget thee. *Aneurin Bevan*

WEST POINT GRADUATION

1831 I want to say that I wish all of you the greatest success. While I say that, I'm not unmindful of the fact that two graduates of the Academy [Grant and Eisenhower] have reached the White House and neither was a member of my party. Until I'm more certain that this trend will be broken, I wish that all of you may be generals and not commanders-in-chief. *John F. Kennedy*

WHITE HOUSE

1832   You have to stand every day three or four hours of visitors. Nine-tenths of them want something they ought not to have. If you keep dead still they will run down in three or four minutes. If you even cough or smile they will start up all over again. *Calvin Coolidge*

WOMAN

1833   The appointment of a woman to office is an innovation for which the public is not prepared, nor am I. *Thomas Jefferson*

1834   A woman is the only thing I am afraid of that I know will not hurt me. *Abraham Lincoln*

WOMEN

1835   A man of sense only trifles with them, plays with them, humors and flatters them, as he does with a sprightly and forward child; but he neither consults them about, nor trusts them with, serious matters. *Lord Chesterfield*

WORK

1836   Wanting to work is so rare a want that it should be encouraged. *Abraham Lincoln*

WORLD

1837   The world is a comedy to those who think, a tragedy to those who feel. *Horace Walpole*

...9...

Pertinent Proverbs

ABSENCE

1838 He that is absent is soon forgotten.

ACTION

1839 Action is the proper fruit of knowledge.

ADVERSITY

1840 Adversity makes a man wise, not rich.

1841 Adversity has no friends. *Cornelius Tacitus*

ADVICE

1842 Fools need advice most, but wise men only are the better for it. *Benjamin Franklin*

1843 When error is committed, good advice comes too late. *Chinese*

1844 Less advice and more hands. *German*

AGE

1845 It is hard to put old heads on young shoulders. Many foxes grow gray, but few grow old. *Benjamin Franklin*

1846 The old forget, the young don't know. *German*

1847 Old age and the wear of time teach many things. *Sophocles*

1848 The old age of an eagle is better than the youth of a sparrow. *Greek*

ALONE

1849 Better be alone than in bad company.

1850 A wise man is never less alone than when alone. *Latin*

AMBITION

1851 Ambition obeys no law but its own appetite. By that sin fell the angels. *William Shakespeare*

1852 Ambition destroys its possessor. *Hebrew*

AMUSEMENT

1853   A dragon stranded in shallow water furnishes amusement for the shrimps. *Chinese*

ANGER

1854   A man in a passion rides a mad horse.

1855   Anger is never without a reason, but seldom with a good one. *Benjamin Franklin*

1856   The greatest remedy for anger is delay. *Lucius Annaeus Seneca*

ANTIQUITY

1857   We praise the past, but use our present years. *Ovid*

APE

1858   The higher the ape goes, the more he shows his tail. *George Herbert*

APPEARANCE

1859   All things are less dreadful than they seem.

APPETITE

1860   One always has a good appetite at another's feast. *Yiddish*

APPLAUSE

1861   Applause is the spur of noble minds, the end and aim of weak ones.

ARGUMENT

1862   A noisy man is always in the right.

1863   You have not converted a man because you have silenced him.

1864   The arguments of the strongest have always the most weight. *French*

ATHEISM

1865   Some are atheists only in fair weather.

AVARICE

1866   He who covets is always poor. *Latin*

BABY

1867   Every baby born into the world is a finer one than the last.

BEARD

1868   If the beard were all, a goat might preach. *Danish*

BELIEF

1869   Men easily believe what they wish to believe. *Latin*

1870   Each man's belief is right in his own eyes.

BOOKS

1871   Books are . . . for wisdom, piety, delight, or use. *John Denham*

1872 Creditors have better memories than debtors.

1873 Borrowing is the mother of trouble. *Hebrew*

BREVITY

1874 Let thy speech be short, comprehending much in few words. *Apocrypha*

BROTHER

1875 Even brothers keep careful accounts. *Chinese*

CAESAR

1876 What millions died—that Caesar might be great! *Thomas Campbell*

1877 Hail Caesar—we who are about to die salute thee! *Latin*

CANDOR

1878 He that speaketh what he will shall hear what he would not.

CARELESS

1879 Throw not the child out with the bath. *Danish*

CAUSE

1880 They never fail who die in a great cause. *Lord Byron*

1881 A bad cause should be silent. *Latin*

CEMETERY

1882 A piece of a churchyard fits everybody.

CHANCE

1883 He who leaves nothing to chance will do few things ill, but he will do very few things. *Lord Halifax*

1884 He that waits for chance is never sure of his dinner. *French*

CHANGE

1885 There is nothing permanent except change. *Greek*

1886 Times change and we change with them. *Latin*

CHARACTER

1887 There is a great deal of unmapped country within us.

1888 A man shows his character by what he laughs at. *German*

1889 It matters not what you are thought to be, but what you are. *Latin*

CHARITY

1890 He that gives to be seen will relieve none in the dark.

1891 Do good and ask not for whom. *Yiddish*

CHEAT

1892 Who cheateth in small things is a fool; in great ones, a rogue.

·CHILDREN

1893 Children are certain cares but uncertain comforts.

1894 Happy is he that is happy in his children.

1895 Just as the twig is bent the tree's inclined. *Alexander Pope*

1896 Little children, little sorrows; big children, big sorrows.

1897 Better the child should cry than the father. *German*

1898 Our neighbor's children are always the worst. *German*

1899 When a child stumbles a good angel puts his hands under. *Yiddish*

CHOICE

1900 If I be hanged, I'll choose my gallows.

1901 There is small choice in rotten apples. *Spanish*

CHURCH

1902 No sooner is a temple built to God, but the Devil builds a chapel hard by.

1903 A church is God between four walls. *French*

CITY

1904 A great city, a great solitude. *Greek*

1905 Unless the Lord keepeth the city, the watchman waketh in vain. *Latin*

CLIMB

1906 He that never climbed never fell.

1907 He that climbs high falls heavily. *German*

COMFORT

1908 When I break my leg it is no comfort to me that another has broken his neck. *Danish*

COMMERCE

1909 Commerce is the great civilizer.

1910 The merchant has no country. *Thomas Jefferson*

COMPANY

1911 He that lies down with dogs will rise up with fleas. *Latin*

1912 He who goes with wolves will learn to howl. *Spanish*

1913 Tell me what company you keep, and I'll tell you who you are. *Spanish*

COMPETITION

1914 In the grave, dust and bones jostle not for the wall.

1915 The only competition worthy a wise man is with himself.

COMPULSION

1916 He that complies against his will,
Is of his own opinion still. *Samuel Butler*

CONCEIT

1917 He is so full of himself that he is quite empty.

CONFESSION

1918 Open confession is good for the soul.
1919 Confession of our faults is the next thing to innocence. *Latin*

CONQUEST

1920 See the conquering hero comes!
1921 We triumph without glory when we conquer without danger. *French*

CONSCIENCE

1922 A clear conscience can bear any trouble.
1923 A guilty conscience never thinks itself safe.
1924 Conscience does make cowards of us all. *William Shakespeare*
1925 Conscience is the voice of God in the soul.

CONSISTENCY

1926 Inconsistency is the only thing in which men are consistent.

COUNTRY

1927 God made the country, and man made the town. *Latin*

COURAGE

1928 The test of courage is to bear defeat without losing heart.
1929 You can't answer for your courage if you have never been in danger. *French*
1930 All are brave when the enemy flies. *Italian*
1931 True courage grapples with misfortune. *Latin*

COW

1932 The cow knows not what her tail is worth till she has lost it.
1933 The cow from afar gives plenty of milk. *French*

COWARDS

1934 Many would be cowards if they had courage enough.

CRITICS

1935 Critics are like brushers of noblemen's clothes.
1936 It is easier to be critical than to be correct.

CROSS

1937 Everyone thinks his own cross is heaviest. *Italian*

1938 A desperate disease must have a desperate cure.

1939 He that fears danger in time seldom feels it.

1940 Fear the goat from the front, the horse from the rear, and man from all sides. *Russian*

1941 No day passeth without some grief.

1942 One of these days is none of these days.

1943 Though the fool waits, the day does not. *French*

1944 A day differs not a whit from eternity. *Lucius Annaeus Seneca*

1945 Every day should be passed as if it were to be our last. *Latin*

1946 Death does not blow a trumpet. *Danish*

1947 As soon as a man is born he begins to die.

1948 Death takes no bribes.

1949 He that once is born, once must die.

1950 He that would die well must always look for death.

1951 Men may live fools, but fools they cannot die.

1952 To live in hearts we leave behind is not to die.

1953 There's no dying by proxy. *French*

1954 Six feet of earth make all men equal. *Italian*

1955 Death—the gate of life. *Latin*

1956 It is uncertain where death may await thee, therefore expect it every-where. *Latin*

1957 Pale Death, with impartial step, knocks at the poor man's cottage and at the palaces of kings. *Horace*

1958 A light debt makes a debtor; a heavy one, an enemy. *Italian*

1959 If a man deceives me once, shame on him; if he deceives me twice, shame on me.

1960 The easiest person to deceive is one's self.

1961 He that handles a nettle tenderly is soonest stung.

1962 He who considers too much will perform little. *German*

DEED

1963 A noble deed is a step toward God.

1964 We live in deeds, not years.

1965 The gods see the deeds of the righteous. *Latin*

DEFECT

1966 Knot in de plank will show through de whitewash. *American Negro*

DELAY

1967 When a man's life is at stake, no delay is too long. *Latin*

DESTINY

1968 One meets his destiny often in the road he takes to avoid it. *French*

DIFFERENCE

1969 It makes a difference whose ox is gored.

DILEMMA

1970 Between Scylla and Charybdis . . . *Greek*

DIPLOMACY

1971 A diplomat is a man who remembers a woman's birthday and forgets her age.

1972 Fling dirt enough, and some will stick. *Latin*

DIVIDE

1973 Who divides honey with the bear gets the lesser share. *Italian*

DO

1974 When a thing is done, make the best of it. *German*

DOCTOR

1975 The doctor can cure the sick, but he cannot cure the dead. *Chinese*

1976 Every doctor thinks his pills the best. *German*

DOG

1977 The dog's kennel is not the place to keep a sausage. *Danish*

1978 Barking dogs never bite.

DOUBT

1979 Doubt makes the mountain which faith can move.

DOWN

1980 He that is down can fall no lower.

DREAM

1981 All men of action are dreamers.

EAGLE

1982 Eagles fly alone.

1983   The morning hour has gold in its mouth. *German*

1984   A person may be educated beyond his intelligence.
1985   Education is an ornament in prosperity and a refuge in adversity.
       Greek
1986   Only the educated are free. *Greek*
1987   There is no royal road to geometry. *Euclid*

1988   We talk little if we do not talk of ourselves.
1989   When a man tries himself, the verdict is in his favor.

1990   Eloquence is the child of knowledge.
1991   Everyone is eloquent in his own cause. *Latin*
1992   It is the heart which makes men eloquent. *Latin*

1993   The longest day has an end.

1994   A man has many enemies when his back is to the wall.

1995   Envy is the sincerest form of flattery.

1996   In the presence of eternity, the mountains are as transient as the
       clouds.

1997   Evil often triumphs but never conquers.
1998   Who does not punish evil invites it. *German*

1999   Example is the school of mankind, and they will learn at no other.
       Edmund Burke

2000   It is costly wisdom that is bought by experience.
2001   Experience is the teacher of fools. *Latin*

2002   Facts do not cease to exist because they are ignored.

FAILURE

2003 Give me the heart to fight and lose.
2004 They went forth to battle but they always fell. *Ossian*

FAITH

2005 What is faith unless it is to believe what you do not see. *St. Augustine*

FAME

2006 Let us now praise famous men. *Apocrypha*
2007 Fame is but an inscription upon a grave.
2008 Fame . . . the last infirmity of noble minds. *John Milton*

FATHER

2009 One father is more than a hundred schoolmasters.

FAULT

2010 Only great men may have great faults. *French*

FEAR

2011 Fear makes lions tame. *German*
2012 Fear is the beginning of wisdom. *Spanish*

FLATTERY

2013 The devil is civil when he is flattered. *German*

FOOL

2014 A fool may ask more questions in an hour than a wise man can answer in seven years.
2015 A fool might be counted wise if he kept his mouth shut.
2016 A fool always finds a bigger fool to admire him. *French*
2017 Unless a fool knows Latin, he is never a great fool. *Spanish*

FREEDOM

2018 Who has lost his freedom has nothing else to lose. *German*

FRIEND

2019 A faithful friend is an image of God. *French*

GLORY

2020 The paths of glory lead but to the grave. *Thomas Gray*

GOD

2021 God does not pay weekly, but he pays at the end. *Dutch*
2022 In the faces of men and women I see God. *Walt Whitman*
2023 God sends nothing but what can be borne. *Italian*
2024 If God be with us, who shall stand against us? *Latin*

GOVERNMENT

2025   A government of laws and not of men. *John Adams*

2026   Every country has the government it deserves. *French*

2027   Republics end through luxury; monarchies through poverty. *Montesquieu*

2028   With how little wisdom is the world governed! *Pope Julius III*

GRADUAL

2029   Feather by feather the goose is plucked.

2030   Little by little the cat eateth up the bacon flickle.

2031   Step by step the ladder is ascended.

GREAT MEN

2032   Towers are measured by their shadows and great men by their calumniators. *Chinese*

2033   Great hopes make great men.

2034   Great men have great faults.

2035   Great men will always pay deference to greater. *Walter Savage Landor*

HONESTY

2036   An honest man's the noblest work of God. *Alexander Pope*

2037   They are all honest men, but my cloak is not to be found. *Spanish*

HONOR

2038   All honor's wounds are self-inflicted. *Andrew Carnegie*

HOSPITALITY

2039   The first day a man is a guest, the second a burden, the third a pest. *French*

HUMILITY

2040   There is no true holiness without humility.

2041   Humble thyself in all things. *Thomas a Kempis*

IGNORANCE

2042   He who knows nothing is confident of everything.

2043   Ignorance is a voluntary misfortune.

IMMORTALITY

2044   All men desire to be immortal.

2045   He hath not lived that lives not after death.

2046   The universe is a stairway leading nowhere unless man is immortal.

2047   The dog that trots about finds a bone.

2048   Justice is truth in action. *Joseph Joubert*

2049   Knowledge in youth is wisdom in age.

2050   Those who really thirst for knowledge always get it.

2051   He who knows nothing never doubts. *Italian*

2052   The gods will sell us all good things at the price of labor. *Greek*

2053   Toil is the sire of fame. *Greek*

2054   God help the sheep when the wolf is judge. *Danish*

2055   Law cannot persuade where it cannot punish.

2056   Laws were made that the stronger might not in all things have his way. *Latin*

2057   Where is there any book of the law so clear to each man as that written in his heart? *Leo Tolstoy*

2058   Eternal vigilance is the price of liberty. *Wendell Phillips*

2059   God grants liberty only to those who love it.

2060   A great library is the diary of the human race.

2061   The web of our life is of mingled yarn, good and ill together. *William Shakespeare*

2062   This life is but a thoroughfare full of woe,
And we but pilgrims passing to and fro. *Geoffrey Chaucer*

2063   Better lose the anchor than the whole ship. *Dutch*

2064   If you've nothing to lose, you can try everything. *Yiddish*

2065   Man is Heaven's masterpiece.

2066   No man is born wise or learned.

2067   Though every prospect pleases,
And only man is vile. *Reginald Heber*

2068   Man is but a reed, the weakest in nature, but he is a thinking reed. *Blaise Pascal*

2069   I am seeking a man. *Diogenes*
2070   We are dust and shadow. *Horace*

MARRIAGE

2071   To marry once is a duty, twice a folly, thrice is madness. *Dutch*
2072   He that marries for money earns it.
2073   Marriage halves our griefs, doubles our joys, and quadruples our expenses.
2074   Marriages are made in heaven and consummated on earth. *French*
2075   I never married and I wish my father never had. *Greek*

MERCY

2076   God strikes with his finger, and not with his arm.

MIGHT

2077   Where might is master, justice is servant. *German*

MISFORTUNE

2078   We all have sufficient strength to bear other people's misfortunes. *François de La Rochefoucauld*
2079   Misfortune is friendless. *Greek*

MISTAKE

2080   He who makes no mistakes makes nothing.

MODERATION

2081   The golden rule in life is moderation in all things. *Latin*

MONEY

2082   Bad money drives out good money. (Gresham's Law)
2083   Money is honey, my little sonny,
        And a rich man's joke is always funny.
2084   Public money is like holy water: everyone helps himself to it. *Italian*
2085   When money speaks, truth keeps silent. *Russian*

MONUMENT

2086   Those only deserve a monument who do not need one.
2087   The monuments of noble men are their virtues. *Greek*

MOTHER

2088   Mother is the name for God in the lips and hearts of little children. *William Makepeace Thackeray*
2089   Simply having children does not make mothers.
2090   Who takes the child by the hand takes the mother by the heart. *German*

2091   God could not be everywhere and therefore he made mothers. *Hebrew*

MOUNTAIN

2092   If the mountain will not go to Mohamet, Mohamet must go to the mountain.

MUSIC

2093   Music is the speech of angels. *Thomas Carlyle*

2094   Music—the only universal tongue.

NAME

2095   What's in a name? that which we call a rose
By any other name would smell as sweet. *William Shakespeare*

NATURE

2096   Nature is a volume of which God is the author.

2097   Nature's rules have no exceptions.

2098   Nature is the art of God. *Latin*

OBEDIENCE

2099   Obedience alone gives the right to command. *Ralph Waldo Emerson*

2100   Learn to obey before you command. *Greek*

2101   No one can rule except one who can be ruled. *Latin*

ONCE

2102   Once upon a time is no time. *German*

OPINION

2103   Those who never retract their opinions love themselves more than they love truth. *French*

2104   A man's own opinion is never wrong. *Italian*

2105   There is a tide in the affairs of men
Which taken at the flood leads on to fortune. *William Shakespeare*

ORATORY

2106   A man becomes an orator; he is born eloquent. *French*

2107   An orator's virtue is to speak the truth. *Greek*

PAIN

2108   Faint is the bliss that never passed through pain.

2109   No matter which finger you bite, it will hurt. *Russian*

PARENT

2110   No fathers or mothers think their children ugly. *Spanish*

2111   Parents can give everything but common sense. *Yiddish*

PAST

2112   The mill cannot grind with the water that is past.

PATIENCE

2113   He preacheth patience that never knew pain.
2114   He that can have patience can have what he will.

PEOPLE

2115   The mob has many heads but no brains.
2116   No man who depends upon the caprice of the ignorant rabble can be accounted great. *Marcus Tullius Cicero*
2117   Nothing is so uncertain as the judgments of the mob. *Latin*
2118   The voice of the people is the voice of God.

PHILANTHROPY

2119   He who bestows his goods upon the poor,
       Shall have as much again, and ten times more. *Bunyan*
2120   In nothing do men more nearly approach the gods than in doing good to their fellow men. *Marcus Tullius Cicero*

PLEASURE

2121   Pleasures are transient, honors are immortal. *Greek*

POLITICS

2122   Public office is a public trust.
2123   There is no gambling like politics. *Benjamin Disraeli*

POVERTY

2124   Poverty: the mother of temperance. *Greek*
2125   No man should praise poverty but he who is poor. *St. Bernard*
2126   Poverty is no disgrace—but it is no great honor either. *Yiddish*

POWER

2127   Lust of power is the strongest of all passions. *Latin*

PRAISE

2128   Praise the child, and you make love to the mother.
2129   Praise yourself daringly, something always sticks. *Latin*
2130   It is not befitting to praise yourself—but it does no harm. *Yiddish*

PRAYER

2131   And Satan trembles when he sees
       The weakest saint upon his knees. *William Cowper*
2132   God warms his hands at man's heart when he prays. *John Masefield*
2133   More things are wrought by prayer
       Than this world dreams of. *Lord Tennyson*

2134 Prejudice is the child of ignorance.

2135 Prosperity is a great teacher; adversity, a greater.

2136 Prosperity makes friends, adversity tries them. *Latin*

2137 The prosperous man is never sure that he is loved for himself. *Latin*

2138 Call the bear "Uncle" till you are safe across the bridge. *Turkish*

2139 Hard questions must have hard answers. *Greek*

2140 I quote others only the better to express myself. *Michel de Montaigne*

2141 Every reform movement has a lunatic fringe. *Theodore Roosevelt*

2142 The more things a man is ashamed of, the more respectable he is. *George Bernard Shaw*

2143 The noblest vengeance is to forgive.

2144 To forget a wrong is the best revenge.

2145 Every revolution was first a thought in one man's mind. *Ralph Waldo Emerson*

2146 If Heaven had looked upon riches to be a valuable thing, he would not have given them to such a scoundrel. *Jonathan Swift*

2147 A man in the right with God on his side is in the majority. *Henry Ward Beecher*

2148 The way of this world is to praise dead saints and persecute living ones.

2149 For age and want save while you may:
No morning sun lasts a whole day.

2150 There is nothing that can't be made worse by telling. *Latin*

2151   The sea hath no king but God alone.
2152   When the sea is calm the careless sailor takes his ease. *Latin*

2153   It is a blind goose that comes to the fox's sermon.

2154   They serve God well who serve his creatures.

2155   The sheep has no choice when in the jaws of the wolf. *Chinese*
2156   The sheep does not bite the wolf. *German*

2157   The chamber of sickness is the chapel of devotion.
2158   In time of sickness the soul collects itself anew. *Latin*
2159   Sickness shows us what we are. *Latin*

2160   Even silence may be eloquent.
2161   Silence is a final jewel for a woman, but it's little worn.
2162   When you have nothing to say, say nothing.
2163   Wise men say nothing in dangerous times.
2164   It is sad when men have neither wit to speak, nor judgment to hold
        their tongues. *French*
2165   Silence is also speech. *Yiddish*

2166   Every man carries the bundle of his sins upon his own back.
2167   I am a man more sinned against than sinning. *William Shakespeare*
2168   The cat shuts its eyes while it steals cream.
2169   Sin writes histories; goodness is silent. *Johann Wolfgang von Goethe*

2170   I hate the man who builds his name
        On ruins of another's fame. *John Gay*
2171   Slander leaves a scar behind it. *Latin*

2172   A man is not always asleep when his eyes are shut.
2173   Sleep is a short death; death, a longer sleep.
2174   Sleep that knits up the ravelled sleave of care. *William Shakespeare*
2175   While we are asleep, we are all equal. *Spanish*

2176   Solitude is often the best society.

2177   Man is a social animal. *Latin*

SOLITUDE

2178   Solitude is the best nurse of wisdom.

2179   The strongest man in the world is he who stands alone. *Henrik Ibsen*

SORROW

2180   Earth has no sorrow that Heaven cannot heal.

2181   The longest sorrow finds at last relief.

2182   When sorrows come, they come not single spies,
       But in battalions. *William Shakespeare*

2183   Small sorrows speak; great ones are silent. *Latin*

SPEECH

2184   Blessed is the man who, having nothing to say, abstains from giving
       us wordy evidence of the fact. *George Eliot*

2185   Discretion of speech is more than eloquence.

2186   He that speaks much is much mistaken.

2187   Speaking without thinking is shooting without aiming.

2188   To speak much is one thing, to speak well, another. *Greek*

STAR

2189   He that looks for a star puts out his candle.

2190   Those blessed candles of the night . . . *William Shakespeare*

2191   Too low they build, who build beneath the stars. *Edward Young*

STEALING

2192   Who steals a calf steals a cow. *German*

STOMACH

2193   The stomach is a bad counselor. *German*

2194   The stomach rules the head. *German*

STRENGTH

2195   He who has great strength should use it lightly. *Latin*

STUPIDITY

2196   He is not only dull himself, but the cause of dullness in others.

2197   Against stupidity the gods themselves contend in vain. *Friedrich von
       Schiller*

SUCCESS

2198   Nothing is so impudent as success.

2199   Everything is subservient to success. *French*

2200 He that knows not how to hold his tongue knows not how to talk.
2201 So much they talked, so very little said.

2202 In tears was I born, and after tears I die. *Greek*
2203 The tribute of a tear is all I crave. *Homer*

2204 The profound thinker always suspects that he may be superficial. *Benjamin Disraeli*
2205 Men suffer from thinking more than from anything else. *Leo Tolstoy*

2206 God stands winding His lonely horn,
      And time and the world are ever in flight. *William Butler Yeats*
2207 Naught treads so silent as the foot of time.
2208 Time is a river of passing events—a rushing torrent. *Greek*
2209 Nothing is ours except time. *Lucius Annaeus Seneca*
2210 In time even a bear can be taught to dance. *Yiddish*

2211 Tomorrow every fault is to be amended, but that tomorrow never comes.

2212 A traveler may lie with authority.
2213 Traveling makes a man wiser, but less happy.
2214 See one mountain, one sea, one river—and see all. *Greek*
2215 He who never leaves his country is full of prejudices. *Italian*

2216 Individuals may perish; but truth is eternal. *French*
2217 To fool the world, tell the truth. *Otto von Bismarck*
2218 Time discovers truth. *Latin*

2219 Tyranny is a lovely eminence, but there is no way down from it. *Solon*

2220 What we do not understand we do not possess. *Johann Wolfgang von Goethe*

2221 A university is a place where pebbles are polished and diamonds are dimmed. *Robert G. Ingersoll*

UNLUCKY

2222 He falls on his back and breaks his nose. *French*

VICE

2223 Never open the door to a little vice lest a great one enter with it.

VICTORY

2224 Victory and defeat are each of the same price.

2225 He conquers twice who upon victory conquers himself. *Latin*

VIRTUE

2226 He who dies for virtue does not perish. *Latin*

2227 Virtue unites man with God. *Latin*

WANT

2228 Man wants but little here below, nor wants that little long.

2229 To have no wants is divine. *Socrates*

2230 If you can't get what you want, you must want what you get. *Yiddish*

WAR

2231 War never leaves where it found a nation. *Edmund Burke*

2232 In war it is not permitted to make a mistake twice. *Greek*

2233 War loves to seek its victims in the young. *Greek*

WEALTH

2234 Who has, is. *Italian*

WIFE

2235 An expensive wife makes a pensive husband.

2236 An obedient wife commands her husband.

2237 The wife that loves the looking glass hates the saucepan.

WISDOM

2238 That man is wisest who realizes that his wisdom is worthless. *Socrates*

2239 Wisdom comes by suffering. *Greek*

2240 There is often wisdom under a shabby cloak. *Latin*

WISE

2241 No man is the only wise man. *Latin*

2242 What's the good of being wise when foolishness serves? *Yiddish*

WIT

2243 Wit does not take the place of knowledge.

2244 Wit is the salt of conversation, not the food.

WOLF

2245 No matter how much you feed a wolf, he will always return to the forest. *Russian*

2246 The wolf will hire himself off very cheaply as a shepherd. *Russian*

2247 The three virtues of a woman: Obey the father, obey the husband, obey the son. *Chinese*

2248 A woman can be anything the man who loves her would have her be. *James M. Barrie*

2249 Women have many faults but the worst of them all is that they are too pleased with themselves and take too little pains to please the men. *Plautus*

2250 A woman who looks much in the glass spins but little. *French*

2251 A handsome woman is always right. *German*

2252 Silence gives grace to a woman. *Sophocles*

2253 It is a sad house where the hen crows louder than the rooster. *Italian*

2254 Blessed is he who has found his work; let him ask no other blessedness. *Thomas Carlyle*

2255 The gods sell us all good things for hard work. *Greek*

2256 Great is work which lends dignity to man. *Hebrew*

2257 He who would rest must work. *Italian*

2258 When I die, may I be taken in the midst of work. *Ovid*

2259 I am a citizen of the world. *Diogenes*

2260 The whole world is the temple of the immortal gods. *Lucius Annaeus Seneca*

2261 Old wounds easily bleed. *German*

2262 Look in thy heart and write. *Philip Sidney*

2263 What comes from the heart goes to the heart.

2264 Writing is the language of the hand. *Hebrew*

2265 The years of a man's life pass like a dream. *Yiddish*

2266 Ask the young; they know everything. *French*

2267 And all our yesterdays have lighted fools
The way to dusty death. *William Shakespeare*

2268   Youth is the season of hope.

2269   The majority of men employ the first portion of their life in making the other portion miserable. *Jean de La Bruyère*

2270   Youth is a continual intoxication, it is the fever of reason. *François de La Rochefoucauld*

2271   Youth holds no society with grief. *Aristotle*

2272   Zeal without knowledge is the sister of folly.

2273   Blind zeal can only do harm. *German*

... 10 ...

Great Thoughts of Distinguished Americans

THE VALIDITY OF OUR SOCIETY

2274 What I am concerned about is not that your son should feel that I, or the Administration, or the Government is right on any particular issue. It is good that he should question whether the steps we are taking are right or are wrong. But what is important is that he feel, and that all our young people feel, a strong faith in the validity and the reality of the ideals on which this country was founded and on which it now endeavors to guide its actions. So long as our young people are steadfast in their faith, we can be assured of the vitality of our society, and its ability to go on meeting the challenges of the future. *Dean Acheson*

TEACHER

2275 A teacher affects eternity; he can never tell where his influence stops. *Henry Adams*

THE GREATEST QUESTION

2276 Yesterday the greatest question was decided which ever was debated in America; and a greater perhaps never was, nor will be, decided among men. A resolution was passed without one dissenting colony, that those United Colonies have, and of right ought to have, full power to make war, conclude peace, establish commerce, and to do all other acts and things which other States may rightfully do. You will see in a few days a Declaration setting forth the causes which have impelled us to this mighty revolution, and the reasons which will justify it in the sight of God and man. A plan of confederation will be taken up in a few days. You will think me transported with enthusiasm, but I am not. I am well aware of the toil, and blood, and treasure, that it will cost us to maintain this declaration, and support and defend these States. Yet, through all the gloom, I can see the rays of ravishing light and glory. I can say that the end is more than worth all the means, and that posterity will triumph in that day's transaction, even though we should rue it, which I trust in God we shall not. . . .

The second day of July, 1776, will be the most memorable epoch in the history of America. I am apt to believe that it will be celebrated by succeeding generations as the great anniversary festival. It ought to be commemorated as the day of deliverance, by solemn acts of devotion to God Almighty. It ought to be solemnized with pomp and parade, with shows, games, sports, guns, bells, bonfires, and illuminations from one end of this continent to the other, from this time forward forever more. *John Adams*

NEED TO BE ADMONISHED

2277 I feel myself to be a frequent sinner before God, and I need to be often admonished of it, and exhorted to virtue. This is administered in all the forms of Christian worship, and I am sure of receiving it with whatever denomination of Christian worshipers I associate to obtain it. *John Quincy Adams*

MANNERS AND CHARACTER

2278 Manners carry for the moment, character for all time. *A. Bronson Alcott*

LIBERTY

2279 Ever since I arrived at the state of manhood and acquainted myself with the general history of mankind, I have felt a sincere passion for liberty. The history of nations, doomed to perpetual slavery, in consequence of yielding up to tyrants their natural-born liberties, I read with a sort of philosophical horror; so that the first systematical and bloody attempt, at Lexington, to enslave America, thoroughly electrified my mind and fully determined me to take part with my country. *Ethan Allen*

ELDER STATESMAN

2280 An elder statesman is somebody old enough to know his own mind and keep quiet about it. *Bernard M. Baruch*

GREATNESS

2281 Greatness, after all, in spite of its name, . . . may be present in lives whose range is very small. *Phillips Brooks*

TRUTH

2282 Truth, crushed to earth, shall rise again;
The eternal years of God are hers;
But Error, wounded, writhes in pain,
And dies among his worshipers. *William Cullen Bryant*

WEALTH

2283   The only noble use of surplus wealth is this: That it be regarded as a sacred trust, to be administered by its possessor, into whose hands it flows, for the highest good of the people. *Andrew Carnegie*

NATURE

2284   I love to think of nature as an unlimited broadcasting station, through which God speaks to us every hour, if we will only tune in. *George Washington Carver*

GOVERNMENT

2285   The office of government is not to confer happiness, but to give men opportunity to work out happiness for themselves. *William Ellery Channing*

MY COUNTRY

2286   And in respect to my country. The honorable senator speaks of Virginia as being my country. This Union is my country; the thirty States are my country; Kentucky is my country, and Virginia no more than any other of the States of the Union. She has created on my part obligation and feelings and duties toward her in my private character which nothing upon earth would induce me to forfeit or vitiate. But even if it were my own State should raise the standard of dissension against the residue of the Union, I would go against her. *Henry Clay*

BEHAVIOR

2287   Behavior which appears superficially correct but is intrinsically corrupt always irritates those who see below the surface. *James Bryant Conant*

ONE GOOD OLD MAN

2288   I think that to have known one good old man—one man who, through the chances and rubs of a long life, has carried his heart in his hand, like a palm branch, waving all discords into peace, helps our faith in God, in ourselves, and in each other, more than many sermons. *George W. Curtis*

EVIL

2289   It is one thing to recognize evil as a fact. It is another thing to take evil to one's breast and call it good. *John Foster Dulles*

DEFENSE

2290   We will play our part in collective defense of the area but we are not going to play gladiator for the world. *Ibid.*

LIFE

2291   Life, itself, without the assistance of colleges and universities, is becoming an advanced institution of learning. *Thomas Alva Edison*

THOUGHT

2292　I think and think for months and years. Ninety-nine times, the conclusion is false. The hundredth time I am right. *Albert Einstein*

THE SOURCE OF FREEDOM

2293　No government can inoculate its people against the fatal materialism that plagues our age. Happily, our people, though blessed with more material goods than any people in history, have always reserved their first allegiance to the kingdom of spirit, which is the true source of that freedom we value above all material things. *Dwight D. Eisenhower*

FAITH IN AMERICA

2294　The world is suffering from a multiplicity of fears. . . . There is a little element of truth in each, a little element of danger in each, and that means that finally there is left a little residue that you can meet only by faith, a faith in the destiny of America. *Ibid.*

THE SMALL TOWN

2295　For any American who had the great and priceless privilege of being raised in a small town there always remains with him nostalgic memories of those days. And the older he grows the more he senses what he owed to the simple honesty and neighborliness, the integrity that he saw all around him in those days. *Ibid.*

WHAT WE HAVE IN COMMON

2296　It is probably a pity that every citizen of each state cannot visit all the others, to see the differences, to learn what we have in common, and to come back with a richer, fuller understanding of America—in all its beauty, in all its dignity, in all its strength, in support of moral principle. *Ibid.*

LOVE

2297　Love, and you shall be loved. All love is mathematically just, as much as the two sides of an algebraic equation. *Ralph Waldo Emerson*

GREATNESS

2298　What I must do is all that concerns me, not what the people think. This rule, equally arduous in actual and in intellectual life, may serve for the whole distinction between greatness and meanness. It is the harder because you will always find those who think they know what is your duty better than you know it. It is easy in the world to live after the world's opinion; it is easy in solitude to live after our own; but the great man is he who in the midst of the crowd keeps with perfect sweetness the independence of solitude. *Ibid.*

GIFTS

2299　We wish to be self-sustained. We do not quite forgive a giver. The hand that feeds us is in some danger of being bitten. *Ibid.*

IMPOSSIBLE TO BE CHEATED

2300 Men suffer all their life long under the foolish superstition that they can be cheated. But it is impossible for a man to be cheated by anyone but himself. There is a third silent party to all our bargains. The nature and soul of things takes on itself the guaranty of the fulfillment of every contract, so that honest service cannot come to loss. If you serve an ungrateful master, serve him the more. Put God in your debt. Every stroke shall be repaid. The longer the payment is withholden, the better for you, for compound interest on compound interest is the rate and usage of this exchequer. *Ibid.*

A NEW DAY

2301 Finish each day and be done with it. You have done what you could. Some blunders and absurdities no doubt crept in; forget them as soon as you can. Tomorrow is a new day; begin it well and serenely, and with too high a spirit to be cumbered with your old nonsense. *Ibid.*

MONEY

2302 The use of money is all the advantage there is in having money. *Benjamin Franklin*

POOR

2303 'Tis hard (but glorious) to be poor and honest: an empty sack can hardly stand upright; but if it does, 'tis a stout one. *Ibid.*

FALSE ESTIMATES OF VALUE

2304 If I know a miser, who gave up every kind of comfortable living, all the pleasure of doing good to others, all the esteem of his fellow citizens, and the joys of benevolent friendship, for the sake of accumulating wealth, Poor man, said I, you pay too much for your whistle. . . . In short, I conceive that great part of the miseries of mankind are brought upon them by false estimates they have made of the value of things, and by their giving too much for their whistles. *Ibid.*

TO YOUNG MEN

2305 The best business you can go into you will find on your father's farm or in his workshop. If you have no family or friends to aid you, and no prospect open to you there, turn your face to the great West, and there build up a home and fortune. *Horace Greeley*

WISDOM

2306 Wisdom is never dear, provided the article be genuine. *Ibid.*

YOUR COUNTRY

2307 Behind all these men you have to do with, behind officers, and government, and people even, there is the Country Herself, your Country, and . . . you belong to Her as you belong to your own mother.

Stand by Her, boy, as you would stand by your mother. *Edward Everett Hale*

POWER

2308   A power over a man's subsistence amounts to a power over his will. *Alexander Hamilton*

IMMORTAL

2309   Our Creator would never have made such lovely days, and have given us the deep hearts to enjoy them, above and beyond all thought, unless we were meant to be immortal. *Nathaniel Hawthorne*

ONE'S SELF

2310   What other dungeon is so dark as one's own heart!
        What jailer is so inexorable as one's self! *Ibid.*

LONELINESS

2311   Writing, at its best, is a lonely life. Organizations for writers palliate the writer's loneliness, but I doubt if they improve his writing. He grows in public stature as he sheds his loneliness and after his work deteriorates. For he does his work alone and if he is a good enough writer he must face eternity, or the lack of it, each day. *Ernest Hemingway*

CREDULITY

2312   Our credulity is greatest concerning the things we know least about. And since we know least about ourselves, we are ready to believe all that is said about us. Hence the mysterious power of both flattery and calumny. *Eric Hoffer*

FAME AND FRIENDSHIP

2313   Fame is the scentless sunflower, with gaudy crown of gold;
        But friendship is the breathing rose, with sweets in every fold. *Oliver Wendell Holmes*

RETIREMENT

2314   There is no joy to be had from retirement except by some kind of productive work. Otherwise, you degenerate into talking to everybody about your pains and pills and income tax. Any oldster who keeps at even part-time work has something worthwhile talking about. He has a zest for the morning paper and his three meals a day. The point of all this is not to retire from work or you will shrivel up into a nuisance to all mankind. *Herbert Hoover*

EFFICIENT MANAGEMENT

2315   I think what I am trying to do is do the same thing for all of America that each good American tries to do in his own home. We are trying to live within our income; we are trying to cut out waste; we are trying to have an efficient management; we are trying to improve our position as we go along. . . . *George Humphrey*

LOVE OF COUNTRY

2316   The man who loves his country on its own account and not merely for its trappings of interest or power can never be divorced from it, can never refuse to come forward when he finds that she is engaged in dangers which he has the means of warding off. *Thomas Jefferson*

DISHONEST

2317   The man who is dishonest as a statesman would be a dishonest man in any station. *Ibid.*

NEVER ALONE AGAIN

2318   It is a moment I shall never forget. I was alone and unable to communicate with anyone. I did not know the names of anything. I did not even know things had names. Then one day, after she had tried a number of approaches, my teacher held my hand under the water pump on our farm. As the cool water ran over my hand, and arm, she spelled the word water into my other hand. She spelled it over and over, and suddenly, I knew there was a name for things and that I would never be completely alone again. *Helen Keller*

ART

2319   Art is a complex riddle of life. You can't define it, the complexity of things. Every day the artist is a different man. He may be better or worse. If he tries to tell you what he is, he isn't being honest. For he doesn't know himself. I have never even been able to say if I did or didn't play well. *Fritz Kreisler*

TRUTH AND MANLINESS

2320   Private and public life are subject to the same rules; and truth and manliness are two qualities that will carry you through this world much better than policy, or tact, or expediency, or any other word that was ever devised to conceal or mystify a deviation from a straight line. *Robert E. Lee*

GOD'S HELP

2321   I propose that God should be openly and audibly invoked at the United Nations in accordance with any one of the religious faiths which are represented here. I do so in the conviction that we cannot make the United Nations into a successful instrument of God's peace without God's help—and that with His help we cannot fail. To this end I propose that we ask for that help. *Henry Cabot Lodge, Jr.*

TO LIVE

2322   I would rather be ashes than dust! I would rather that my spark should burn out in a brilliant blaze than it should be stifled by dry rot. I would rather be a superb meteor, every atom of me in magnificent glow, than a sleepy and permanent planet. The proper function of man is to live, not to exist. I shall not waste my days in trying to prolong them. I shall use my time. *Jack London*

GREAT MEN

2323 The heights by great men reached and kept
Were not attained by sudden flight,
But they, while their companions slept,
Were toiling upward in the night. *Henry Wadsworth Longfellow*

THE COMMON FATE

2324 Be still, sad heart! and cease repining;
Behind the clouds is the sun still shining;
Thy fate is the common fate of all,
Into each life some rain must fall,
Some days must be dark and dreary. *Ibid.*

AGE

2325 For age is opportunity no less
Than youth itself, though in another dress,
And as the evening twilight fades away
The sky is filled with stars, invisible by day. *Ibid.*

TRIUMPH AND DEFEAT

2326 Not in the clamor of the crowded street,
Not in the shouts and plaudits of the throng,
But in ourselves, are triumph and defeat. *Ibid.*

SIMPLICITY

2327 In character, in manners, in style, in all things, the supreme excellence is simplicity. *Ibid.*

SORROW

2328 If we could read the secret history of our enemies, we should find in each man's life sorrow and suffering enough to disarm all hostility. *Ibid.*

THE ONLY FAITH

2329 The only faith that wears well and holds its color in all weathers is that which is woven of conviction and set with the sharp mordant of experience. Enthusiasm is good material for the orator, but the statesman needs something more durable to work in—must be able to rely on the deliberate reason and consequent firmness of the people, without which that presence of mind, no less essential in times of moral than of material peril, will be wanting at the critical moment. *James Russell Lowell*

AGE AND YOUTH

2330   He must be a born leader or misleader of men, or must have been sent into the world unfurnished with that modulating and restraining balance wheel which we call a sense of humor, who, in old age, has as strong a confidence in his opinions and in the necessity of bringing the universe into conformity with them as he had in youth. *Ibid.*

BE OF GOOD CHEER

2331   Let us be of good cheer, however, remembering that the misfortunes hardest to bear are those which never come. The world has outlived much, and will outlive a great deal more, and men have contrived to be happy in it. It has shown the strength of its constitution in nothing more than in surviving the quack medicines it has tried. *Ibid.*

A FATHER

2332   By profession I am a soldier and take pride in that fact. But I am prouder—infinitely prouder—to be a father. A soldier destroys in order to build; the father only builds, never destroys. The one has the potentiality of death; the other embodies creation and life. And while the hordes of death are mighty, the battalions of life are mightier still. It is my hope that my son, when I am gone, will remember me not from the battle but in the home repeating with him our simple daily prayer, "Our Father Who Art in Heaven." *Douglas MacArthur*

THE GUNS ARE SILENT

2333   Today the guns are silent. A great tragedy has ended. A great victory has been won. The skies no longer rain death—the seas bear only commerce—men everywhere walk upright in the sunlight. The entire world is quietly at peace. The holy mission has been completed. And in reporting this to you, the people, I speak for the thousands of silent lips, forever stilled among the jungles and the beaches and in the deep waters of the Pacific which marked the way. I speak for the unnamed brave millions homeward bound to take up the challenge of that future which they did so much to salvage from the brink of disaster. *Ibid.*

OLD SOLDIERS NEVER DIE

2334   I am closing my fifty-two years of military service. When I joined the Army, even before the turn of the century, it was the fulfillment of all my boyish hopes and dreams. The world has turned over many times since I took the oath on the Plain at West Point, and the hopes and dreams have all since vanished, but I still remember the refrain of one of the most popular barracks ballads of that day, which proclaimed most proudly that old soldiers never die; they just fade away. And like the old soldier of that ballad, I now close my military career and just fade away, an old soldier who tried to do his duty as God gave him the light to see that duty. Good-bye. *Ibid.*

2335   Build me a son, O Lord, who will be strong enough to know when he
is weak, and brave enough to face himself when he is afraid, one who
will be proud and unbending in honest defeat, and humble and gentle
in victory.

Build me a son whose wishes will not take the place of deeds; a son
who will know Thee—and that to know himself is the foundation
stone of knowledge.

Lead him, I pray, not in the path of ease and comfort, but under
the stress and spur of difficulties and challenge. Here let him learn to
stand up in the storm; here let him learn compassion for those who
fail.

Build me a son whose heart will be clear, whose goal will be high;
a son who will master himself before he seeks to master other men;
one who will reach into the future, yet never forget the past.

And after all these things are his, add, I pray, enough of a sense of
humor, so that he may always be serious, yet never take himself too
seriously. Give him humility, so that he may always remember the
simplicity of true greatness, the open mind of true wisdom, and the
meekness of true strength.

Then, I, his father, will dare to whisper, "I have not lived in vain."
Ibid.

2336   The accumulation of all powers, legislative, executive, and judiciary,
in the same hands, whether of one, a few, or many, and whether
hereditary, self-appointed, or elective, may justly be pronounced the
very definition of tyranny. *James Madison*

2337   There are more instances of the abridgment of the freedom of the
people by gradual and silent encroachments of those in power than
by violent and sudden usurpation. *Ibid.*

2338   There is a destiny that makes us brothers,
None goes his way alone:
All that we send into the lives of others
Comes back into our own. *Edwin Markham*

2339   I have come to regard this matter of Fame as the most transparent
of all vanities. *Herman Melville*

2340   A democracy—that is, a government of all the people, by all the
people, for all the people; of course, a government of the principles

of eternal justice, the unchanging law of God; for shortness' sake, I will call it the idea of Freedom. *Theodore Parker*

THINK TWICE BEFORE YOU SPEAK

2341   If Thou thinkest twice, before thou speakest once, thou wilt speak twice the better for it.

Better say nothing than not to the Purpose. And to speak pertinently, consider both what is fit, and when it is fit to speak.

In all Debates, let Truth be thy Aim, not Victory, or an unjust Interest: And endeavor to gain, rather than to expose thy Antagonist. *William Penn*

DELAY

2342   Our Law says well, to delay Justice is Injustice. *Ibid.*

MODERN CAPITALISM

2343   The fundamental idea of modern capitalism is not the right of the individual to possess and enjoy what he has earned, but the thesis that the exercise of this right redounds to the general good. *Ralph Barton Perry*

THE PURITANS

2344   What the Puritans gave the world was not thought, but action. *Wendell Phillips*

SELF-KNOWLEDGE

2345   At the height of our power we hesitate because we can see in a terrifying self-knowledge the necessity of putting reason before will, persuasion before assertiveness, asking before answering, concern before self-regard. *Nathan Pusey*

WHAT OUR PEOPLE EXPECT

2346   The basic things expected by our people of their political and economic systems are simple. They are:

Equality of opportunity for youth and others.

Jobs for those who can work.

Security for those who need it.

The ending of special privilege for the few.

The preservation of civil liberties for all.

The enjoyment of the fruits of scientific progress in a wider and constantly rising standard of living. *Franklin D. Roosevelt*

VALOR

2347   Valor is a gift. Those having it never know for sure whether they have it till the test comes. And those having it in one test never know for sure if they will have it when the next test comes. *Carl Sandburg*

MENTAL NEUTERS

2348   While I am not in favor of maladjustment, I view this cultivation of neutrality, this breeding of mental neuters, this hostility to eccentricity and controversy with grave misgiving. One looks back with dismay at the possibility of a Shakespeare perfectly adjusted to bourgeois life in Stratford, a Wesley contentedly administering a country parish, George Washington going to London to receive a barony from George III, or Abraham Lincoln prospering in Springfield with nary a concern for the preservation of the crumbling Union. *Adlai Stevenson*

A NEW AMERICA

2349   History's headlong course has brought us, I devoutly believe, to the threshold of a new America—to the America of the great ideals and noble visions which are the stuff our future must be made of. I mean a new America where poverty is abolished and our abundance is used to enrich the lives of every family. I mean a new America where freedom is made real for all without regard to race or belief or economic condition. I mean a new America which everlastingly attacks the ancient idea that men can solve their differences by killing each other. *Ibid.*

A PRAYER

2350   Great God, I ask thee for no meaner pelf
Than that I may not disappoint myself,
That in my action I may soar as high
As I can now discern with this clear eye.
Henry David Thoreau

ON TRIAL

2351   One is never more on trial than in the moment of excessive good fortune. *Lew Wallace*

LEAVING A RECORD

2352   I resolved that because I had no ancestry myself I would leave a record of which my children would be proud, and which might encourage them to still higher effort. *Booker T. Washington*

FREEDOM

2353   The time is now near at hand which must probably determine whether Americans are to be freemen or slaves; whether they are to have any property they can call their own; whether their houses and farms are to be pillaged and destroyed, and themselves consigned to a state of wretchedness from which no human efforts will deliver them. The fate of unborn millions will now depend, under God, on the courage and conduct of this army. . . . We have, therefore, to resolve to conquer or to die. *George Washington*

(Speech delivered to his army before the battle of Long Island, 1776)

GOD

2354   No people can be bound to acknowledge and adore the invisible hand which conducts the affairs of men more than the people of the United States. Every step by which they have advanced to the character of an independent nation seems to have been distinguished by some token of providential agency. *Ibid.*

THE ETERNAL RULES

2355   There is no truth more thoroughly established than that there exists in the economy and course of nature an indissoluble union between virtue and happiness, between duty and advantage, between the genuine maxims of an honest and magnanimous policy, and the solid rewards of public prosperity and felicity. . . . The propitious smiles of Heaven can never be expected on a nation that disregards the eternal rules of order and right, which Heaven itself has ordained. *Ibid.*

LIBERTY

2356   Interwoven as is the love of liberty with every ligament of your hearts, no recommendation of mine is necessary to fortify or confirm the attachment.

The Unity of the Government, which constitutes you one people, is also now dear to you. It is justly so; for it is a main Pillar in the Edifice of your real independence; the support of your tranquillity at home; your peace abroad; of your safety; of your prosperity in every shape; of that very Liberty, which you so highly prize. *Ibid.*

RELIGION

2357   Of all the dispositions and habits which lead to political prosperity, Religion and Morality are indispensable. In vain would that man claim the tribute of Patriotism, who should labor to subvert these great pillars of human happiness, these firmest props of the duties of Men and Citizens. *Ibid.*

PUBLIC OPINION

2358   In proportion as the structure of a government gives force to public opinion, it is essential that public opinion should be enlightened. *Ibid.*

CONFIDENCE

2359   Be courteous to all, but intimate with few; and let those few be well tried before you give them your confidence. *Ibid.*

A TRUST

2360   And the civilized world seems at last to be proceeding to the conviction of that fundamental and manifest truth, that the powers of government are but a trust, and that they cannot be lawfully exercised but for the good of the community. As knowledge is more and more extended, this conviction becomes more and more general. *Daniel Webster*

MOTHERS

2361   Mothers are, indeed, the affectionate and effective teachers of the human race. . . . They work, not upon the canvas that shall perish, nor the marble that shall crumble into dust, but upon mind, upon spirit, which is to last forever, and which is to bear, for good or evil, throughout its duration, the impress of a mother's plastic hand. *Ibid.*

WHAT THEIR HEARTS HOLD

2362   Put fear out of your heart. This nation will survive, this state will prosper, the orderly business of life will go forward if only men can speak in whatever way given them to utter what their hearts hold— by voice, by postcard, by letter, or by press. Reason never has failed men. Only force and oppression have made the wrecks in the world. *William Allen White*

FAITH

2363   When Faith is lost, when honor dies
        The man is dead! *John Greenleaf Whittier*

FOR THE RIGHT

2364   The right is more precious than peace, and we shall fight for the things which we have always carried nearest our hearts—for democracy, for the right of those who submit to authority to have a voice in their own government, for the rights and liberties of small nations, for a universal dominion of right by such a concert of free people as shall bring peace and safety to all nations and make the world itself at last free. *Woodrow Wilson*

...11...

Selections from Speeches of Herbert Victor Prochnow

THREE GREAT STRUGGLES
(Chicago, Illinois, 1967)

2365   We need on this significant day to renew our faith in those abiding values which have made our achievements possible. We need to reaffirm our stand on the principles that motivated our people in their struggle to greatness.

The history of this nation is the history of three great struggles:

First, the struggle for political freedom and against tyranny;

Second, the struggle for economic freedom and against poverty;

Third, the struggle for intellectual freedom and against ignorance.

These are the three freedoms which liberate humanity from tyranny, poverty, and ignorance.

RESPECT FOR THE LAW

2366   Are we witnessing a widespread spiritual and social disintegration? Have we forgotten that respect for the law is the foundation of a free society and the only assurance that men can remain free?

It is observance of the law that enables communities, cities, states, and the nation itself to function. It is the law which assures men and women that they may in confidence purchase homes, own life insurance, and buy an automobile. It is the law which assures us that we may protect our rights in pensions and in the ownership of hard-earned savings. It is the law which protects us in a thousand simple commitments in life. It is the law which assures the equality of men and makes life a vital experience. Respect for the law is essential to the survival of freedom.

INDEPENDENCE DAY AND THE GOOD CITIZEN
(Chicago, Illinois, 1967)

2367   On this Independence Day, you and I have certain responsibilities if we are to be good citizens.

For example, if you demand balanced budgets of your government, you must not advocate expenditures which, when demanded by all citizens, bring unbalanced budgets. Every dollar which a government spends comes finally from the toil and taxes of its citizens.

If you demand that crime be in the cell and not in the saddle, you must support honest law enforcement in your community without any personal privileges or exceptions for yourself.

If you demand free speech, you must not suppress it in others, or use violence to deny the right of free speech to those with whom you disagree.

If you wish your savings and property to be free from seizure, destruction, or theft, you must zealously protect and secure these rights for every citizen.

If you believe in a society of free men with government of the people, by the people, and for the people, you must exercise faithfully your right to vote at the ballot box.

If you demand that the government give you complete economic security, you must not forget that a nation's greatest strength comes when each person to the best of his ability stands on his own feet and courageously seeks to discharge his responsibilities.

If you would like to live in a community in which you may have pride, then dedicate yourself in a spirit of humility to your responsibilities in that community. These are practical ways in which to live the good life as a citizen.

You may say that this is the counsel of perfection. This is the good life of the good citizen. And so it is. On this Independence Day, the person who lives it may say with joy, "I have fought the good fight. I have kept the faith as a good citizen."

THE LAST GREAT EMPIRES
(Chicago, Illinois, 1962)

2368   One night in August, 1914, the members of the British Cabinet waited, hour after hour, as the deadline approached for the German reply to the British ultimatum. At last there fell upon their ears the deep boom of Big Ben, the great clock above the Parliament buildings, as it sounded the midnight hour. Then Lloyd George, his voice heavy with emotion, uttered the fateful words, "It's war."

Lloyd George said in his autobiography that the heavy boom of Big Ben sounded like doom to him through the stillness of that August night. Lloyd George was right. It was the doom of the world as we then knew it. By the end of the first World War, great empires began to totter. Communist revolutions erupted. Dictatorships sprang up. Currencies collapsed. Economic depression overtook the world. Then, unbelievably, came the second World War with its disastrous consequences, engulfing almost all of mankind. War recruits emotional energies as it seeks to justify its motives with subtle hypocrisies and flaming phrases promising a brave new world in the future. Then it proceeds ruthlessly to destroy what mankind has achieved in a slow and painful struggle upward through the centuries. Winston Churchill could say at the end of World War II: "What is Europe now? It is a rubble heap, a charnel house, a breeding ground of pestilence and hate."

Those were dark and disillusioning days as men awakened from their wartime dreams and surveyed the dismal wreckage. There were few grounds for courage. And yet, as we now know, the raw materials of economic and social renewal were present in Western Europe, waiting only to be given the leadership that was in less than two decades to make this one of the great areas of strength in the world.

At the outset of World War II in 1939, Soviet Russia was the only country in the world controlled by communists. Then a relentless drift to socialism and communism began. Ten years later communism had swept over one-third of the world's population, one-fourth of the earth's surface and a number of nations.

In 1945, in one of his less prophetic moments, Churchill declared: "I have not become His Majesty's First Minister to preside over the liquidation of the British Empire." But his successors were so to preside. During the nineteenth and the first half of the twentieth centuries, Britain, France, Belgium, Holland, and Portugal maintained order in a large part of Asia, the Middle East, and Africa. At the end of World War I, the Austro-Hungarian and Ottoman empires came to an end. By the end of World War II, the winds of political freedom were blowing fiercely through the corridors of all the old colonial empires.

THE FOUNDERS OF THIS REPUBLIC

2369   With victory in the War for Independence, the founders of this Republic met in Philadelphia in 1787 in one of the most distinguished gatherings in history. Despite the fact that the fifty-five men who composed that group were chosen from a new nation of only three million people, it would be extremely difficult today to bring together any political or economic assembly that would match it in clear grasp of principles and in unquestioned integrity of statesmanlike purpose. Washington presided. Benjamin Franklin quietly placed all the weight of his wisdom and experience at the service of the nation he was founding. Robert Morris, financier of the Revolution, was there to add his judgment. Hamilton swayed the assembly with his genius for clear thought. James Madison, the chief drafter of the Constitution, wrote with a clarity that no political subterfuge could honestly mistake. Within ninety days, these men completed the first written

Constitution ever to be offered to any nation. With this charter defining the rights of free men to govern themselves, the United States began as a nation with George Washington as President, Thomas Jefferson as Secretary of State, and Alexander Hamilton as Secretary of the Treasury. The Constitution and the Bill of Rights erected perhaps the strongest defenses against tyranny ever devised by free men. The struggle for political freedom had been won.

THE GROWTH OF A NATION
(Chicago, Illinois, 1962)

2370 The iron plow and the reaper took their toll from the prairies. Foundations were laid for vast new industries. Where men have political freedom, progress is never confined to material things but runs the gamut of all man's accomplishments. It was true in this nation. Such achievements as Washington Irving's *Sketch Book*, Emerson's *Essays*, Melville's *Moby Dick*, and Hawthorne's *Scarlet Letter* began to appear. Free men were beginning to write free thoughts. Ignorance was regarded from the very beginning of this nation as an enemy of democracy. The little red schoolhouse and the little white church sprang up on ten thousand hills.

There were booms and depressions, the tragedy of a Civil War, crop failures, and crises that shook the nation to its foundations. Life was hard. Hours of labor were long. Children worked in the factories and on the farms. Even as late as 1900 the life expectancy for a child of a laborer was thirty-four years, but today that child has the same life expectancy as any American child. Whereas 90 percent of the people had lived on farms when the nation was first established, by 1860 there were 140,000 manufacturing plants and our people were producing more goods by machine than by hand. A great industrial machine economy had been brought into existence by hard work, thrift, and investment. New processes were revolutionizing industry, and striking mechanization and new equipment were remaking the American economy and thrusting it dramatically forward in the world. The struggles against poverty and ignorance were being won.

THE VALUE OF INCENTIVES
(Los Angeles, Cal., 1960)

2371 It cannot be too strongly emphasized that in every economic system the people must work, save, and invest. If the people of a communist nation are willing to work hard, they can accelerate the economic growth of their country. If the people of a communist nation save, they can invest their savings in factories and machinery to expand their industry. In the Soviet system the state decides what must be produced, how long men and women must work, what must be saved and how the savings will be invested. In our system private individuals have the freedom to decide what they will produce, how much they will save, and how much they will invest. The fundamental distinction in the communist system is the right of the state to make the decisions regarding work, saving, and investment, in contrast to our society, where it is the right of free men to make the decisions. The underlying issue is the freedom of man. On this issue, Dostoyevsky once stated that even "tragic freedom" is preferable to "compulsory happiness."

The communist system has clearly recognized that the incentives of our capitalist system have great value, and it rewards labor on an incentive basis for increasing production. In a visit recently with two government officials in a Soviet satellite nation, I was told the communist system favors incentives. They said, "We are strong believers in incentives for increased production. Production must be encouraged by giving men incentives." I said, "When you commend incentives as a means of increasing production, you apparently do not agree with the communist doctrine 'From each according to his ability and to each according to his need.'" There was an embarrassing silence. Then one official replied, "We were speaking in economic terms and not in political terms."

The superintendent of a Soviet factory in southern Russia proudly said to me, "Our profits last year were very good in this factory. The state returned part of these profits to us so we could give extra payments to the most productive workers. We also got part of the profits returned to us by the state so we could invest in new plant and equipment." Even the communists recognize how necessary incentives are to encourage their people to work hard, to save, and to invest.

VAST NEW WORLD PROBLEMS
(Chicago, Illinois, 1966)

2372 Our position of leadership of the free world has brought with it another responsibility we had neither anticipated nor sought. With the shattering of all the great empires following two world wars, forty new nations with a population of one billion have emerged. These people are engaged in a struggle against poverty and ignorance. They stir uneasily in their hopes and dreams. They constitute a continuing threat to the peace of the world which we cannot safely ignore. And yet, it is a serious question whether this nation with only 200 million persons can possibly solve problems of poverty, illiteracy, disease, inadequate tax systems, persistent inflation, and land reform for 1,000 million people of the world. Six hundred million people with problems of this kind live in India, Pakistan, Indonesia, and Southeast Asia, over 50 million in the Middle East, 235 million in Africa, and 230 million in Latin America.

How can we assure that these nations, many of which are largely unprepared for self-government, do not endanger the peace of the world through revolutions and violence? How can we give educational facilities to hundreds of millions who are illiterate, when tens of millions of their children, even of primary age, do not have school facilities of any kind? How can we assure the necessary food to millions suffering from malnutrition, when per capita food production now in various areas is probably less than it was before World War II? How can we eliminate widespread disease in the underdeveloped nations and add even five years to the life expectancy of these people, many of whom live only thirty or forty years? How can we provide pure water supplies and drainage systems for hundreds of millions who are sick because of impure water and improper sanitation? How can we supply means of transportation, communication, and power to many countries that are almost completely without such facilities? There is not sufficient available capital in the entire world to accomplish these objectives within a reasonably short time. Under these conditions it seems inevitable that we shall face for many years a turbulent and politically unstable world.

LATIN AMERICA

2373 We must recognize that it is no easy task for governments in some Latin American countries in their present stage of economic development and with widespread illiteracy and poverty to follow middle-of-the-road policies that satisfy the radical elements, the military groups, the large landowners, and businessmen. As they soberly analyze their grave problems, the leaders of many of these countries feel impelled to speak the language of economic urgency and to adopt policies of expediency rather than wisdom.

ADMINISTRATION OF FOREIGN AID

2374 The administration of foreign aid might be better also if we used an organization of the major powers of the free world to which we would contribute, along with contributions from other free nations. The United Nations would not be the logical agency to administer these funds; for one reason, it represents both the lenders and the borrowers. This organization could have a highly technical staff to evaluate aid and loan projects, and this should result in a reduction in our own staffs. The aid projects would represent the joint efforts of the major nations of the free world. The underdeveloped nations would come to recognize more clearly than they now do that the United States with 200 million people cannot possibly assure one billion people the substantial economic progress they expect to attain in a short time. Under this arrangement, the total aid might be larger, but our own costs should be less. We have nothing to lose by examining these approaches or by bringing some entirely new ideas to these programs.

BIG CHALLENGES PRESENTED

2375   We are witnessing an economic, political, and social struggle of such magnitude that it may determine the character of the world's governments and institutions for decades. The underdeveloped nations already have an important voice in world affairs. With experience in self-government their power will increase. Their choice of communism or democracy, regimentation or freedom, collectivism or private enterprise, may determine the character of civilization in large areas of the world.

INDUSTRIALIZATION
(Chicago, Illinois, 1964)

2376   The underdeveloped nations seem determined to industrialize their economies. They hope that industrialization will raise living standards more rapidly. They also feel that it improves their international status. A large steel mill is one expression of this desire. National pride, and not economic realism, seems to demand an international airline as a status symbol.

Industrialization requires vast sums of capital, technical knowledge, more skilled workers, more productive agriculture which frees labor for industry, and governments qualified to guide economies in which the population is shifting from self-sufficient agricultural areas to the cities. Savings, investment, work skills, and all the disciplines and techniques of an industrial society are not readily acquired. The impact of these far-reaching economic shifts in nations with unskilled, illiterate people is almost certain to bring economic and political turmoil.

LATIN AMERICA
(Hollywood, Florida, 1964)

2377   Consider briefly the situation in Latin America, an area especially important to us, and in South America in particular. The overall picture is one of a continent having an isolated interior with practically no population. The result is a concentration of population within one hundred to two hundred miles of the coast. South America is a continent of striking contrasts of wealth and poverty, luxury and misery, great cosmopolitan centers and small backward villages where the masses are illiterate, the children without schools, and the people without tools for productive work.

WORLD LEADERSHIP

2378   The survival of a society upon which the mantle of world leadership has fallen depends upon hard work and not leisure, thrift and not extravagance, personal sacrifice and not personal indulgence. Economic discipline is an essential for a nation's greatness.

THE CHILDREN OF PROGRESS
(Chamber of Commerce of the United States, Washington, D.C., 1965)

2379 Those who built this nation to its present greatness may not have
been the children of perfection, but they were the children of progress. They believed in the invincibility of intelligence, economy, and
hard work. Guided by Providence, they entered a wilderness with
vision, industry, and courage. They took the forked stick and made
a steel plow. They took the rude sickle and made a reaper. They took
the wagon and made an engine, an automobile, an airplane, a tractor.
They made an iron thread into an ocean cable, rough type into great
color printing presses, and steel beams into soaring skyscrapers. They
made forest trails into magnificent highways. They put the little red
schoolhouse and the little white church on a thousand hills.

Soon a wilderness poured forth its riches from farm and factory,
and the vast solitude of a continent became a great dynamic nation.
There rose the noise of industry, the halls of science and learning, and
the temples of religion. If our feet have rested sometimes upon the
clods, our forehead has grazed the stars.

Once, a relatively few pioneers followed faint trails through the
American wilderness. Today, there are hundreds of millions of people
on the broad highways of the world who are determined to leave
behind them their mud huts, their illiteracy, their disease, and their
poverty.

Other ages and times have had their triumphs and their defeats.
The fifteenth century stands for the revival of arts and letters, the
sixteenth century for discovery, the seventeenth for the rise of liberty, the eighteenth for the fall of tyranny, and the nineteenth for
man's industrial upsurge. The century in which we now live is witnessing a tremendous social, economic, and political upheaval. In our
time, there is no place for those who are at ease. Our greatness will
rest upon the heroic qualities of character, industry, and self-discipline we bring to the difficult problems of our time.

PRIORITIES

2380 When we do not have the self-discipline in a period of prosperity to
balance our budget, ought we not at least to set down our priorities
for expenditures? If we cannot do everything, which things come
first? In what order do we place defense, highways, schools, housing,
health, welfare, transportation, the conservation of water resources,
agriculture, and space programs? We need to establish clearly which
are the most urgent budget priorities.

RESPONSIBILITY FOR ORDER

2381 Can this nation alone ever be sufficiently powerful to maintain order
wherever trouble may arise in the entire world? If not, what are the

dimensions of our responsibility? What course do we choose to follow? Where do we stand on this issue?

A TIME FOR DECISION

2382 These are great issues which confront us. They are issues on which we must make a choice. There is a time for the discussion of such issues. But there also is a time when we must firmly choose the course we will follow, or the relentless drift of events will make the decision. The time to choose where we stand is here.

PROGRESS
(Nashville, Tennessee, 1964)

2383 In 1789, it took George Washington eight days to travel the two hundred-odd miles from his home, Mount Vernon, to the scene of his inauguration as President in New York City.

The fact that it required eight days is not significant. The important fact is that the time it took was the same as it would have taken two thousand years before. No real progress had been made in transportation in twenty centuries. Moses or Nebuchadnezzar could have traveled just as rapidly.

Ninety percent of the people lived on farms. Life in the 1700s was not greatly different from life in the first century. Candles and oil lamps were used for light, fireplaces for heat, horses and sailing ships for travel. The federal budget was a little over one million dollars. Julius Caesar could have stepped from the first century into the nineteenth century more easily than Benjamin Franklin or Mark Twain could have stepped into 1970. But for the first time in history no man now dies in the historical epoch in which he was born.

THE FINAL MEASURE OF GREATNESS
(Chicago, Illinois, 1963)

2384 We have a responsibility of far-reaching importance in our own communities. It is tempting to discuss international and national affairs. The problems of Calcutta and Caracas seem more challenging than those of Chicago and Cincinnati. The illiteracy of Peru is more interesting than the school dropouts in Peoria. But how can we bring understanding and leadership to the solution of the nation's problems unless there is economic strength, civic character, and spiritual depth in the local communities in which our people live?

Have you and I therefore given to our communities the kind of dedicated and devoted concern that would give even the smallest community distinction? To paraphrase Seneca, a wise Roman philosopher, "No city ever becomes great by chance."

What, specifically, are you and I doing to meet the problems of our communities and to give them the distinction and civic greatness that could be theirs? A mountain range culminates in great peaks. Towns and cities culminate in men and women who are great citizens. Leadership in a city does not spring from groups. It springs first from individuals within groups. As A. Whitney Griswold, the late president of Yale University, put it: "The divine spark leaps from the finger of God to the finger of Adam."

There are in every community men and women with great talents. Perhaps there is needed the renewal of a personal dedication to build in the cities in which we live, the good city, for out of the good city come the good state and the good nation—and finally the good society for all mankind. . . .

Someone has said that the major problem which confronts the American people in this critical period in history is how to be great on a full stomach. Have we, despite the narcotic of increasing leisure, easier living, and all the distractions of the most affluent society in history, the will and the character to meet our responsibilities as the children of Providence?

The ultimate purpose of man is not merely to fly from Chicago to London in seven hours—eating a ten-course dinner en route. The great goal of free men is not simply to create a sleek and self-satisfied culture of comfort, leisure, and fun. The lasting achievement of mankind is not even the size of its fallout shelters or the destructiveness of its bombs.

The final measure of greatness is whether you and I, by our individual lives, have increased the freedom of man, enhanced his dignity, and brought him nearer to the nobility of the divine image in which he was created.

LOOKING AHEAD
(University of Notre Dame, Notre Dame, Indiana, 1968)

2385 On the evening of December 31, 1899, the most powerful man in American business, John Pierpont Morgan, sat in the mahogany-paneled library of his large brownstone house at the corner of Madison Avenue and Thirty-sixth Street, New York, playing solitaire. The old year was coming to a close. As the bells and horns at midnight proclaimed the beginning of the New Year, Mr. Morgan was looking forward to the great possibilities of the new century. Andrew Carnegie, the steelmaster, with income that would be over 23 million dollars in 1900, and with no income tax to pay, could also await the New Year with eager anticipation, for he was to create the greatest corporation in the world and own almost 60 percent of its stock.

Horatio Alger, Jr., whose books about the rise of hard-working boys from rags to riches had sold 20 million copies, had just died without achieving riches himself, but having had a significant influence on our thinking in those years.

Business leaders could look forward with reasonable confidence to a period of stability. They could not possibly have foreseen the changes that would drive this nation to world leadership and to the most productive economy with the widest distribution of wealth in history.

THE ROLE OF BUSINESS

2386   We need also to recognize more clearly that it is not government, but modern, private industry with its massive power-driven equipment producing a continuous flow of goods, which is a major instrument for the social and economic enrichment of man and for his personal emancipation from drudgery, poverty, and insecurity. The real revolutionists of our times are businessmen creating wealth for the masses. It is within the power of businessmen to have the relative role of government decline, if they continue their amazing record of raising the standard of living of our people.

COMBINING BEAUTY AND UTILITY
(Philadelphia, Pennsylvania, 1969)

2387   The critics of business have said that you cannot have massive power-driven factories without quantity production. You cannot have standardization of the material adjuncts of life without standardization of human conduct, thought, and opinion. They say that standardization of the processes of production stamps a sterile sameness upon men's lives as well as upon their commodities. Ugliness becomes synonymous with utility. They say we have lost fine craftsmanship. These criticisms of business are the common property of the superficial thinkers of our time. The facts are that our industrial economy has passed through its adolescence. Industry has followed the same evolution from crude production to refinement and beauty that hand production followed. Gradually with the increasing level of demand of consumers and the severe competition among manufacturers, industry is combining beauty and utility. Even a mass-produced kitchen range now has a beauty never possessed by an old kitchen stove or a cast-iron, soot-covered pot hanging in a smoky fireplace. Our machine industry has emancipated mankind from drudgery and has augmented the leisure, affirmed the dignity, and made more certain the independence of the individual worker. In addition, as it grows in stature, imagination, and vision, industry is bringing increasing beauty in fabric and form to the wealth of material goods it produces. An automobile today not only runs well. It also looks good.

INDIVIDUAL MEN

2388   America is great because individual men have freedom and equality, because individual men have been given the incentive to create, to work, and to save, because individual men have been rewarded for their labor with a generous share of the goods they helped to produce. America has taken its place among the great civilizations of history because the cornerstone upon which the republic rests is the social, economic, and spiritual betterment of individual men. In this achievement American business has played a significant role. Government has its proper functions in a society, but the ultimate greatness of a people must rest finally in the creative energies of the individual men and women who constitute the society.

There is genius enough in those who direct the business structure of this nation to give us in material well-being and social and spiritual enrichment a future that will exceed even the amazing progress of the past.

THE UNDERDEVELOPED NATIONS
(University of North Dakota, Grand Forks, N.D., 1966)

2389 We know who the 1.5 billion people of the underdeveloped nations are. They are the millions who suffer from illiteracy, poverty, and malnutrition. They are the millions who are born but never live. But we do not know what they may become in only a few years when they constitute 80 percent of the world's population. We do not even know what Red China will become a generation from now when she has 1.5 billion people and when she also has further developed destructive nuclear capacity.

Will these nations, many of which are largely unprepared for self-government, constantly endanger the peace of the world through revolutions and violence? Will there in the foreseeable future be educational facilities for the hundreds of millions who are illiterate?

It is no easy task for governments in these nations in their present state of development and with widespread illiteracy and poverty to follow middle-of-the-road policies that satisfy the radical elements, the military groups, the large landowners, and businessmen. The leaders of many of these countries who are constantly facing crises feel impelled to speak the language of economic urgency and to adopt policies of expediency rather than wisdom. Governments will be considered politically inadequate if they are not economically responsive to need.

We know the magnitude of these problems now. But we do not know how great they will be in the future, and whether they will challenge all of Western civilization. The underdeveloped nations are falling increasingly behind the more advanced nations in income. The gap is widening. Will these trends continue so that we shall face increasing turbulence and widespread violence in the world?

We are now the most powerful nation in the world, but we do not know whether we shall be sufficiently powerful to maintain law and order everywhere in this kind of restless world.

WHAT WE MAY BE
(Indiana Central College, Indianapolis, Indiana, 1969)

2390   You and I know what we are personally, but have we really thought as the successive years crumble under our feet what we might become. Achievement sleeps in many minds. To the great disadvantage of some young people, I once taught university classes. I often thought that if I could lead only one student out of hundreds to decide that he would become the greatest authority in the world in some field it would be a far-reaching achievement. It might be economics, law, accounting, literature, medicine, science, or any other field. He would be ruthless in eliminating from his life every unnecessary activity. Five years after he had finished his formal education he would know a little about his field. In ten years he would begin to be informed. In twenty years he would be able. In twenty-five years he would become an authority with national recognition. In thirty years he might become distinguished as one of the great men of the world in his field. Young men know what they are now, but do they really realize what they might become with a complete dedication to some great objective?

TWO GREAT PRINCIPLES
(Lansing, Michigan, 1967)

2391   In our dedication to the commendable objective of eliminating economic poverty, we have forgotten that a people may suffer even more from spiritual poverty. They may suffer from poverty of character. They may suffer from poverty in moral standards. Is there any clear assurance that with our remarkable economic progress we have had a comparable advance in things that are spiritual? Is there any assurance that with higher and higher standards of living we have had higher and higher moral standards? Is there any assurance that with more material things we have greater respect for law? Is there any assurance that with greater affluence we have come to esteem more those abiding values in a civilization that lie beyond butter and guns?

Perhaps we need to reaffirm our stand on two great principles that have strongly motivated the conduct of our people throughout our history. The first principle is our recognition of the sovereignty of God. We need to reemphasize that man is not the center of the universe. Pleasure is not the goal of the people. Power is not the goal of government. Expediency is not the guiding principle of conduct. It is Providence that is sovereign and gives the ultimate objectives and goal to mankind. It is the City of God, as St. Augustine said, that man is to build on earth. In a nation where faith in Providence dies, literature loses its inspiration, art its beauty, government its consecration, business its ideals, and labor its dignity.

The second great principle we need to reemphasize is the divine worth of man. We believe in the independence and dignity of every man, for he was made in the image of God and is overshadowed only by Him.

In a world beset by bewildering uncertainty, we need to renew our allegiance to the two great principles of the sovereignty of God and the divine worth of man.

As the Old Testament prophet said: "Choose this day where you will stand."

WHAT YOU ARE

2392 You may remember the play *The Green Pastures*. In that play, Noah said to the Lord, "I ain't very much, but I'm all I've got."

Well, you and I are all we've got. The question is "What are we going to do with what we've got?" You know what you are, but you do not know what you may be. Will you press for the goal of a great and good life? Will you use yourself to make life richer, better, nobler? This is the vision I bring to you.

Someone may say that this is the counsel of perfection. This is the good life. And so it is. The person who lives it will be able to say with joy:

"I have fought the good fight, I have finished my course, I have kept the faith."

Subject Index

(see also **Names and Places Index**)

Names and Places Index

(see also **Subject Index**)

71 72 73 10 9 8 7 6 5 4 3 2 1